Home Schooling in Full View

A Reader

Home Schooling in Full View

A Reader

Edited by

Bruce S. Cooper
Fordham University

INFORMATION AGE
PUBLISHING

Greenwich, Connecticut • www.infoagepub.com

Cover art by Daphne Maeglin

Library of Congress Cataloging-in-Publication Data

Homeschooling in full view : a reader / edited by Bruce S. Cooper.
    p. cm.
  Includes bibliographical references.
  ISBN 1-59311-338-2 (pbk.) -- ISBN 1-59311-339-0 (hardcover)
  1. Home schooling. I. Cooper, Bruce S.
  LC40.H669 2005
  371.04'2--dc22

                                2005009103

Dedicated to a devoted cousin and friend—

Carol Anne Leblang Forde
(1956-2005)

CONTENTS

PREFACE

An Introduction to Homeschooling

Bruce S. Cooper

So much is happening that a book is warranted, one that captures the incredible life and vibrancy of the oldest, and in some ways newest, form of education. Parents, educating their children at home, or *homeschooling*, has come out of the shadows and stands tall and *in full view*, next to other types of education: public schools, private and religious schools, charter schools, and now homeschools!

This, a first full-scale edited book, is a reader that describes, discusses and analyses homeschooling from an array of different and international perspectives. We portray the energy of this movement in this volume, looking at the history of *education writ large*, in a larger social, political and religious context, one for placing homeschooling in perspective. Like most movements in education, this one is both a reaction to the problems and inadequacies of existing schools, and a new direction in schooling that stands on its own.

This book grew out of the efforts of Associates for Research on Private Education (ARPE), an international organization of scholars and practitioners affiliated with the American Education Research Association (AERA), which has spurred interest and research on private schools for over 30 years. ARPE publishes quarterly, the *Private School MONITOR,* as a means for highlighting the newest developments in the field of private education.

And the *MONITOR* published an article on the legalization of home-schooling by Scott Somerville, and was going to print a few more key articles on homeschoolers' performance on the SAT (the major college admission test). This outpouring of writing and interests shortly became this book. We would like to thank a long-time ARPE member, Tom Hunt, of University of Dayton, who directed us to George Johnson, the publisher at Information Age Publishers, who accepted our proposal. We all are feeling the interest in and excitement about recent research on home-schooling—and this book is the result.

As such, *Homeschooling in Full View: A Reader*, seeks to portray the richness and diversity of homeschooling—from an educational, religious, social, and political perspective. Some chapters are highly scholarly, based on research: for example, analysis of how well homeschooled kids do on college entrance exams (SATs) and processes of gaining access to the prestigious Ivy League colleges. Other chapters are more philosophical, or more highly personal—a mother who writes about her feelings and concerns.

THE AUDIENCES

We conceive of several audiences for this book: First, university professors and their students are becoming interested in privatization as a growing policy issue, including private schools and issues around homeschooling. This book is the perfect course reader, presenting ideas that will stimulate discussion and research for courses on social and religious thought and key familial-institutional developments in education.

This reader has collected under one cover a range of issues: nesting homeschooling in the history and development of education; the complex relationship between compulsory, universal education, the rights and roles of parents in the education of their children; and the *approved values* (e.g., no religion taught in public schools) of the government that affect the upbringing of our children.

Second, researchers and policy analysts will find this book useful since it includes articles on the philosophy, history, politics, sociology, and theology of homeschooling. Who would have thought that something as simple as teaching one's own children at home—bothering no one and relieving the government of having to educate these children at public expense—would create so much thought, discussion and research?

And third, public educators will find more and more homeschoolers in their districts and states, and may not know quite what to make of them. Yet in many states, the local public school superintendents have some responsibility for these children, may want to reintegrate some of them back into the system, or if the parents so choose, may offer public services and programs (e.g., sports, psychological assistance, and use of school facilities) to homeschool families. It's to the advantage of every educator to know and understand the causes, needs, and goals of homeschool children and parents. After all, these families are tax-paying, voting, active, and well-organized citizens of their community.

BACKGROUND

It is probably a testimony to the insecurity of the nation's largest public monopoly, the public schools with their 49 million children in over 13,000 school districts, that such a small and harmless experiment in education (homeschooling) should generate national, and now international, controversy. We are so accustomed as a society to being *institutionalized* in everything we do—from health to education to business to politics—that taking the simple private, family approach to education is foreign to many Americans.

Perhaps, homeschool activists—parents, church leaders, and educators—may not find this book terribly revolutionary or all that revealing. After all, these parents live what we are writing about here. But, at the same time, homeschoolers will take great comfort in knowing that a fascinating collection of excellent writers, thinkers, and teachers (the authors in this book) produced such an exciting reader that brings so many themes and ideas together. Perhaps the closer one is to a personal life event—like teaching one's own child—the less one can fully comprehend the breadth of the discussion surrounding something as simple as home education.

Together, then, the audiences for this book are potentially extensive: educators, parents, religious people, and those who want to keep pace with the latest developments in educational and social/religious life.

TERMS

English is in part a Germanic language, one in which words are drawn, or blended together to form new ones. "Home schooling" (likewise, "home school", and "home schooler") was two separate words. Common usage led to the hyphenization of these terms, such as *home-schooling*, to the blending of the words into one new word: homeschooling. (Similar fusion pressures show up with words like *policy maker, policy-maker,* and now *policymaker.*) And even the most important book on teachers, that by Dan Lortie (1970), became *Schoolteacher: A Sociological Study,* the blending of school teacher into school-teacher into schoolteacher.

Some authors in this book prefer the fully-blended version of the term, while others use "home schooling" as two distinct words. Whatever the final and best form, one could argue that the newness and energy of the phenomenon, and its development, have led to changes in the structure of the nouns and adjectives themselves: homeschooling, homeschooler, homeschool, or homeschooled, although my *spell check* ("spell check," "spell-check," "spellcheck"?) rejects the blended form of the terms. It is time to up-date/update these terms to keep pace with common usages.

THE CHAPTERS

This book comes at homeschooling from many different perspectives, exposing the considerable variety and richness of the phenomenon and the thoughts and enthusiasm that this kind of education creates, even from it critics (perhaps particularly from its detractors). We seek to explore and discuss homeschooling as a social movement, in reaction to changes in public life and education; as a worldwide movement that affects many nations; and as a point of some controversy in American education.

Brian Ray, one of the major leaders, researchers, and spokespeople for the homeschool movement in the United States, contributes the first chapter, placing homeschooling in a national context. Once the context of homeschooling is established, Ray brings us up to date on the current status of homeschooling in the United States, as the numbers top a million children out of about 53 million K-12 school students in all 50 states and the District of Columbia. His analysis explains the organization and actions of homeschooling parents, and their community of supporters. Ironically, the smallest, most atomistic units of education—families—are also among the most well networked, organized, and politically powerful. Read the No Child Left Behind Act of 2001 and note that homeschoolers are specifically exempted from many of the law's testing requirements. Politicians have learned the hard way not to take on the well-organized homeschool and church-related lobbies that wanted to limit the intrusion of the federal government into the private and religious lives of church, parents and children.

The ability of the homeschool lobby to clog the White House switchboard in a matter of hours testifies to the strength, commitment, and level of networking that underpins the homeschooling effort. Parents are at home as teachers and mentors, which allows them to contact other parents and lobbying groups—a strong voice that protects the rights of families to homeschool their children.

Brian Ray's association, the Home School Education Network, works overtime to enlarge and enhance communications amongst homeschooling parents and their friends, churches, associations, and interest groups.

Ray shows just how exciting the business of homeschooling has become, and how these groups support one another in times of need and crisis. Donald Erickson's chapter places homeschooling in the sociopolitical context of compulsion: government requirements leading to the "one best system" (Tyack, 1974), a unified, unitary educational establishment, if not monopoly. And like most monopolies, they struggle and eventually go out of business or change—as public education is doing now.

Charles Glenn (Boston University) takes Erickson's argument the next step, showing how homeschooling and compulsory education go hand-in-hand, not only in the United States but in many modern nations of the world (Glenn, 1983; Tyack, 1974). Glenn goes nation to nation, with a brief history of the building of public common education, often, in his words, "to render education secular and uniform." Both forced secularism and uniformity are bound to upset some parents who want a religious education—and feel that uniformity is not suitable for each unique child (theirs).

He then explains which nations permit homeschooling (or not) and which ones monitor the effort or not, which ones forbid it but make exceptions (e.g., Spain, Greece, Israel, Uruguay). Finally, Germany, Argentina, Cuba, Brazil and others have compulsory public education—not allowing parents to homeschool their children at all. Interesting contrasts.

Glenn takes us back to the beginnings of education, to give a running leap between the middle ages in Europe and the early period in the United States, where the role of government in education was small and circumscribed, through the origins of the "one best system" in the nineteeth century, its formalization and routinization in the middle and late twentieth century, and its current controls. We get a running jump on what appears in historical terms to be a natural, basic, almost tribal form of education—children taught by lessons and examples by their parents and by their communities. Glenn does not dismiss the role or responsibility of governments in society; only that citizens be aware of the state's role and control it. Glenn concludes his analysis of choice in society with the assertion:

> that we need to move beyond singing the praises of parent choice of schools and think very seriously about the terms on which and the constraints within which such choice is exercised. There are those who argue that government should simply cease to concern itself with education, but I am convinced that this is profoundly unrealistic and not desirable; our goal should be *to limit the role of government* to setting the ground rules within which schools as civil society institutions provide education, and to providing the public funding which make this education universally and adequately available.

Tom Smedley looks at homeschooling from a personal and societal perspective, "for liberty" and for the love of our children. He poses the interesting question: Is homeschooling "hard work" for parents. Yes, he answers, it is "hard but not a hardship", as Smedley sees the rights of the family, and their role in educating children most essential, a means for containing the costs of public education. After all, we know that even children attending public schools still do much if not most of their essential learning in the family.

Michael Apple, in his chapter, takes a critical (and critical theory) perspective on homeschooling. He mounts a massive attack on the process, based on four different arguments. First, Apple questions the "defensive religious posture" of homeschool supporters, relating this stance to the general move in society toward a "private consciousness", a kind of suburbanization of life and education. Second, at the root of the Apple critique is the sense to many that the state is intervening in everyone's lives—fear, in Clarke and Newman (1997), words of the "managerial state." Third, Apple fears the fracturing of a sense of community, the "health of the public sphere," and potential for homeschooling to contribute to great societal stratification and racial separation. This "cocooning," to use his term, makes for interesting reading and sheds light—in a contrasting, negative way—on what many of the other chapters see as homeschooler's attempt to preserve their beliefs and families.

The chapter by Nicky Hardenbergh is a formal response to Michael Apple and another critic of homeschooling, Rob Reich (his chapter follows), in which she reviews the attacks on homeschooling and refutes the over simplicity of some of their arguments. That is, while many homeschoolers are conservative, and religious, a strong minority of these families is more concerned about doing what is right for their children, than whether they have a different ideology. She explains, "There is, however, one point toward which the views of virtually all homeschoolers converge: the conviction that the full responsibility for our children's education properly rests with the family, rather than with public officials." Her critique of Apple is essential: we are to understand—as this book explains— that "compulsory school attendance" is not synonymous with learning or education, for that matter. Children learn in all sorts of ways and places: at home, at church, synagogue or mosque.

Rob Reich in Chapter 7 makes a cogent argument for *regulating* but not preventing homeschooling, since he favors family choice, opportunity and parental involvement in their children's education. What concerns Reich is giving parents (or anyone/any organization) total control over the lives of children. Further, he is concerned about "civic ethics" of education within a larger argument for citizenship. He acknowledges that "the diversity of pluralistic democracy" can be threatening to some parents, while it is important to children in their total education. For, to Reich, isolation is the opposite of "getting an education." In effect, he seeks a healthy balance between the rights and concerns of parents, and the authority of the state and the public in "cultivating citizenship as part of children's education."

Venus Taylor's chapter analyzes the growth of homeschooling among the nation's African American families, related to the very basic problems faced by Blacks in our society: the failure of the *Brown v. Board of Education* decision over 50 years ago to end the black-white achievement gap. School leaders talk about smaller classes, more relevant curriculum, sensitive teachers, and the equal treatment for all. Yet homeschooling, Taylor explains, can provide all of these qualities, and more, while public schools continue to fail Black kids. For, as Nancy Kober, of the Center on Education Policy, starkly reiterates: "[T]he average 1999 reading score of Black students at age 17 was about the same as that of White students at age 13. In science, the average scores of Black and Hispanic students at age 13 were lower than the average score of White students at age 9."

Chapter 9 by Scott Somerville of the Homeschool Legal Defense Association testifies to the incredible political clout of homeschoolers, teamed up with other key lobby groups (e.g., Christian schools associations), to bring homeschooling from an underground, hidden, forbidden activity to one in full view, legalized in all 50 states. And once the courts acted, then so did the states, as laws were passed making homeschooling legal. And the striking moment came when the U.S. Congress passed the most dramatic revision to the federal education act (No Child Left Behind, NCLB) seen since 1965 (with the passage of the Elementary and Secondary Education Act), but specifically left homeschoolers out of the requirements and testing under NCLB. Few members of Congress wanted to tangle with the well-organized homeschool lobby that could clog the phone banks of Congress or the White House in a matter of hours.

Rarely has any group altered state laws so systematically; and Somerville, a Harvard law school graduate, and a homeschooling parent of six himself, has participated in, and written about, a major sociopolitical revolution in his chapter. Homeschoolers bring the same dedication and discipline to their political affairs as to the teaching of their children.

Chapter 10 by Steven F. Duvall describes the homeschooling efforts of families with special needs children. He compared the behavior of special education teachers (in public schools) with those efforts by parents; the gains of home- and school-educated special needs students; and the performance of homeschool versus public school children with disabilities. Not only are the teaching methods compared, but so are the results and the gains, and the differences. Critical to the whole process, Duvall found, was Academic Engaged Time (AET), those specific learning behaviors that engage students of all abilities and needs. It seems that homeschool parents, once they understand the importance of AET, can concentrate on helping their children to learn for longer time periods than a schoolteacher who must look out for 15 to 25 students at the same time. One-on-one (parent and child) can really make a difference, even for (perhaps, more for) children with disabilities.

One argument against homeschooling is that parents cannot possibly prepare their children on an equal footing to public schools for advanced studies, college preparation, successfully taking the SATs, and gaining college admissions. In response to this argument, Clive Belfield in Chapter 11 compares the SAT (college entry test) scores for about 6,000 homeschoolers with those of other public school children, to test the notion that children taught at home cannot easily keep up with public schoolers. He found that homeschool students showed a combined total average score of 1,093, compared to public school students at 1,012.6. And on verbal, homeschoolers achieved a 566.6 against public schoolers' 502.6. However, these are raw differences, which do not adequately control for family background or differential rates of SAT test taking by public school students and homeschoolers.

Chapter 12 by Joy Marean, Marc Ott, and Matthew Rush is perhaps the most useful to practicing homeschool families, when it is time to consider college access, giving advice on applying to university, insight into what the Ivy League admissions departments expect when reviewing a homeschooler's application, and how many of these students who applied to these colleges (Dartmouth, Yale, Harvard, Pennsylvania) and were admitted in 2002

For example, what do these students do without an "official" transcript and letters from a school guidance director on their behalf? Marean, Ott, and Rush give some useful suggestions such as: (1) make one's own transcript, (2) keep work samples on hand; (3) create lists of books read and curricular materials used; (4) file the grade reports and transcripts issued by any homeschooling umbrella organization, a local school or community college; (5) note all extracurricular activities pursued, part-time jobs held, and internships completed; (6) record the results of all standardized tests taken; and (7) log the amount of time spent on each academic subject at home.

And get friends and adults who know the student to write letters of support, which led to Columbia University's receiving 22 homeschoolers' applications, admitting four with one enrolling; its admission rate was 18% for the homeschoolers and 12% for the general population. Dartmouth College had 25 applicants, 6 admissions, and 4 enrolled, with a yield of 67% and an admissions rate of 24%. This chapter reassures homeschoolers that colleges, even the most selective, are open and willing to review and admit them.

Chapters 13 and 14 pick up again on the international homeschooling theme (introduced earlier by Charles Glenn in Chapter 4). First, Sean Gabb provides in Chapter 13 an historical overview of the development of homeschooling in England, Scotland, and Northern Ireland, where the aristocracy knew only homeschooling, including the royal family. In modern times, the laws protect the rights of families to keep their children home for instruction, as Gabb explains. In fact, the United Kingdom probably has the most liberal laws on school attendance, giving homeschoolers there full rights. For example, the 1986 law in Northern Ireland states that "the parent of every child of compulsory school age shall cause him to receive efficient full-time education suitable to his [her] age, ability, and aptitude, and to any special education needs he may have, *either by regular attendance or otherwise.*" He also presents the statistics of the homeschooling population in the United Kingdom, no easy task, given that parents are not required to report to any official authority: about 84,000 homeschoolers is one good guess.

Finally, in Chapter 14, Tom Burkard and Dennis O'Keeffe examine the primary force preserving the failing public system of education: compulsory education. They make the salient point in this volume: were it not for compulsory attendance laws, "home schooling" would not be an issue. Further, even with compulsory education, students cut and skip school (are truant) in rising numbers, testifying to the failure of required attendance policies in the United Kingdom and the United States, as explored in Guare and Cooper's new book, *Truancy Revisited* (2003).

Buckard and O'Keeffe then go on to analyze the key arguments for compulsion (and thus against homeschooling), including the economic rationale: we need schools to build our industrial/commercial systems, to weld our society together (the "melting pot"), to improve social adjustment and cohesion, and to ensure that children do not join cults. It is the same force that has brought the federal government into every U.S. school that talks down the rights of families and communities to educate their own children. Thus, this chapter brings us full circle: from family to society to government to school, and back home again. For as they explain the essential argument: "if compulsory schooling laws were repealed, it would allow for the growth of alternatives which met the needs of students, as opposed to those who have a vested interest in maintaining existing schools."

Tom Buckard and Dennis O'Keeffe's chapter takes a libertarian view, questioning the requirements of compulsory education, the very laws that made U.S. homeschooling families until quite recently lawbreakers. They stand with E. G. West and Murray Rothbard in examining the arguments for required attendance at schools and the unintended results of mixing kids who want to be in school with those who hate it.

Their work on truancy (see Stoffer & O'Keeffe, 1989), along with ours, (see Guare & Cooper, 2003) indicates that despite a web of laws and regulations, students still exert their take-or-leave-it authority by "bunking off," the British term, cutting class, or not attending school at all. (No one has studied the students who are physically present but mentally and spiritually absent, although we do see kids with their heads down, napping in the class—at least they are quiet and nondisruptive; and other students with the glazed over look, barely following the lesson.)

CONCLUSION

My BMW repair man has a profoundly gifted son, to use his term, who freaked out during the first few weeks of public education; now, instead, the boy stays home, studies his own ideas, pursues his own interests, and learns way ahead of his peers, working closely with his parents and friends. An interest in birds led this young ornithologist to engage in long email conversations about new bird species with professors of biology; little did these experts realize that they were conversing professionally over the Internet with a 10-year-old homeschooler.

Another key stimulant for many families to homeschool their children was the conscious removal of religious beliefs and practices from public education: no more prayer, no more Bible study, and no more consideration of the Biblical view of creation (as compared to theories of evolution). This stripping away of religion even has its humorous side. For example, walking down the hall, a public school principal comes upon seven or eight students huddled together against one wall. The principal sticks his head into the crowd, looks, and says, "Oh, it's okay, you're only shooting dice; I thought you might be praying."

For not only are some homeschool families upset by the antireligious tone of many public schools, but the curriculum to many is downright negative toward Bible and religion, and firmly against teaching the Biblical accounts of creation. Why, some parents wonder, can children be required to read *Lord of the Flies* but not the Book of Ruth, one of the greatest Biblical stories of intergenerational loyalty and family life, as two women (in-laws) bond together after the deaths of their husbands. Homeschooling, for some, reinforces the basic human and familial values, bolstering the family just at the time when the vast majority of parents are both working, and children are placed in child-care earlier and longer.

Research shows that homeschool families have more children, breast feed their babies longer, and spend much more time working on educational issues and concerns than regular school families. And homeschooling is taking on international importance as well. For example, in countries like Russia, where Chechans laid waste to a school that led to the death of 330 children, parents are afraid to send their offspring to school. The *Baltimore Sun* ("Terrorized Russians," 2004) published a story about a U.S. private school supplying materials to Russian parents:

> The Calvert Schools, an internationally known supplier of educational materials for parents who teach their children at home, is seeing a surge of online inquiries from families in Russia, where a school in the southern city of Beslan was stormed by militants last month, and elsewhere in Eastern Europe. Its nonprofit home instruction division sells textbooks, lesson plans and other educational materials.

Calvert has received 75 inquiries from Russia—compared with 12 in the past year—11 from Belarus, nine from the Ukraine, two from Uzbekistan, and a handful from Estonia and Latvia. Pat Lines, an expert on homeschooling, says she was not surprised: "Home-schooling has been growing all over the world," Lines continues that: "Whenever people think public education is missing something, they'll turn to another option. Sometimes that's a private school option and sometimes that's a home-schooling option."

REFERENCES

Clark, J., & Newman, J. (1997). *The managerial state.* Thousand Oaks, CA: Sage.

Glenn, C. D. (1988). *The myth of the common school.* Amherst, MA: University of Massachusetts Press.

Guare, R. E., & Cooper, B. S. (2003). *Truancy revisited: Students as school consumers.* Lanham, MD: Scarecrow Education Book.

Stoffer, P., & O'Keeffe, D. (1989). *Officially present: An investigation into post-registration truancy in nine maintained schools.* London: The Education Unit, Institute for Economic Affairs.

Terrorized Russians try Calvert curriculum: Homeschooling's popular after attack by Chechans. (2004, September 24). *Baltimore Sun,* p. 3.

Tyack, D. B. (1974). *The one best system: This history of American urban education.* Cambridge, MA: Harvard University Press.

CHAPTER 1

A HOMESCHOOL RESEARCH STORY

Brian D. Ray

INTRODUCTION

A Dutch education law association devotes its annual meeting in 2004 to the thorny topic. A daily newspaper in the state of Ohio devotes 7 days of articles in November 2004 to investigating the educational movement, concluding, among other things, that an "untold number" of suspicious concepts and activities are associated with it (e.g., Oplinger & Willard, 2004a, 2004b; Willard & Oplinger, 2004). And German families continue to flee to other countries because this schooling choice they have made for their children is outlawed in their nation. Now about 25 years after the modern homeschool movement emerged in the United States, what does research tell the world about this age-old pedagogical practice?

Many people, based on a few experiences or anecdotes, have come to believe that homeschool parents are either move-to-the-country anarchist goat-herders, or right-wing Bible thumpers, and that their children are either mathematically limited, due to mama's fear of math, or child prodigies in rocket science who are unthinkably socially hindered. Although one can find statistical deviants in every group, homeschool research tells

Home Schooling in Full View: A Reader, 1–19
Copyright © 2005 by Information Age Publishing
All rights of reproduction in any form reserved.

1

a different story from the experience-based stereotypes and philosophical biases concerning those involved in home-based education.[1]

BRIEF HISTORY AND DEMOGRAPHICS

Parent-led home-based education is a millennia-old practice. By the late 1970s, however, only about 13,000 grades K-12 students were being homeschooled in the United States (Lines, 1991). The practice of homeschooling was specially rekindled during the 1980s, promoted by individual parents and educational thinkers with a variety of backgrounds in pedagogical philosophies and religious worldviews. Growing at 7% to 12% per annum and with an estimated 1,700,000 to 2,100,000 K-12 students home-educated during the 2002–2003 institutional school year (Ray, 2003; c.f., Princiotta, Bielick, & Chapman, 2004), home-based education is now arguably the fastest growing form of education, compared to public and private institutional schooling.

Although measures of central tendency mask the variety of people involved in homeschooling, the following descriptions give a glimpse of the current homeschool population, especially those in the United States (c.f., Ray's 2005 more comprehensive list):

1. Both parents are actively involved in home-based education, with the mother/homemaker usually as the main academic teacher. Fathers do some of the formal academic teaching of the children and are engaged in other ways in their lives.

2. The learning program is flexible and highly individualized, involving both homemade and purchased curriculum materials.

3. Some families purchase complete curriculum packages for their children, while others approach homeschooling with only a small degree of preplanned structure: this is often called "lifestyle of learning," "relaxed homeschooling," or "unschooling."

4. As a rule, home-educated students have relatively little interaction with state-run schools or their services. A minority participate in public-school interscholastic activities such as sports and music ensembles, and some occasionally take an academic course in local schools or enroll in state-school-controlled distance programs.

5. Children study a wide range of conventional subjects, with an emphasis on reading, writing, math, science, and integrating faith with living.

6. Many students take advantage of the flexibility provided by home education to participate in special studies and events, such as volunteer community work, political internships, travel, missionary excursions, animal husbandry, gardening, and national competitions (e.g., homeschoolers have won the National Spelling Bee a number of times in recent years).

7. Most homeschool children are taught at home for at least 4 to 5 years. Most parents intend to home educate their youths through the high school years, and a high percentage do so.

8. They have larger-than-average families. On average, these families have about three children in the U.S. (over 50% above the U.S. mean), and it is not uncommon for homeschool families to have four to six children.

9. Male and female students are equally represented.

10. A married couple head at least 95% of homeschooling families.

11. The typical homeschooling parent has attended or graduated from college (or university). About half of home educators have earned a bachelor's degree or higher. Significant numbers, however, have only a high school education.

12. The total annual household income is under $25,000 for about 18% of the families; $25,000–49,000 for about 44%; $50,000–74,000 for about 25%, and $75,000 or more for about 13%. This is close to the median (typical) income for American families.

13. In terms of faith, a wide variety (over 75%) of parents and families who homeschool regularly attend religious services. The majority are Christian and place a strong emphasis on orthodox and conservative biblical doctrine. Those other than Christians have always been a part of the modern homeschool movement. Furthermore, an increasing proportion of agnostics, atheists, Buddhists, Jews, Mormons, Muslims, and New Agers are homeschooling their children.

14. In terms of racial/ethnic background, about 85% are white/non-Hispanic, but a rapidly increasing portion of minorities are engaging in home-based education. See chapter 8 of this book for a discussion of African American homeschool families.

HOMESCHOOL STUDENTS' ACADEMIC PERFORMANCE

Since most of the public thinks that schooling is supposed to have something to do with learning to read, write, and do arithmetic and know some basic science and history, researchers have naturally asked, "Does home-schooling work, academically?" Many policy makers, educators, school administrators, and parents wonder whether ordinary mothers and fathers, who are not government-certified teachers, are capable of teaching their children after age five. Is it possible for adults without specialized, university-level training in teaching to help their children learn what they need to learn?

Studies done by dozens of researchers during the past 20 years examined the academic achievement of the home-educated (see reviews, e.g., Ray, 2000b, 2005). Examples of these studies range from a multi-year study in Washington State to three nationwide studies across the United States to two nationwide studies in Canada (Ray, 1994, 1997, 2001c; Rudner, 1999; Van Pelt, 2003; Wartes, 1991). In study after study, the home-schooled have scored, on average, at the 65th to 80th percentile on standardized academic achievement tests in the United States and Canada, compared to the public school average of the 50th percentile.

Researchers, wondering if only certain families—in which the parents have a high educational attainment or family income—are able to home-school such that their children score high on achievement tests, show that children in homeschool families with low income and in which the parents have little education are scoring, on average, above state-school averages (Ray, 2000, 2005, chapter 4). In addition, research shows that whether the parents have ever been certified teachers has little to no relationship to their children's academic achievement; and that the degree of state control of homeschooling (e.g., regulations) has no relationship to academic achievement (Ray, 2005).

Homeschool Students' Social, Emotional, and Psychological Development

Homeschool parents call it the "S question." *Socialization* questions are asked of nearly every homeschool parent and every homeschool teenager. Some of them tire of the questions; others receive them as an opportunity to spread the word about one of their favorite topics. These questions arise mainly in societies in which the institutionalization of children is the norm for children during the ages of 6 to 18.

More specifically, the first part of the S question usually asks if the child will experience healthy social, emotional, and psychological development. Numerous studies, employing various psychological constructs and measures, show the home educated are developing at least as well, and often better than, those who attend institutional schools (Medlin, 2000; Ray, 2005, chapter 4). No research to date contravenes this conclusion.

For example, regarding self-concept in the psychological development of children, several studies have revealed that the self-concept of home-schooled students is significantly higher than that of public school students. As another example, Shyers (1992) found the only significant childhood social-interaction difference between the institutionally schooled and homeschoolers was that the institutionally schooled had higher behavior problem scores. The second question related to socialization is how the homeschooled child will do in the real world.

HOMESCHOOLERS IN THE "REAL WORLD" OF ADULTHOOD

The real world is defined by many as the world of adulthood, in which one is responsible for obtaining one's own food, shelter, and clothing. For some college students, the real world is still 4 years away. Others are already in the real world, because, in addition to taking classes, they work to provide their own food and shelter. To simplify the matter for this article, the real world is defined as life after the secondary-school years.

Linda Montgomery (1989), a principal of a private high school, was one of the first to look to the future and adulthood of the home-educated. She investigated the extent to which homeschooled students were experiencing more conditions that fostered leadership in children and adolescents than students who attended institutional schools. Her findings on 10- to 21-year-olds showed that the home educated were certainly not isolated from social and group activities with other youth and adults. They were quite involved in youth group and other church activities, jobs, sports, summer camps, music lessons, and recitals. She concluded that homeschooling nurtured leadership at least as well as does the conventional system.

Susannah Sheffer (1995) talked with homeschooled adolescent girls moving into adulthood. Sheffer began her report by citing the work of Carol Gilligan and her colleagues in the Harvard Project on Women's Psychology and Girls' Development who, lamenting, "have written about girls 'loss of voice' and increasing distrust of their own perceptions." Sheffer suggested that the great difference in structure and function—the way things work, the relationships people have, expected behaviors, and the roles people play—between homeschooling and conventional schooling may have explained why she found so many of these home-educated adolescents to have not lost their voice and sense of identity. Meredith, a 14-year-old in Sheffer's study, said, "I was worried that I would become a typical teenager if I went to school" and "I think some people would have seen [school] as my opportunity to 'be like everybody else.' But I didn't want to be like everybody else." Sheffer concluded, "Throughout this book the homeschooled girls I've interviewed have echoed these statements. They have talked about trusting themselves, pursuing their own goals, maintaining friendships even when their friends differ from them or disagree with them." Finally, these home-educated girls maintain their self-confidence as they pass into womanhood.

Sheffer's findings regarding adolescent girls might explain some of the successes that other researchers have found, regarding young adults who were homeschooled. In a study that categorized college students as either home, public or private schooled, and examined their aptitude for achievement in college English, Galloway and Sutton (1995) found that homeschooled students demonstrated similar academic preparedness for college and similar academic achievement in college as students who had attended conventional schools. In a similar vein, Oliveira, Watson and Sutton (1994) found that home-educated college students had a slightly higher overall mean critical thinking score than did students from public schools, Christian schools, and ACE (private) schools but the differences were not statistically significant.

Similarly, Jones and Gloeckner (2004) cited three studies (Gray, 1998; Jenkins, 1998; Mexcur, 1993) as showing the home educated to be performing as well or better than institutional-school graduates at the college level. Jones and Gloeckner, in their own study, concluded: "The academic performance analyses indicate that home school graduates are as ready for college as traditional high school graduates and that they perform as well on national college assessment tests as traditional high school graduates" (p. 20).

The ACT and SAT are the best-known tests used as predictors of success in university or college in America. Both the SAT and ACT publishers have descriptively reported for several years that the scores of the homeschooled are higher, on average, than those from public schools (see Chapter 11 by Belfield in this volume on SAT scores). For example, for the 1999–2000 school year, the home educated scored an average of 568 in verbal while the state-school (i.e., public-school) average was 501, and 532 in math while the state-school average was 510 (G. Barber, personal communication, February 20, 2001).

Sutton and Galloway (2000) compared homeschool, public-school, and private-school graduates who were then in college in terms of success (i.e., academic achievement, leadership, professional aptitude, social behavior, and physical activity). There were no significant differences among the three groups in most of the studied variables. Results from multivariate analysis of variance showed, however, that college graduates from homeschooling "held significantly more leadership posts for significantly greater periods of time than did the private school group" while there was no significant difference on these variables between the homeschooled and public-schooled (p. 137).

Although over the past 2 decades some college and university personnel have shown animosity toward the homeschooling process, it appears that most are now interested in welcoming the home educated (e.g., Barnebey, 1986; Home School Legal Defense Association, 2004). A recent survey asked many questions of 34 college admission officers in Ohio, who averaged 10 years of experience in college admission work and of whom 88% had personal experience working with homeschooled students (Ray, 2001b). For example, they were asked how homeschooled students at their institution compared to their general student population in terms of academic success. About 9% said "far more academically successful," 22% reported "somewhat more academically successful," 38% said "academically about average," 0% reported "somewhat less academically successful," 0% said "far less academically successful," and 31% said "don't know." On a five-point, strongly agree–strongly disagree scale, the admission officers were nearly symmetrical in their responses to the statement, "As the primary instructors, parents should be recognized as capable of evaluating their student's academic competence in letters of recommendation" (i.e., 32% agree, 24% neither, and 32% disagree). To the item, "The majority of homeschooled students are at least as socially well adjusted as are public schooled students," 44% agreed or strongly agreed, 35% responded "neither," and 21% disagreed or strongly disagreed. Likewise, Irene Prue's (1997, p. 62) nationwide study of college admission personnel revealed that " homeschoolers are academically, emotionally, and socially prepared to succeed in college."

Several colleges think so well of home-educated students that they have been actively recruiting them for several years (e.g., Biola University, Boston University, Nyack College). Christopher Klicka's (1998, p. 3) survey of college admission officers found a Dartmouth College admission officer saying, "The applications [from homeschoolers] I've come across are outstanding. Homeschoolers have a distinct advantage because of the individualized instruction they have received." This individualized instruction, combined with homeschooled students' experience in studying and pursuing goals on their own, may be showing long-lasting effects. Admission officers at Stanford University think they are seeing an unusually high occurrence of a key ingredient, which they term "intellectual vitality," in homeschool graduates (Foster, 2000). They link it to the practice of self-teaching prevalent in these young people, as a result of their homeschool environment.

Sutton (2002) wrote in Brown University's alumni magazine, "Although the number of homeschoolers applying to college is still small, it represents only the first wave. The next homeschooled generation—the real boom—is just hitting puberty." *The Chronicle of Higher Education* headlined another article, ìHomeschooling: Growing Force in Higher Educationî

(Morgan, 2003). Sixty-two percent of college admission officers agreed îthe homeschool movement is having or will have a significant impact on higher educationî (Ray, 2001a).

A few researchers have examined adults who were home educated without necessarily linking them to the college scene. J. Gary Knowles (Knowles & de Olivares, 1991; Knowles & Muchmore, 1995) was the first to focus research on adults who were home educated, collecting extensive data from a group who were home educated an average of about 6 years before they were 17 years old. He found that they tended to be involved in entrepreneurial and professional occupations, were fiercely independent, and strongly emphasized the importance of family. Furthermore, they were glad they had been home educated, would recommend homeschooling to others, and had no grossly negative perceptions of living in a pluralistic society.

Ray (2004a) recently conducted the largest nationwide study of home-educated adults. The target population was all homeschooled adults in the U.S. Most of his findings were consistent with what Knowles and his colleagues (Knowles & de Olivares, 1991; Knowles & Muchmore, 1995) found. Of 7,306 adults who had been homeschooled participating, 5,254 had been homeschooled for 7 or more years during K-12. This subset of participants had several qualities in common:

1. Their average age was 21.
2. They were homeschooled for an average of 11 years.
3. Regarding the primary method of instruction used during their homeschool years (of nine listed in the survey), 34% selected "more than one of the above" nine methods, 25% chose "traditional textbooks and assignments," and 22% responded "eclectic, directed by parent."
4. A higher percent of them had taken some college courses than the general U.S. population of similar age, and a higher percent of the home-educated already had a baccalaureate.
5. Less homeschoolers (61%) read a newspaper at least once a week than do U.S. adults of similar age (82%).
6. More of the home-educated (98%) read a book in the past six months than did the general population (69%).
7. More of the homeschooled (100%) read one or more magazines on a regular basis than the general population (89%).
8. Seventy-one percent of the homeschooled "participate in any ongoing community service activity" compared to 37% of the general population.

9. With the statement, "politics and government are too complicated to understand," 4% of the home educated agree while 35%
   of the general population agree.

10. For those of age 18 to 24, 76% of the homeschooled voted in the
    past 5 years while 29% of the same-age general population in the
    U.S. voted.

11. Of those ages 18 to 24, 14% of the home-educated participated in
    a protest or boycott during the past 12 months while 7% of the
    general population did so.

In essence and on average, the home educated were very positive about
their homeschool experiences actively involved in their local communities, keeping abreast of current affairs, highly civically engaged, going on
to college at a higher rate than the national average, tolerant of others'
expressing their viewpoints, religiously active, but wide-ranging in their
worldview beliefs, holding worldview beliefs similar to those of their parents, and largely home-educating their own children. The study did, however, include adults who did not fit this profile.

These home-educated adults' degree of community and civic involvement supports some ideas that Patricia Lines, formerly a researcher with
the United States Department of Education, expressed about homeschoolers over a decade earlier (1994). She asked whether homeschooling
parents and their children were withdrawing from the larger public
debate about education and, more generally, from social discourse that
was an integral part of a liberty-loving republic. In a sense, she addressed
whether these children and youth were being prepared to be a significant
part of society. Lines (1994) concluded:

> Although [homeschool parents] have turned their backs on a widespread
> and hallowed practice of sending children to a school located in a particular
> building, adhering to a particular schedule and program, they have not
> turned their backs on the broader social contract as understood at the time
> of the Founding [of the United States].... Like the Anti-federalists, these
> homeschoolers are asserting their historic individual rights so that they may
> form more meaningful bonds with family and community. In doing so, they
> are not abdicating from the American agreement. To the contrary, they are
> affirming it.

The data on the degree of community involvement and civic engagement of adults who were homeschooled are not shocking. After all,
researchers Smith and Sikkink (1999) found that homeschool parents, the
main models for their children, were highly civically engaged. In a survey
examining the rate at which parents were engaged in public civic activities, Smith and Sikkink used data from the 1996 National Household

Education Survey conducted by the U.S. Department of Education, which differentiates between students educated in public, Catholic, non-Catholic church-related, and nonreligious private schools, and homeschool students. Parents were asked about the extent of family involvements in a variety of civic activities. The researchers concluded:

> Far from being privatized and isolated, home schooling families are typically very well networked and quite civically active. The empirical evidence is clear and decisive: private schoolers and home schoolers are considerably more civically involved in the public square than are public schoolers, even when the effects of differences in education, income, and other related factors are removed from the equation. Indeed, we have reason to believe that the organizations and practices involved in private and home schooling, in themselves, tend to foster public participation in civic affairs ... the challenges, responsibilities, and practices that private schooling and home education normally entail for their participants may actually help reinvigorate America's civic culture and the participation of her citizens in the public square.

Findings on homeschoolers in New Mexico (Ray, 2001a) and Ohio (Ray, 2001b) are consistent with those of Smith and Sikkink. The aforementioned recent study of adults who were home educated, therefore, implies that the modeling of their parents with respect to civic activity is having a long-lasting impact on homeschool children and youth.

BUT WHAT DOES ALL THIS TELL US?

Scholars repeatedly find positive or good measurable results (e.g., high academic achievement, positive self-concept, high frequency of voting) associated with homeschooling. Some of these scholars have also, rightfully, pointed out the limitations of their studies. For example, Ray (2000b) wrote: "this is not a causal-comparative study ... background variables in this ex-post-facto study are not controlled in such a way as to make possible conclusions about the causes of academic test scores being higher or lower than those of students in conventional schools" and "one should keep in mind the limitations of representativeness and generalizability" in this study" (p. 81). Rudner (1999), likewise, concluded his report on the high academic achievement of the home-education by writing: "This was not a controlled experiment.... This study does not demonstrate that home schooling is superior to public or private schools.... This study simply shows that those parents choosing to make a commitment to home schooling are able to provide a very successful academic environment" (p. 11).

Welner and Welner (1999), although criticizing Rudner on some matters, agreed with him by writing: "This is not to say that these [homeschool] parents did not do a good job teaching their children; it is only to say that a comparable sample within the public or private schools may have scored just as well" (p. 13).

In other words, the design of most research to date does not allow for the conclusion that homeschooling necessarily causes higher academic achievement than does public (or private) institutional schooling. On the other hand, research designs and findings to date do not refute the hypothesis that homeschooling causes more positive effects than does institutional public (or private) schooling. Along these lines, Ray (2000b), after reviewing many studies on homeschooling and conducting several himself, gingerly wrote: "Assuming, for the sake of discussion and based on a multitude of studies, that home schooling is associated with high academic achievement (and possibly causes it), one could ask whether there is any link between the preceding list of positive factors and the nature of the educational 'treatment' known as home schooling" (p. 92).

Although scholars who have conducted the studies have not claimed that research shows homeschooling causes higher achievement (or healthier social and emotional development), others have attempted to use research to attack obliquely both researchers of and advocates of homeschooling. Typically, the attacks are verbal and not published in writing.[2] One written example was newspaper reporters Oplinger and Willard (2004a, 2004b) using the alleged comments of scholars to claim that in reality little is known about whether homeschooling is associated with positive outcomes. They quoted (2004a) one academic as saying that a researcher who published a study in 1999 "was the first mover on this. Before this, there was no story, basically." If the academic was accurately quoted and presented, then he was blatantly wrong and ignored about 20 years of research and the "story" that preceded the 1999 study. More subtly, Reich wrote in 2001, "recent studies of homeschooled children show that they often outperform their public and private school counterparts in scholastic achievement," and with respect to the child's and the state's "shared interest in academic achievement, homeschools can sometimes be more effective than traditional campus-based schools" (p. 27). More accurately, however, Reich should have written that in virtually every study done the home-educated performed as well and usually better than those in public schools. Later Reich (2003) hedged on what he wrote earlier and claimed that no, or close to no, dependable research findings support the proposition that homeschool students outperform their peers in institutional public schools in terms of academic achievement.

Here, then, is a summary to this point. The body of research to date is clear that homeschooling is associated with positive or desirable outcomes that researchers have measured (i.e., academic achievement, social and emotional development, civic involvement). The research to date, by its design, does not substantiate a causal link between homeschooling and these positive results. Nevertheless, some researchers and journalists insinuate that little is really known about homeschooling's effects or that there are probably some serious deleterious effects on the home educated and society that no one has revealed via research on homeschooling.

It is true that the designs of studies to date leave room for theorizing about why positive things are associated with home-based education. Exploration should be done, however, regarding the pall that some attempt to cast on research on homeschooling and on homeschooling itself. After many years of research and following the homeschool movement, this author infers that most of the negative casting emerges from a couple of springs. One spring is philosophical, political, and religious theorizing based on various worldviews that are prostatism, pro-Marxism, procommunitarianism, or prohumanism and generally antilibertarian and antitheistic (i.e., against those holding orthodox or traditional understandings of Christianity, Judaism, or Islam) with respect to parental jurisdiction, responsibility, and authority regarding the education of children (in its broadest sense). The second spring is the propagation of a covey of logical fallacies.

From the first spring of philosophy and worldview, several academics have claimed that (a) homeschool parents are selfish for home educating their children (Apple, 2000; Lubienski, 2000), (b) homeschool parents are antistate (Apple, 2000), (c) homeschool parents and their children are removing themselves from basic and essential participation in the democratic processes of the U.S. republic and they neglect social responsibilities (Lubienski, 2000; Reich, 2002), and (d) the home educated will be socially isolated and likely not learn to be decent, civil and respectful and to work and live well with others from diverse backgrounds (Apple, 2000; Evans, 2003; Reich, 2002). These scholars, however, neither clearly define terms such as *antistate* or *civil* nor offer any empirical evidence that these claims are true. Research findings have, in fact, contradicted their claims.

For example, to date almost a dozen investigations address home-educated adults and show that the home educated are more highly involved in community life, civic activities, democratic processes, and exhibiting leadership traits and are decent, civil, and respectful (references provided earlier). This is not to say, of course, that every homeschool graduate is brilliant, attractive, and destined for success. It simply means that, on average, they appear to be doing well in the real world of adulthood because the environment in which they were educated—in the broad sense, academically, mentally, morally, civically, and aesthetically—apparently gave them sound academic skills, a solid and confident social and emotional nurturance, respect for others, a stable worldview, and a zest for learning.

Another example has to do with the claim that homeschoolers are self-ish. Some argue that homeschoolers reap the benefit of free public education but are unwilling to bear their share of the cost by sending their own children to school (read Lubienski, 2000 for more detail). It *is* true that homeschoolers avoid some inconvenience or ill effects to their own children by not putting them in public schools, but it *is not* true that this creates extra costs for others; in fact, it reduces them, because children who are not in tax-funded schools make fewer demands on public resources, thereby freeing up resources to meet other children's, or other persons', needs. [3]

The second spring provides four logical fallacies that regularly surface in discussions about homeschooling. First is the argument from ignorance (a.k.a., proof by lack of evidence), that is, the mistaken assumption that a claim is true because there is no proof that it is false. Oplinger and Willard's (2004) articles hold many examples of this erroneous thinking. Others imply that if research based on experimental designs does not exist, then there is likely something negative associated with homeschooling. When Lubienski (2000) claimed that homeschooling is "a flight from the public production of values" (p. 228) and Reich (2002, p. 58) suggested that the homeschooled would not become civil, decent, and respectful after research (e.g., Galloway & Sutton, 1999; Knowles & de Olivares, 1991; Knowles & Muchmore, 1995; Lines, 1994, 2000; Montgomery, 1989; Ray, 2001a, 2001b; Romm, 1993; Sikkink, 2001; Smith & Sikkink, 1999; Sutton & Galloway, 2000; Welner, 1999) had already been published that contradicted, if anything, their assertions, then they were either arguing from ignorance, ignoring research, or behaving in an anti-research fashion.

Academics such as Apple (2000), Evans (2003), Lubienski (2000), and Reich (2002) have chosen to ignore research on educational constructs such as academic achievement while making debatable philosophical arguments and claims that the production of social values (in other words, the values, beliefs, and worldview of individual students who comprise a society) and development of civility (while not clearly defining this term) should be controlled more by the state and the gatekeepers and influencers (teachers, peers, and entire curriculum) in state-run (public) institutional schools. Nor have these critics of homeschooling offered empirical evidence to support their philosophical arguments.

A corollary to the argument from ignorance is an attempt to put the burden of proof on parents and children who practice homeschooling, or on researchers who study homeschooling and find positive things associated with it. In other words, these two categories of persons are expected, since they practice or study a minority pedagogical approach, to offer more-than-adequate empirical evidence that what they do or study causes effects (e.g., high achievement, healthy psychological development, high civic engagement, decent and civil persons) that are as good or better than the effects associated with public institutional schooling. This author has not seen anyone publicly provide (e.g., in articles, books, courts, legislatures) a rationale for this attempt of placing of the burden of proof on those who practice or study homeschooling.

The is/ought fallacy—the mistaken belief that something should exist solely because it does exist—is the second fallacy implied or used. The unstated thinking goes something like this: the United States is a pretty good place, most children and youth attended state-controlled schools in which government-licensed persons teach during the past several decades, and most attend public schools today, so state control of children's education must be the best way to ensure that the people are properly educated. This author has heard adults say it something like this: "Well, I went to public schools and I turned out okay ... didn't I?" This fallacious thinking begs a lot of questions and ignores both important philosophical discussions and fact-based evidence. For example, what convincing evidence is there that state-run institutional schools have reduced poverty, racism, crime, use of harmful illegal drugs, births out of wedlock, or discrimination or have increased decency, civility, respect, harmony, peace, or joy in America over the past 100 years? Or, why would a people that values free-thinking, freedom, and democratic republicanism want a majority, or any, of its citizens spending large portions of their days in state-controlled institutions of teaching, training, and indoctrination rather than in ones that are controlled by free association, choice in how to spend money, and charity amongst community members?

The third fallacy is poisoning the well and its corollary, sweetening the well. Scholars and journalists often imply or catalyze the rejection of the findings or ideas of homeschool researchers or advocates of homeschooling solely because of the researcher's or advocate's circumstances or position in life. For example, reporting that a researcher who has found positive things associated with homeschooling is a homeschool father but not reporting that a critic of homeschooling is a former public-school teacher, a man who is past-president of a public-school teachers' union, a professor in a school of education that makes its money by training public-school teachers, and an employee who is paid by taxpayers' money at a state university (e.g., Oplinger & Willard, 2004a; Willard & Oplinger, 2004b) are poisoning and sweetening wells.

Another example is reporting that one study with positive findings about homeschooling was largely funded by a homeschool organization but not reporting that another study with positive findings was conducted by a researcher who is a veteran public-school counselor (e.g., Stevens, 2001, p. 13). A third example is Belfield (2004) writing "[t]here may also be issues of publication bias: many studies are reported in sympathetic journals" while not noting that the vast majority of education journals and those who publish in them have clear financial and other vested interests in tax-funded public schooling.

Innuendo—an oblique allusion, veiled or equivocal reflection on character or reputation, or a propaganda technique that uses subtle and misleading language to manipulate minds—is a fourth fallacy that is employed by antihomeschool scholars and writers. For example, Apple (2000, p. 262) linked homeschoolers with "cocooning" with getting away from "the Other" with segregation by race with desires for "purity," while never explicitly claiming that racism or bigotry are involved in the motives and behaviors of homeschoolers. Another example was Reich (2002) claiming the potential "peril" of homeschooling customizing a child's education "down to the tiniest degree" and insinuating that this would not "cultivate democratic citizenship" (p. 59), while neither philosophically nor empirically exploring the degree to which a state-run education may customize a child's education "down to the tiniest degree" and whether public schooling in fact cultivates democratic citizenship any more than do private schooling or homeschooling.

NOT AN EPHEMERAL FAD

Parent-led home-based education is growing and will continue to grow around the world (Ray, 2005). For example, based on current information and rates of growth, there may be 3 million homeschool students in grade levels kindergarten through 12 in the United States by 2010 (Ray, 2004a, 2004b). Researchers and educators find that homeschooling lends itself, systemically, to several practices found to be desirable in classroom schooling. Many philosophers, sociologists, and historians find homeschooling to have beneficial influences on children, families, and societies. To date, the body of empirical research on homeschooling repeatedly reveals, typically and on average, positive things associated with homeschooling.

Practically no research has found negative effects associated with homeschooling. Regardless of the lack of actual negative findings, however, some scholars and others continue philosophical and theoretical arguments against parent-led home-based education without offering empirical premises for their claims and assertions.

Many researchers have called for more methodologically rigorous causal-comparative and statistical empirical studies. If they are conducted and show any negative findings or a tempering of the degree of positive findings, it will be of interest to see how advocates of homeschooling respond. If such studies are conducted and continue to show positive findings related to parent-led home-based education, it will be fascinating to see whether it quiets the critics of homeschooling and research on homeschooling or simply motivates them to metamorphose their philosophical and political objections into new forms and directions.

NOTES

1. This synoptic review of research is based on the author's in-depth and long-term tracking of research on homeschooling. The reader who would like to access more of the primary sources on which the author relies might consult the following documents: McDowell & Ray (2000), Medlin (2000), Ray (2000a, 2000b, 2004, 2004b), and Rudner (1999).

2. The author can only substantiate this claim by his experience listening to and reading radio, television, and print-media interviews and not being able to locate many published attacks during his approximately 22 years of following discussions and debates about homeschooling.

3. The author thanks Charles L. Howell, PhD, of Minnesota State University at Moorehead, for his help at this point in this chapters.

REFERENCES

Apple, M. W. (2000). The cultural politics of home schooling. *Peabody Journal of Education*, 75(1 & 2), 256-271.

Barnebey, L. F. (1986). American university admission requirements for home schooled applicants, in 1984. *Dissertation Abstracts International*, 47(3), 798A.

Belfield, C. R. (2004, January). *Home-schooling in the U.S.* Occasional Paper No. 88 from the National Center for the Study of Privatization in Education Teachers College, Columbia University. New York: National Center for the Study of Privatization in Education Teachers College, Columbia University. Retrieved January 23, 2004, from http://www.ncspe.org/readrel.php?set= pub&cat=90

Evans, D. L. (2003, September 2). *Home is no place for school*. Retrieved September 3, 2003, from http://www.usatoday.com/news/opinion/editorials/2003-09-02-opposee x.htm

Foster, C. (2000, November/December). In a class by themselves. *Stanford Magazine*. Retrieved December 4, 2000, from http://www.stanfordalumni.org/jg/mig/news_magazine/magazine/novdec00/articles/homeschooling.html

Galloway, R. A., & Sutton, J. P. (1995). Home schooled and conventionally schooled high school graduates: A comparison of aptitude for and achievement in college English. *Home School Researcher*, 11(1), 1-9.

Galloway, R. S., & Sutton, J. P. (1999). Are adults who were home educated experiencing success in their adulthood? *Private School Monitor, 20*(3), 4-6.

Gray, D. W. (1998). A study of the academic achievement of homeschooled students who have matriculated into post-secondary institutions. *Dissertation Abstracts International, 59,* 021.

Home School Legal Defense Association. (2004). *Rating colleges & universities by their homeschool admission policies.* Retrieved May 28, 2004, from http://hslda.org/docs/nche/000002/00000241.asp

Jenkins, T. P. (1998). *The performance of home schooled students in community colleges.* Unpublished doctoral dissertation, Texas A & M University-Commerce.

Jones, P., & Gloeckner, G. (2004, Spring). A study of home school graduates and traditional school graduates. *The Journal of College Admission, 183,* 17-20.

Klicka, C. J. (1998). *Homeschool students excel in college (special report).* Purcellville, VA: Home School Legal Defense Association.

Knowles, J. G., & de Olivares, K. (1991, April). *"Now we are adults": Attitudes, beliefs, and status of adults who were home-educated as children.* Paper presented at the Annual Meeting of the American Educational Research Association, Chicago, IL.

Knowles, J. G., & Muchmore, J. A. (1995). Yep! We're grown-up home-school kids—and we're doing just fine, thank you. *Journal of Research on Christian Education, 4*(1), 35-56.

Lines, P. M. (1991, October). *Estimating the home schooled population* (working paper OR 91-537). Washington DC: Office of Educational Research and Improvement, U.S. Department of Education.

Lines, P. M. (1994, February). Homeschooling: Private choices and public obligations. *Home School Researcher, 10*(3), 9-26.

Lines, P. M. (2000, Summer). Homeschooling comes of age. *The Public Interest, 140,* 74-85.

Lubienski, C. (2000). Whither the common good?: A critique of home schooling. *Peabody Journal of Education, 75*(1 & 2), 207-232.

McDowell, S. A., & Ray, B. D. (Eds.). (2000). The home education movement in context, practice, and theory: Editors' introduction [Special double issue]. *Peabody Journal of Education, 75*(1 & 2), 1-7.

Medlin, R. G. (2000). Home schooling and the question of socialization. *Peabody Journal of Education, 75*(1 & 2), 107-123.

Mexcur, D. (1993). *A comparison of academic performance among public school graduates, conventional Christian school graduates, accelerated Christian school graduates, and home school graduates in three Christian colleges.* Unpublished doctoral dissertation, Bob Jones University, Greenville, SC.

Montgomery, L. R. (1989). The effect of home schooling on the leadership skills of home schooled students. *Home School Researcher, 5*(1), 1-10.

Morgan, R.. (2003, January 17). Homeschooling: Growing force in higher education. *Chronicle of Higher Education.* Retrieved May 5, 2004, from http://hslda.org/docs/news/hslda/200301/200301161.asp

Oliveira, P. C. M. de, Watson, T. G., & Sutton, J. P. (1994). Differences in critical thinking skills among students educated in public schools, Christian schools, and home schools. *Home School Researcher, 10*(4), 1-8.

Oplinger, D., & Willard, D. J. (2004a, November 15). Claims of academic success rely on anecdotes, flawed data analysis. *Akron Beacon Journal*. Retrieved November 17, 2004, from http://www.ohio.com/mld/ohio/news/special_packages/home_schooling/10185099.htm

Oplinger, D., & Willard, D. J. (2004b, November 16). Socialization study inaccurately promoted, researcher says. *Akron Beacon Journal*. Retrieved November 11, 2004, from http://www.ohio.com/mld/beaconjournal/news/local/10193424.htm

Princiotta, D., Bielick, S., & Chapman, C. (2004, July). *1.1 million homeschooled students in the United States in 2003* [NCES 2004–115]. Washington, DC: U.S. Department of Education, Institute of Education Sciences.

Prue, I. M. (1997). *A nation-wide survey of admissions personnel's knowledge, attitudes, and experiences with home schooled applicants*. Unpublished doctoral dissertation, University of Georgia, Athens.

Ray, B. D. (1994). *A nationwide study of home education in Canada: Family characteristics, student achievement, and other topics*. Salem, OR: National Education Research Institute, www.nheri.org

Ray, B. D. (1997). *Strengths of their own—Home schoolers across America: Academic achievement, family characteristics, and longitudinal traits*. Salem, OR: National Home Education Research Institute, www.nheri.org

Ray, B. D. (2000a). Home schooling for individuals' gain and society's common good. *Peabody Journal of Education, 75*(1 & 2), 272-293.

Ray, B. D. (2000b). Home schooling: The ameliorator of negative influences on learning? *Peabody Journal of Education, 75*(1 & 2), 71-106.

Ray, B. D. (2001a). *Home education in New Mexico: Family characteristics, academic achievement, and social and civic activities*. Salem, OR: National Home Education Research Institute, www.nheri.org

Ray, B. D. (2001b). *Home education in Ohio: Family characteristics, academic achievement, social and civic activities, and college admissions officers' thoughts*. Salem, OR: National Home Education Research Institute, www.nheri.org

Ray, B. D. (2001c). Homeschooling in Canada. *Education Canada, 41*(1), 28-31.

Ray, B. D. (2003, February). *Facts on homeschooling*. Retrieved May 5, 2004, from http://www.nheri.org/modules.php?name=Content&pa=showpage&pid=21

Ray, B. D. (2005). *Home centered learning annotated bibliography*. Salem, OR: National Home Education Research Institute, www.nheri.org

Ray, B. D. (2004a). *Home educated and now adults: Their community and civic involvement, views about homeschooling, and other traits*. Salem, OR: National Home Education Research Institute www.nheri.org

Ray, B. D. (2004b, Fall). Homeschoolers on to college: What research shows us. *Journal of College Admission, 185*, 5-11.

Ray, B. D. (2005). *Worldwide guide to homeschooling, 2005-2006*. Nashville, TN: Broadman & Holman.

Reich, R. (2001, August 30-September 2). *Testing the boundaries of parental authority over education: The case of homeschooling*. Paper prepared for delivery at the meeting of the American Political Science Association, San Francisco.

Reich, R. (2002). The civic perils of homeschooling. *Educational Leadership, 59*(7), 56-59.

Reich, R. (2003, April 21-25). Comments made on the panel discussion titled "Home Schooling: The Ultimate in Educational Quality Accountability?" at the Annual Meeting of the American Educational Research Association, Chicago, Illinois.

Romm, T. (1993). *Home schooling and the transmission of civic culture*. Unpublished doctoral (EdD) dissertation, Clark Atlanta University, Atlanta, GA.

Rudner, L. M. (1999). Scholastic achievement and demographic characteristics of homeschool students in 1998. *Educational Policy Analysis Archives, 7*(8). Retrieved August 14, 2003, August 2, 2001, & April 4, 2000 & earlier, from http://epaa.asu.edu/epaa/v7n8

Sheffer, S. (1995). *A sense of self: Listening to homeschooled adolescent girls*. Portsmouth, NH: Boynton/Cook, Heinemann.

Shyers, L. E. (1992). A comparison of social adjustment between home and traditionally schooled students. *Home School Researcher, 8*(3), 1-8.

Sikkink, D. H. (2001, April 10-14). *The shape of homeschoolers' political action*. Paper presented at the Annual Meeting of the American Educational Research Association, Seattle, WA.

Smith, C., & Sikkink, D. (1999, April). Is private schooling privatizing? *First Things, 92*, 16-20. Retrieved July 31, 2000, from http://www.firstthings.com/ftissues/ft9904/articles/smith.html

Stevens, M. L. (2001). *Kingdom of children: Culture and controversy in the homeschooling movement*. Princeton, NJ: Princeton University Press.

Sutton, J. (2002, January/February). *Homeschooling comes of age*. Retrieved May 28, 2004, from http://www.brownalumnimagazine.com/storyDetail.cfm?ID=672

Sutton, J. P., & Galloway, R. (2000). College success of students from three high school settings. *Journal of Research and Development in Education, 33*(3), 137-146.

Van Pelt, D. (2003). *Home education in Canada: A report on the pan-Canadian study on home education 2003*. Medicine Hat, Alberta: Canadian Centre for Home Education.

Wartes, J. (1991, December). *Five years of homeschool testing within Washington State*. (Available from the Washington Homeschool Research Project at 16109 N. E. 169 Pl., Woodinville, WA, 98072).

Welner, K. M. (1999. April 19-23). *Homeschooling and democracy: Exploring the tension between the state and parents* (working draft). Paper presented on at the Annual Meeting of the American Educational Research Association, Montreal, Quebec, Canada.

Welner, K. M., & K. G. (1999). Contextualizing homeschooling data: A response to Rudner. *Education Policy Analysis Archives, 7*(13). Retieved April 13, 2000, from http://epaa.asu.edu/epaa/v7n13.html

Willard, D. J., & Oplinger, D. (2004, November 16). *Parents want to control influences; Critics see need for wide exposure*. Retrieved November 17, 2004, from http://www.ohio.com/mld/ohio/news/special_packages/home_schooling/10193415.htm

CHAPTER 2

HOMESCHOOLING AND THE COMMON SCHOOL NIGHTMARE

Donald A. Erickson

Homeschooling parents are sometimes depicted as selfish and withdrawn, preoccupied with their insular world. They withhold their young, and probably their moral support, from the famously beneficial common school, the place where, according to Levin and Belfield (2003, p. 136), children get the common experience that prepares them for civic responsibilities and cohesion. Levin and Belfield provide an impressive analysis, from one point of view, of the common school's citizenship-building functions, and of what the public and private sectors in general can contribute. I discuss in this chapter a quite different view—especially of what homeschooling offers.

Levin and Belfield discuss evidence that "private schools produce more community service, civic skills, civic confidence, political knowledge, and political tolerance than public schools." How can that happen if the common (public) school is the major source of those qualities, and if private agencies are, almost by definition in the minds of some people, neglectful of public needs?

Could a firm sense of personal identity, developed through private schools, homeschooling, and other expressions of specialness, be more conducive to good citizenship than common experiences in the current public school? Don't we best participate in mass society via institutions small in scale, close at hand, and cohesive in outlook—structures that mediate between the otherwise isolated individual and big government (Berger & Neuhaus, 1977)?

It is erroneous, furthermore, to depict homeschooling as dismissal of schools, of their beneficial functions, and of the public forum itself. We know that homeschoolers are extensively involved in the political sphere (Belz, 1997). Many youngsters identified as homeschoolers are enrolled full-time in public or private schools while learning a lot, systematically, elsewhere; and their parents interact constructively with professionals in those schools, according to several reports, including an excellent one by Patricia M. Lines (2003). Many purported homeschoolers are enrolled in schools part-time, in similarly interactive arrangements. Some get very little of their academic instruction at home. An unknown number of homeschoolers pursue studies mostly or exclusively at home, but *their* parents, especially, contribute to the common good. Even more than other homeschoolers, they are proactive in the education of their children, resuscitating parenthood while death rattles in its throat. Homeschooling provides instructional differentiation that is taboo in many public schools, and that is often impossible within the physical confines of schools of any type.

HOMESCHOOLING AND STULTIFICATION

The best way to learn differs from learner to learner, including kids who are hyperactive in classrooms but learn just fine at home, graduate students, and bankers.

Why bankers? Because for instance, Bankers Trust (BT), a huge international company, lost woefully on investments called derivatives in the early 1990s because its traders were inadequately prepared (Rothfeder, 1998). So BT developed high-quality lectures and videos, plus a thick manual, and ordered many of its bright young traders to get busy and learn. Almost all of them got bored and dropped out.

When youngsters flunk or drop out, most educators try to improve school strategies—demanding that all teachers be fully certified, "diversifying" classrooms, cutting class size, testing better and oftener, trying to make instruction more "constructivist," and so forth. BT, not hung up on schooling, developed a computerized game called *Straight Shooter!* in which "derivatives traders travel in cyberspace from New York to London to Hong Kong, navigating around … bulls and bears in New York, were-wolves in London, and tigers in Hong Kong." When the beasties attack with question-rockets, traders blast back with answer-missiles from cell phones. When the missiles are accurate, the player scores points. A player whose answers are inaccurate hears "Go back to business school!" or something even worse.

The game, unlike the fancy lectures, worked remarkably well. Would similar games work with many ghetto kids who go berserk in classrooms? Electronic games are not a general-purpose solution to educational problems, but classrooms are not either.

I doubt that many homeschoolers are aware of Philip Jackson's (1968) study of the abnormal nature (often abhorrent nature, I would say) of the classroom, but many homeschool parents act as if they are. Homeschoolers in general reject the assumption (maybe I should say, religious doctrine) that the classroom is the divinely ordained setting for acquiring understandings and skills. The insistence of homeschoolers on the right to pick and choose from a wider smorgasbord of educational resources may help de-stultify American education.

Stultification is particularly evident in classrooms where the train wreck called "de-tracking" sprawls. De-tracking places fast and slow learners (and often cooperative and rebellious learners) in the same classrooms (not different classrooms, as tracking would do), on the assumption that all children have substantially the same capacity and willingness to learn, and thus will be equally successful academically if we give the same challenging, accelerated instruction to them all.

Evidence that basic intelligence is not entirely set into concrete at birth is interpreted by de-trackers to mean that intelligence is infinitely and readily malleable, or something close to that, if society just stops being wicked—so if youngsters differ in intelligence when they enter the common school, educators must rectify the unfairness. Since that interpretation does not survive much analysis, a frequent solution is the sleight-of-hand known as "multiple intelligences theory" (MI) (Gardner, 1983). What MI does, essentially, is obscure the fact that the general factor (g) of intelligence in mountains of research not only differs greatly among humans but has formidable consequences in many spheres of life with a cognitive thrust (Jensen, 1998). The truth is obscured by attaching the moniker "intelligence," and by implication the label of "g-factor intelligence," to many human abilities that plainly are not g-factor intelligence, such as musical talent, facility at visualizing spatial relationships, and social skill—so all youngsters can be regarded as gifted cognitively. With similar logic, you could note that both spades and fiddles make noises and are manipulated by hands, you could call them both violins, and you could conclude that diggers, if treated fairly, would render Bach partitas with consummate skill.

When academic failure is blamed on tracking and other presumed oppression, failing students acquire a great excuse—often called victimism—for not trying; and many of the rest of us suffer what Paul Johnson (1998) calls that corrosive vice of the civil world during the twentieth century—guilt. Johnson means that minds can corrode into confusion—the de-tracking murk, for instance—when people are reproached for social woes they cannot totally cure (students who cannot keep up with classmates, for instance).

The same claim to being discriminated against can be used to justify students who disrupt classrooms and prevent classmates from learning. In an article coauthored with Amy Stuart Wells (Wells & Oakes, 1996), my UCLA colleague Jeannie Oakes, probably the most famous advocate of de-tracking, is on written record praising classroom rebellion as a heartening sign that disadvantaged kids not only recognize classroom oppression but refuse to go along with it. It is great that they rebel, according to Oakes, and if nasty, unfair parents would just get lost, people like her would make schools morally "good." (Oakes may mean well, but her comments are reminiscent of the anti-parental prattle of policy elites, described later, during the twentieth century's first half.) In de-tracked classrooms I have seen, many earnest kids cannot learn because they must sit beside half-stoned gangsters on the prowl, many fast learners are so bored by slow instruction that they drop out (as I did for more than 6 years), and many students fail who might have done well under the right circumstances.

Kids who relish video games for amusement, but go berserk in classrooms, might also do well with video games for learning. I wonder how many youngsters who are academic flops would flourish if we switched our imaginations on and our taboos (like de-tracking) off. When students rebel and disrupt in a conventional classroom, we should try something else, greatly different if necessary. If nothing works, we should consider removing youngsters from the usual academic settings and getting their attention in some other positive enterprise, on the understanding that plugging back into academics is permissible whenever people mellowed by age are ready to take their studies (in whatever form) seriously.

By adopting unusual educational methods and producing superior results in the process, homeschoolers may inspire rebellion in fed-up citizens. Take the saga of Blair Hornstine, which got front-page treatment in newspapers coast-to-coast in May, 2003. In her final year at Moorestown High School (a "National School of Excellence" in New Jersey), Blair was stricken with fatigue so severe her doctor ordered her to stay home and rest half of every school day. Perhaps she had worked too hard as captain of the school's moot-court team; or cofounding a program that gave needy people 30,000 pounds of food; or raising money to provide 10 cleft-palate Chinese orphans with corrective surgery; or becoming a National Merit Scholar, Toyota Community Scholar, and Coca-Cola scholar.

Worried that Blair might lose out academically, her parents hired tutors to lead her through courses at home whenever she had enough energy. With that homeschooling arrangement, she polished off the courses, qualified to be valedictorian of her graduating class, and was accepted for admission by top universities.

Realizing how undereducated many U.S. students of robust health appear in international comparisons, Moorestown High administrators mounted a plaque inside the school's main entrance, to commemorate Blair's accomplishments. The student body president, quivering with emotion over the public address system, said he hoped Blair's example would inspire her peers to control their hormones and take their studies seriously. If more moms and dads followed the example of the Hornstine family, the mayor declaimed on TV, city schools would suffer less bullying, gang activity, violence, drug addiction, and teen-age pregnancy. Grateful citizens tossed flowers on the Hornstine lawn, cheered, and sent congratulatory e-mails.

Just kidding. Moorestown High administrators, moaning that Blair had "unfair advantages" (tutors some families could ill afford, instead of the same educational treatment as everyone else), demoted her from valedictorian to co-valedictorian. Townspeople bombarded the Hornstine residence with eggs and insulting phone calls.

The high school's administrators apparently wondered whether they had botched something when their action against Blair was reversed in court. Their biggest blunder was to advertise that being deprived of much instruction in a renowned high school does not transform top students into academic dwarfs, and that tailoring educational opportunities to fit individual needs can do a lot of good. I wonder how many parents from coast to coast were prompted by this incident, or even by homeschooling neighbors, to provide their young with tutoring and other instructional advantages never before considered, or even to pull their offspring out of wasted sessions in schools to master musical instruments, pursue naturalist interests, do compassionate community work, and a lot more.

WRESTING POWER FROM PARENTS

I think the American public was tragically ill-advised, in the eighteenth and nineteenth centuries, to agree that the common school, soon defined clearly as a government thing, would assume major responsibility for turning children into good citizens, for government thought molding has prostituted the dream, turning it into the nightmare we face today. The common school movement has weakened parenthood for more than a century, now threatens to obliterate it, and has done huge damage to youth and our future.

In the Colonial Era, before citizens ratified the common school dream, the nation had an astonishing variety of educational arrangements, according to James Carper (2001), including early versions of home-schooling; town schools of different types; "dame schools—where women taught reading skills in their homes for a small fee; ... private venture schools of New England; ... various denominational, charity, and pay schools of the Middle Colonies; ... missionary efforts in the South [by the Society for the Propagation of the Gospel in Foreign Parts]; [and] ... academies that appeared throughout the provinces." There was no consistent distinction between public and private. Educational institutions as a whole, including denominational ones, relied on public and private sources of funding. Sometimes parents were charged fees and sometimes not. Though rarely compelled in practice, attendance was virtually universal in some areas. No state departments of education or city-wide boards of education dictated how children must be taught.

Some economists and historians think we gained substantially nothing, and may have lost a great deal, by insisting later that public schools, and only public schools, be supported by taxation, that all youngsters be compelled to attend schools during a specified age span, and that government be empowered to determine what would be inserted into student heads (and in what manner) (West, 1965; MacDonald, 2004). MacDonald thinks, considering the quality of public dialog at the time, that a higher proportion of American citizens probably were more literate then than now.

Since no system is perfect, why abandon one that seemed to work so well? In the explanation and comment that follows, I draw primarily on Tyack (1974) and Tyack and Cuban (1995), with whom I disagree now and then. Their biggest flaw is neglect of parenthood. Citizens who ratified the common school proposal were reacting, Tyack (1974) explains, to threats to the fabric of society, the authority of the state; mobs and violence; corruption and radical ideas in politics; vice and immorality as village constraints broke down; immigrants who refused to become assimilated; conflict between labor and capital; and highly visible crime, poverty, and disease (p. 34). Horace Mann, often called the father of public education, warned audiences of the social hell that lay before them if they did not achieve salvation through the common school (Tyack & Cuban, 1995, p. 57).

A huge immigration of impoverished Irish with a scary religion (Catholicism) and a propensity for illegal activity alarmed the Protestant U.S. majority, who had hoped America would become their nifty version of God's kingdom. Major political thinkers feared that alien ideas from Europe would doom the great American experiment unless something perdurable, like the public school, sold democratic principles to each new generation.

Some citizens may have approved the common school idea in the hope, Carper suggests, that young people would thereby get a better shot at economic success. Many may have regarded the common school, in its initial local form, not as an agency of distant government, which hordes in this nation feared because of experiences in Europe, but as an extension of the family, much like any local private school. In this view, it probably did not seem dangerous to set up a legal framework in which the state would dictate, but presumably only pro forma, what and how all children must be taught, for the people making that determination, for all practical purpose, would be the local good guys, whom we could easily control. State departments of education, when first introduced, had only one or two people in their offices, so apparently did not terrify the general public.

As in much human history, power handed to good guys in government, so they would do the things we liked, eventually fell into the grasp of bad guys, who did what we feared and despised. The destruction of public school localism, among other developments, wrested power over the education of the young from parents, thus triggering much trouble, including warfare on parenthood itself. Between 1852 and 1918, every state began to require all children to attend a public school (or some school defined, in various ambiguous ways, as similar or equivalent). More and more tax money was extracted from citizens to support the common school dream.

There are radically different, constantly changing conceptions of the common school dream, and especially of the kind of citizen the common school should manufacture. But since government determines which conception is the right one, government by consent of the governed turns out to be government by consent that government itself grafts into youthful craniums (see comments on this point long ago, by estimable legal scholar Alexander Meikeljohn, in Arons, 1983).

Tyack and Cuban describe the common school dream as repeatedly "renegotiated." On the contrary, the dream has been repeatedly distorted and redistorted with little regard for what ordinary citizens think, and often in blatant contempt of them.

Power was wrested from parents largely through the installation, during a lengthy period, of a system of school governance foreign to what citizens originally agreed upon. Since the period was indeed lengthy, and since citizens plopped into graves in neat actuarial sequence along the way, only historians and their loyal readers had enough perspective to realize what was happening. Otherwise there might have been a reaction far more widespread than the parental choice movement, and much earlier. I also think the reaction would have been earlier and more severe if public school classrooms had been sufficiently open to scrutiny by scholars and common citizens. And if scholars who did observe classrooms and corridors had peered around with open minds (you can see a lot by looking, as Yogi Berra says), rather than gathering prespecified bits and pieces of information known as "variables"—grist for number crunching. I have often concluded, when visiting classrooms, that much professional education literature does not describe that world at all.

According to Tyack and Cuban, citizens thought they were getting schools dependably responsive to local preferences; and accordingly, they got, but just initially, a congeries of village schools, even in big cities. Even after it became legally clear that states had ultimate (plenary) authority over public schools, the practical powerlessness of state departments of education left virtually all operational authority in the hands of local school boards, and in many cities, in the hands of many sub-boards (or "ward boards") in various neighborhoods. The boards and sub-boards, furthermore, were generally large, providing many ears bendable by local men and women, and had jurisdiction over geographic areas so small and sensitively arranged (much like villages) as to comprise, in the majority of cases, communities of considerable agreement, so boards and educators could identify what the local majority wanted. School superintendents, when they first appeared on the scene, were little more than clerks to school boards and subboards.

The movement called "scientific management" insisted that all organizations, public and private, should be run by administrators acquainted with scientific findings, not by yahoos exercising what passed as common sense (Ravitch, 2000; Lagemann, 2000). The reform movement called "progressivism" similarly demanded that public agencies, especially, be rescued from local wheeling-and-dealing, and be entrusted to professionals operating under the distinctly limited guidance of selective board members. Later, the spookiness of parental repression was emphasized by the Dr. Spocks of this world, and on many occasions public schools encouraged students to distrust the guidance, especially in the form of discipline, of their own parents.

Arrogance was the rule in the school reform Sanhedrin at that time, convinced as it was that it had science-based answers to most (if not all) educational problems created by backward school boards. The Sanhedrin shaped school reform "more powerfully from 1900 to 1950 than any other group has done before or since," according to Tyack and Cuban. Policy elites, apparently convinced that they knew how to create great schools, dictated more and more specifications, including teacher qualifications, courses of study, playground apparatus, musical equipment, drinking fountains with water coming out exclusively on a slant, buildings "entirely free of stains [and] ... odors" (even in home economics rooms where girls baked cookies?), and the correct arrangement of flags and other wall hangings. The California State Department of Education expanded its school code from 200 pages in 1900 to more than 2,600 by 1985.

My professors at the University of Chicago from 1958 to 1962, many of whom were my colleagues later, were far more skeptical about the knowledge base for running schools. Take Philip Jackson, a heretic who said that since nobody in the United States knew how to train teachers properly, as far as he could see, the University of Chicago should venture into that activity only on a very limited experimental basis.

The prevailing U.S. method of training teachers still demonstrates well the fallacy of regarding education, and especially pedagogy (which relates to the methods of teaching, in contrast to knowledge of subjects taught), as applied science, for the nation producing the most effective teachers (Japan), according to videotaped samples of teaching in several countries, adopts no such pretense (Stigler & Stevenson, 1991). While fledgling Japanese teachers study lesson plans developed and polished by their predecessors, and are rewarded later for honing and adapting the plans still further, and for developing new ones that any teacher may use, many U.S. teachers, after undergoing courses in educational psychology, sociology, history, etc., are exhorted to go forth triumphantly and put the stuff to innovative use. If taught by competent people the stuff can't hoit, as they say in Brooklyn, but is not a good substitute for pedagogical skills.

Similar logic would say to equip fledgling, caterwauling musicians with scientific knowledge about acoustics and the anatomy of the human hand, rather than with performance techniques perfected for generations. The demonstrable incompetence of many U.S. teachers (in comparison with teachers elsewhere) is a price we pay for letting some professors of teacher education pose as scientifically sophisticated.

For a demonstration of how difficult it is to translate research findings into classroom practice, I recommend a book (Cohen, McLaughlin, & Talbert, 1993) in which intelligent professors describe how they and the teachers under their guidance attempt, on the basis of empirical evidence (of how students develop understanding in their own heads), to develop a new instructional method called "teaching for understanding." At many points in the book, the earnest professors and teachers seem like bumbling Keystone Kops. They could have saved themselves (and their students) a lot of trouble if they had started, instead, with lesson plans perfected by the Japanese teachers mentioned earlier, who are adept at helping students understand complex concepts. Classroom teaching is closer to performance artistry than to applied science, I am convinced, though while artistic performances feature mainly emotional expression, instructional performances must focus mainly on cognition.

When "scientific" experts surged forward to improve American schools, big changes occurred. The typical public high school at the beginning of the twentieth century had approximately 100 students, but in response to allegedly scientific formulas (by wizards like James Conant (1959), who later in his life admitted making hasty recommendations about school size), more than half of all high schools had at least 1,000 students by 1986, vastly increasing depersonalization and insulation from local demands. Parents got big schools whether they wanted them or not. By 1930, as Callahan (1962) demonstrates, public school administration was extensively dedicated to a "cult of efficiency," rather than responding to local preferences. A superintendent of schools in Portland, Oregon, could brag that he knew exactly what page of a textbook each classroom would be studying at a given hour. Teachers, now given "professional" training, were urged to counteract the extremes of localism—dish out instruction considered cosmopolitan and uplifting, not what parents wanted for their children. Sub-boards of education in cities were abolished to rid education of parental haggling and inefficiency.

Some 127,531 local school districts in 1932 (including many with only one school each) were reorganized, fierce *resistance of local people notwithstanding*, into 16,960 sprawling ones in 1973, according to Tyack and Cuban, at the behest of experts who saw parents opposing them "as backward yokels who did not know what was good for their children." School boards became much smaller (with fewer bendable ears) and higher-class in makeup. Their members learned (were brainwashed?) to keep their meddling fingers out of the scientific thing called administration, school boards were deprived of their own staffs and thus of much information available to school administrators, soon earning a reputation as rubber stamps. By 1977 it was estimated that 85 percent of policies adopted by U.S. public school boards had been recommended by superintendents, the people who had once been school board clerks. In 1908, the average state department of education had one staff member for every 100, 000 public school students. By 1974, the figure was one for every 2,000.

By the late 1970s, however, almost every aspect of the above-discussed transfer of power, including maltreatment of minorities, had come under attack, especially in the wake of the landmark case of *Brown v. Board of Education* (1954). Education politics became far more complicated. Now we witness an almost ceaseless, bewildering, multistranded tug of war among policy elites, legislators, judges, bureaucrats, teacher unions, and other interest groups. Not one of these combatants has consistent firepower any more, though most are capable, when sufficiently agitated, of stopping something. Notice, however, that public schools have not been relocated. As federal legislation called No Child Left Behind (NCLB, more easily remembered as Antsy Elbee) demonstrates, centralization intensifies. Parents who exercise influence get it the hard way, except when they are rich (more on that later).

My abbreviated discussion of ideational and structural changes could easily imply, I fear, that what we had before we got a corrupted common school dream was a golden ideal. Though what we had previously worked surprisingly well, as I have noted, it was not golden and not ideal. Educational arrangements needed, and still need, major adjustments to cope with shifting needs.

Many of the new arrangements, based on faulty assumptions about gurus and yokels, did far more harm than good, especially as they assaulted parenthood and gave unprecedented influence to politicos, state and federal bureaucrats, researchers concocting scientific evidence that was mostly dogma in disguise, and messiahs pushing garbage as reform. Local schools had serious faults, but reinforcing the family was not one of them, and the ponderous, costly apparatus of public education that replaced them is more alarming. Now a remarkable number of homeschooling parents produce impressive results without the pretense and cost (Rudner, 1999).

Once the common school dream became a nightmare, not only did public school parents have to take whatever messiahs of school reform dished out, with rare exceptions, including much that was wasteful, but religious parents were repeatedly harassed and hauled into court because their private schools were not equivalently convoluted and wasteful, or for failing to send their children to schools for the number of years specified in compulsory attendance statutes. The people of deep faith who probably suffered the most in this regard were the old order Amish, who originally came to the United States because William Penn promised them religious liberty. After decades of being hounded, prosecuted, jailed, and deprived of their property in this country, they negotiated successfully for guarantees of religious freedom with the governments of Brazil and Honduras, which needed skillful farmers, and were fleeing to those nations for the right to abide by their religious convictions when a 1974 decision of the U.S. Supreme Court, in which I testified proudly in their defense, finally rescued them from brutality here.[1]

THOUGHT CONTROL RUN AMOK

Another shameful aspect of rule by school-reform politicos, bureaucrats, and mullahs does not spring directly from pretentious pseudoscience, deadly as that is, but from thought-formation strategies in public schools.

Among many areas of basic outlook I could mention, none is more messed up than our prevailing public school depiction (and prevailing courtroom depiction) of relationships among religion, our national origins, and our current culture.

Religious fervor was prominent in this nation's founding, and the United States possibly is still, except in institutions like courts and public schools, the most religious nation in the modern world. Though the Enlightenment is often depicted as rejection of religion, the United States version of the Enlightenment was distinctly religious, according to Paul Johnson (1997) and Forrest McDonald (2004).

For many years, however, under the influence of experts and the courts, public education has reflected the anti-religious view that religion is so irrelevant to most of life that it can be ignored totally in the routines students undergo hour after hour, day after day, year after year. The best discussion I have seen of the stark contradiction between this view and the theism of our Judeo-Christian heritage is by McCarthy, Oppewal, Peterson, and Spykman (1981).

A great awakening occurred among many Protestants, especially of Evangelical persuasion, when decisions of the U.S. Supreme Court in the 60s banned official prayer and Bible reading from public schools, holding that they violated the religious establishment clause of the federal First Amendment. The shock, as described by Willmore Kendall (1988), was enormous. Complacent about public school centralization to that point, many Christians now felt a major podium of a God-fearing nation had been transformed into a pulpit for secularism. Schools, which had seemed responsive to local opinion, were (suddenly, it seemed) controlled by distant agencies like the U.S. Supreme Court. Kendall thought the decisions on prayer and Bible reading created a deadly breach in the common school consensus, an undermining of the civil peace that would resonate through future years. From that point on, evangelicals established their own private schools by the hundreds and often protested antireligious practices in public schools.

One protest that drew nationwide attention is especially pertinent here, for the attorney defending the religious parents of Hawkins County in East Tennessee was Mike Farris, who later became founder and president of the Home School Legal Defense Association. I recommend the disturbing report by Bates (1993), who makes clear his total disagreement with the religious views of the prosecuted "fundamentalist" parents, as he calls them, but also his disgust with the way they were mistreated.

The Hawkins County controversy involved primarily what was misrepresented as a conflict between evolution and creationism. Since evolution means change, which is continuous in the cosmos, the biased representation of the issue made it easy to ridicule people who reject, not the reality of change but the contention that the universe, in all its complexity, fell into place by chance. Many scientists, including some who say they are definitely not creationists, reject the same Darwinism—like Berlinksi (1996), who says Darwinism could "vanish into the void without affecting the contemporary scientific world view in the slightest." As for representing the other side of the controversy as creationism, that lumps together people with widely divergent views of what creationism means, whether they interpret the book of Genesis entirely literally, entirely figuratively, or somewhere in between, for instance, and thus confuses the debate. The conflict could more accurately and productively be described as between Darwinist cosmology and rejection of Darwinist cosmology. These two interpretations of existing evidence should both be discussed in classrooms, partly because they are both interpretations of scientific evidence, partly because students need to learn that competing interpretations lie at the very heart of science, and partly out of respect for youngsters from religious homes.

There is much additional evidence of anti-religious bias in public schools. Something is wickedly wrong with an interpretation of the common school dream that tramples the tender faith of children for no good reason at all. As for other areas of biased mind molding in government schools, they are often difficult to investigate because they have not been aired in courtrooms or because the classrooms, corridors, offices, and auditoriums in which they occur are protected from much scrutiny. I wish I had space to discuss pertinent classroom observations I have made by virtue of my special access (especially to schools run by my current or previous graduate students), as well as observations by others.

Another way to uncover effects of government thought control in public schools is to learn how high school graduates think about their world, at least partly because of the schooling they have undergone. There is no better analysis of that than *The Closing of the American Mind* (Bloom, 1987), a best-selling sensation when it appeared. Bloom's objects of investigation were graduates of high schools, mostly public, who attended his college classes during his many years as professor at Yale, Cornell, and the University of Chicago. I have seen no indication that things have improved since he wrote, and many reports suggest the opposite. These young people, Bloom says, are "students of comparatively high intelligence, materially and spiritually free to do pretty much what they want with the few years of college they are privileged to have—in short, the kind of young persons who populate the twenty or thirty best universities." They believe firmly in the relativity of all purported truth. They are committed, not to moral standards, but to openness to all human beings, all life-styles, all ideologies. They are incapable of seeking and admiring the best in the human race, for that would amount to identifying what is bad, which they think they must never do. Instead of solid knowledge of American history and its heroes, they hold in their heads "a smattering of facts about other nations or cultures and a saccharine moral [that we]—should all get along." They think this nation's founders were racists, murderers of Indians, and representatives of class interests. If you led them through the Louvre, they would have no clue for understanding what hung on the walls. Classical music is dead among them. Their education has neglected almost everything the common school was established to produce—a citizen who is rational, industrious, honest, law abiding, dedicated to the family, well acquainted with the logic of our basic rights, well informed about the Constitution and American history, and deeply attached to the letter and spirit of the Declaration of Independence. No one secured their parents' assent to this perversion of the common school dream.

Still another way of understanding how the rule of politicians, bureaucrats, and gurus has turned the common school dream into a nightmare is to examine textbooks and standards for various subjects. One daunting example is found in *Losing Our Language* (Stotsky, 1999), a study of the most widely used textbooks called "basal readers"— for teaching children to read. Stotsky's most disturbing revelation is that youngsters exposed to these textbooks are unlikely to encounter the gems of literature many of us remember from childhood. Instead, the textbooks attempt to ensure that each culture in a world-wide collection is represented by some scrap of scribble, no matter how lamentable in quality. Guides that come with the readers exhort teachers to focus on "relations of domination, submission, oppression, and privilege," not qualities of great literature. These notions of what should be emphasized are not surprising, given the contention of multiculturists, who had great influence on the basal readers, that standard English is a weapon privileged groups wield to batter the underprivileged. Many multiculturists, Stotsky observes, think underprivileged students should be encouraged to make errors in grammar and diction as a way of defying linguistic oppression. Where will that get underprivileged youngsters, do you suppose?

We can also investigate thought control in public schools by asking what views predominate in the world of intellectuals that exercises influence over those schools., It is widely acknowledged (see, for example, MacDonald, 2000) that the collection of heavenly visions known as "political correct" is preeminent among U.S. intellectual and artistic leaders, so much so that mainstream journals like *Chronicle of Higher Education* (see especially the issue dated November 12, 2004) discuss the depressed condition of conservative academics.

TRANSPLANTED TIME VERSUS PARENTHOOD

One sure way to diminish parenthood is to place youngsters in schools and similar institutions where parents exercise less influence than do other people, such as classmates, teachers, and the school-reform high priesthood.

The nation has seen dramatic changes in that regard, especially since the late nineteenth century. According to Tyack and Cuban, only *half* of youngsters between 5 and 15 years of age were in schools (K–12) in 1900, but 90% in 1940. Only about 7% of 5-year-olds were in kindergartens in 1900, but 60% in 1970. In 1898, the typical U.S. youth could expect to receive just 5 years of schooling. Now we are upset when youngsters drop out before completing high school, and we would like them all to graduate from college. The average number of days per year that youth spent in schools—during the years when they were there—burgeoned from 99 in 1900 to 158 in 1950.

High schools (public and private) enrolled only a microscopic elite—2% of the nation's 17-year-olds—in 1870, but 79.4% in 1940. Decade after decade, higher proportions of the nation's youth went to school, attended for longer periods of the year, and continued for more years.

For many centuries, most children, even in advanced countries, had grown up in extensive contact with adults, taking deep interest in adult affairs, and often participating (especially on farms) in the work of their parents or other adults. From U.S. colonial times onward, as I indicated earlier, many children were educated at home, especially in isolated areas. After age 12 or 14, many boys stopped going to school altogether, including some of my childhood friends. The concept of a special teen age group called *adolescent* was unknown when, before the twentieth century, youth were largely merged with the adult population. Serious independence and responsibility began early, at a stage of life when many of today's youth sow frivolous oats in college dormitories and fraternity houses.

By the 1960s and 1970s, thinkers began to wonder whether the enormous transplantation of youthful time had been entirely beneficial, despite the educational advances it made possible. Urie Bronfenbrenner (1972), one of the first prominent scholars to examine the phenomenon extensively, thought the school had become "one of the most potent breeding grounds of alienation." Alienation was turning many schools into "quasi-penal institutions in which teachers increasingly function as guards, while pupils are treated as prisoners for whom liberty is a special privilege." If we did not reverse this process and achieve "reunification with our children," we would see "far more rapid and pervasive growth of alienation, apathy, drugs, delinquency, and violence among the young and not-so-young in all segments of our national life."

In 1974, a national Panel on Youth headed by the famous James S. Coleman, after examining school monopolization of youthful time, asked whether it was the best way this nation could devise for preparing its young for adulthood, especially in the light of serious deterioration in youth morality and general well being (Coleman et al., 1974). Not only were the young separated from their parents for unprecedented periods, the separation occurred under conditions that promoted and strengthened previously unknown youth culture, and a huge industry of products and entertainment, often corrupting in nature, had sprung up to capitalize on the new youth market.

Small neighborhood public schools, in which students came mainly from families with similar values, had given way to large public schools, many of which served diverse, culturally disunited constituencies. Private schools, especially when connected with particular churches or temples, were quite different in this respect, for their patrons were there as a matter of choice; and homes, places of worship, and associated private schools often collaborated so tightly as to envelop students within what sociologists call "total institutions" (for an example see Peshkin, 1986).

When court rulings against racial segregation gave way to messy dogma demanding, not the elimination of race, ethnicity, and social class as policy considerations, but deliberate attempts to *diversify* and *be inclusive* along those lines (while simultaneously ignoring distinctions of morality and life style that U.S. families traditionally regarded as important), many public schools were alarmingly transformed. A good many youngsters were drawn then, and still are drawn, into difficulties they likely would have escaped under guidance by parents. Good parents do not hesitate, as *inclusionists* do, to identify influences an impressionable child should not encounter.

The prevailing system of youth socialization, entirely new in human history and still not well understood, now is widely regarded as the beneficial norm. The objection against homeschooling most frequently raised, in my experience, is that young people will suffer inadequate socialization because of it, whereas prevailing youth socialization may actually be the best reasons for letting parents arrange their own youth-socialization systems. Mixing youngsters together is like mixing volatile chemicals. Do it right and you get great results. Do it wrong and you blow up the neighborhood. The most dramatic study of how to blow things up is probably Grant (1988).

Public schools have been further debauched as decent places for growing up by a vast diminution of disciplinary authority, often at the hands of U.S. courts (Arum, 2003). The Panel on Youth suggested *reducing* the purview of the school, though not in a manner approaching what home-schooling often achieves today; providing more educational opportunities outside school walls; and creating organizations that would bring young and old together again. Students could be given more responsibility for people needing help; the school could be limited to academic functions (leaving more room for the family); school and work could be alternated (half a day in one and half a day in the other, or school and work on different days of the week, assuming labor laws were revised to make that possible); business and industry could perform more educational functions; and young people could be encouraged to drop out of school temporarily, for a year or two at some point.

Now we are extending the transplantation of youthful time through an expansion of child care that threatens the virtual death of parenthood. If the elimination of parenthood seems too outlandish to happen, or even to advocate, note that John Rawls (1999), widely regarded as the most influential moral philosopher of the late twentieth century, explicitly said the family might have to be dumped, though he hoped not. Why dumped? Because Rawls, who was dedicated to giving all children an equal start in life, knew the family was the major source of unequal starts.

Another argument for diminishing or eliminating family influence, widely advanced by people building themselves an empire of early childhood services, springs from evidence of the criticality of childhood experiences to everything that follows, and of the existence of much rotten parenthood in this country. Unfortunately, the main reaction of early-childhood empire builders to those realities is to demand, not that steps be taken to inhibit the formation of additional deficient families, but that government step in and influence children in a positive manner, virtually from the moment of birth. Worse still, early childhood services designed to give disadvantaged youngsters a decent start in life are offered increasingly to all families, thus encouraging more parents to be delinquent. But if parents work full-time outside the home while their children are brought up mainly by strangers, Bronfenbrenner asked, who will keep the family going, the principal cradle of morality? Who *will* keep the family going? Who will resuscitate the quaint, dying customs called motherhood, fatherhood, and parenthood?

For evidence of alarming, mindless extension of early childhood services, see frequent reports along that line in almost any newspaper—reports, for example, of governors and legislators seeking to make early-childhood services available to larger proportions of the population, including moms and dads who do not need them but may use them to escape parental responsibility. Also see how a leading early-childhood empire-builder, in the end-of-twentieth-century yearbook of the National Society for the Study of Education, glows about how close he and other common school expansionists have come to a seamless system extending from birth to graduation from college (Goffin, 2001). Note, as well, how public monopolization of student time spreads in the other direction—fattens, so to speak, in the form of Saturday programs, after-school activities, and extended-hour child-care programs. The proliferation looks cancerous to me.

THE OUTLOOK NOW

How can we end the common school nightmare? How can we overthrow pseudo-scientific experts who inflict such harm on American youth? According to the following report, there is hope:

> I have seen the future of public education in the foothills of the Sierras—[in] the kind of personalized public school that will spring up from coast to coast as traditional public schools are forced to narrow their curricula and eliminate programs because of mandated testing [there goes Antsy Elbee's testing craze again!] and budget constraints.... [It] is a flexible, web-like, networked school that is far more effective and far more appealing to parents and students than the rigid, hierarchical factory school design that often typifies public education today.... [Instead of] ... traditional trappings of school, it provides home schooling parents with a network of services. . . [that fit] the student's personal and academic needs, his or her learning style, and the kind of instructional approach *desired by the parent....* [A] mentor-teacher *assists the parent and student* in monitoring the student's progress toward the attainment of *the standards that they set for themselves.... The parents agree to provide a minimum of 4 hours a day of supervised instruction* ... at home, on campus, or in some other venue.... [The school] *replaces a one-size-fits-all mentality with a customer focus, a regulatory environment with a nurturing one....* If public schools hold fast to the old ... way of doing things, their buildings will soon be as empty and forlorn as the steel mills in America's Rust Belt.

The empahsis in the passage is mine. The writer, Wayne Gerson (2003), is not a starry eyed ignoramus about education, for he, before retirement, was a public school superintendent for 22 years, in four different states. The characteristics he describes are echoed by other observers across the land, including Lines, mentioned earlier. What we have in networked schools, in homeschooling more generally, and in other recent arrangements for parental choice, is similar, as Carper aptly notes, to the condition of American education described near the beginning of this chapter—before citizens signed on to common school dream and it transmogrified into a nightmare.

It is whopping rejection of the nightmare that Gerson depicts—dramatic realignment of power play. Could anything be farther from the applied-science pretense of the school reform gang than choices made by common parents in networked schools—made by the same yokels whom gurus spent 50 years disparaging and depriving of power (more than a century disparaging, if you count current de-tracking masterminds)? Note the rejection, in networked schools, of the one-size-fits-all mentality of divines dictating uniformity to get equality. Teachers assist parents in networked schools; parents do not assist teachers by raising bake-sale money for classroom equipment. Learning standards and instructional methods are selected, not by feds, states, and gurus but by parents and students. Networked schools bypass regulation, which often, in the past, came close to driving people of conscience out of their skulls.

The promise in this rebellion does not lie in a naive idea that parents can do no wrong. (Will mistakes be a startling new educational development, do you think?) The promise lies in developing, not in the manner of applied (or faked) science, but primarily through much common-sense trial and error (illuminated by good studies whenever that is feasible), new combinations of educational resources. Start with parenthood. Add, on different occasions, choices from among: virtuoso teachers; tutors; pastors; rabbis; computerized instruction; video games; movies; the Internet; science laboratories in schools; athletic activities in parks; classrooms; auditoriums; libraries; outings of many kinds sponsored by homeschooling groups; sailing lessons; bands, orchestras, and even junior symphonies; art studios and galleries; help for hurt people organized by churches and temples; this pacing and that for learning; specification of learning objectives by different participants and combinations of them, including students, parents, and teachers; brokers who help locate appropriate resources—the outlook today is almost endless. Mix and blend in countless ways, in response to countless needs and interests. Dish out, taste, and modify. Codify what works well. Search for new ingredients. Banish taboos. Tell government and its meddlers to go away. Continue to mix and blend. Is this a new era or what?

Many parents will discover they need the advice of good teachers. Other parents will do well on their own. Some dads and moms will decide that wrapped-up packages called schools are what their children require. Other dads and moms will develop their own instructional packages— right at home. Many chaotic families may have to settle for what some of them get now—the simple option of shifting from one school to another. We will need new modes of intervention for youngsters endangered by choice badly exercised. Teachers will discover that their skills achieve lots more when enveloped in parenthood. Opponents will dig up scandals, produce dishonest research findings, lobby for anti-parental legislation, stage lawsuits.

Gerson fails to note that the networking he describes is also offered by private schools. It is far safer there, because virtually all public schools providing services to homeschoolers collect public money on the basis of homeschooler enrollment, and consequently should not be trusted to continue current practice if lucre gets distributed on a different basis or if laws and regulations are introduced to limit homeschooling liberty or halt the movement altogether.

Ah, there's the rub! The public school networking described by Gerson and others may turn out to be a trap. Once parents are hooked on the benefits, all kinds of new provisos may appear, nullifying most if not all networking liberties now enjoyed. If any form of education given signifi-cant tax-derived benefits has survived for long *anywhere in the world* with-out getting regulation-rigidified, I have seen no evidence of it in decades of searching. If our colonial educational arrangements proved unstable, similar ones today may prove equally unstable. As Mancur Olson (1971) demonstrated long ago, the groups deriving the most direct benefits from public programs (like public school teachers and administrators) can afford intensive, consistent publicity and lobbying (via unions, for instance) that common citizens (like homeschooling parents), who have many other matters to attend to, can seldom manage. Much will depend on how long this nation's homeschoolers sustain the remarkable vigilance and political action described by Somerville (2001). To extend networking freedom far beyond its current, severe geographic limits, homeschoolers will need to *expand* their sphere of influence!

Charter schools (another mechanism of parental choice), despite their elements of promise, are setting a bad precedent, I fear, by agreeing to make their liberty and existence contingent on achieving long lists of objectives dictated by government, including many yet unspecified. (If government demanded of charter schools only demonstrable essentials of good citizenship, which would certainly be few in number and compara-tively easy to demonstrate, that would be quite another matter.) He who calls the accountability tune will toss pipers who toot other ditties! Worse still, once the principle is established that private educational arrange-ments given public largesse must do whatever government says, the prin-ciple could easily be extended to all private educational arrangements, including homeschooling in homes, sans tax-financed networking. It has happened in more than one country. Parental-choice movements should plan and ponder more seriously and cooperatively along these lines.

I hope time will prove my cautionary impulses wrong. Perhaps the common school nightmare, along with recent reactions to it, has so thor-oughly discredited the common school concept that liberty-granting net-works for homeschoolers can be sustained indefinitely, that charter schools can end up dancing to something more musical than legislation like Antsy Elbee, and that even vouchers and tax credits will escape in the United States what they have fallen into everywhere else.

Apart from what homeschooling parents continue to do, then, how can other advocates of educational freedom and de-stultification help shape the future? I would say support, as homeschoolers do, the little state groups that monitor for anti-parental legislation and that alert home-schooling associations accordingly. Support state and federal home-schooling agencies (especially the Home School Legal Defense Association, the closest thing I have seen in many years to a miracle-worker). Support the National Home Education Research Institute in Salem, Oregon. Help bombard legislators with letters when that is appropriate. Join pertinent debate in the public forum. Disabuse kith and kin of common school mythology, which, according to Charles Glenn (1988), has been blabbered indefensibly since the inception of the common school.

More contradictions: If educational experiences during long years of compulsory attendance are essential to maintenance of our democracy, why it is so easy for half-literate, poorly informed immigrants to become American citizens? If children are not reasonably fed, clothed, sheltered, loved, guided, and given medical care, educational experiences are sub-stantially meaningless; so why (if not in response to common school empire-building) does government single education out for detailed dic-tation, while leaving the rest, at least until politicians get inspired by emerging early-childhood empires, to child-abuse law enforcement? How can the rooting out of religious activities and symbols be justified while virtually every other viewpoint on ultimate reality gets free expression? Top attorneys must continue to launch test cases on such matters.

As Susan McDowell suggests in her research, we have scarcely started to plumb what parents, with their unique capabilities, can contribute to the education of the young. Scholars must get busy plumbing it. The state and its experts did not rear heroes in history who never saw the inside of a high school. Parents did. The state may finance and elaborate the cor-rupted common school, but it does not prepare formulas and change dia-pers in the middle of the night. Parents do. The state does not hug children when they are frightened, worry and weep when they are ill, and agonize when they stumble into drugs and bad company. Parents do. Who but a loving parent can gauge a mood by the slightest twitch on a young-ster's face? Is anything more important to guiding instruction than know-ing how the learner responds? Are parental sensitivities priceless or what?

It will prove vital, I predict, to head off the insistence of our federal Antsy Elbee, and of much state legislation, on judging educational endeavors shallowly, in the light of achievement tests. The parental choice movement must articulate, with empirical support, its special contributions not reflected in achievement tests. Some pertinent existing evidence is eloquent on that point, but we need more detail and depth.

I am thinking of a videotape from a homeschooling father who wanted me to testify in his behalf. He had made the tape by setting up a video camera, atop a tripod, at the side of his living room, pointing to the area where many homeschooling activities took place. He kept the control module in his pocket. It was clear, I thought, that the camera had been present for so long that his two little girls, one approximately 11 years old and one 3 or 4 years of age, had become oblivious to it. In one scene, the father sat on the sofa, with a daughter snuggled on each side, discussing a mathematical problem with the 11-year-old. I found the mixture of tranquility, affection, trust, and absorption in the subject stunning.

Something was going on, I concluded, that would have lifelong consequences for family connections, beneficial self-concepts, and interest in learning, but had never been mentioned in any educational publication I had read. I was similarly stunned by another scene, in which the 11-year-old played a cello accurately and expressively, her face reflecting deep emotion, while her father accompanied her on the piano and the 3-or-4-year-old sat entranced. The spirit in the room was unlike any classroom I had ever observed. Someone should finance the planning and collection of hundreds of unstaged video tapings by homeschooling families, and put them into digital library. Psychologist James Stigler at University of California at Los Angeles has developed software that makes analysis of such material far more efficient than formerly. Analysis of such tapes could yield priceless, unprecedented evidence. It could help prevent another common school nightmare.

NOTES

1. Wisconsin v. Yoder, 405 U.S. 205 (1972). For descriptions of rather similar cases, see www.expertwitness-on-education.com.

REFERENCES

Arons, S. (1983). *Compelling belief: The culture of American schooling*. New York: McGraw-Hill.

Arum, R. (2003). *Judging school discipline*. Cambridge, MA: Harvard University Press.

Bates, S. (1993). *Battleground: One mother's crusade, the religious rght, and the struggle for control of our classrooms*. New York: Poseidon Press.

Belz, J. (1997). Rebels of the best kind: As educational structures change, keep your eyes on the homeschoolers. *World, 12*(23), 5.

Berger, P. L., & Neuhaus, R. J. (1977). *To empower people: The role of mediating structures in public policy.* Washington DC: American Enterprise Institute for Public Policy Research1.

Berlinski, D. (1996, January). The soul of man under physics. *Commentary, 101,* 38-46.

Bloom, A. (1987). *The closing of the American mind.* New York: Simon & Schuster.

Bronfenbrenner, U. (1972, July). Reunification with our children. *Inequality in Education,* 10-20.

Callahan, R. E. (1962). *Education and the cult of efficiency.* Chicago: University of Chicago Press.

Carper, J. C. (2001, Spring). The changing landscape of U. S. education. *Kappa Delta Pi Record,* pp. 106-110.

Cohen, D. K., McLaughlin, M. W., & Talbert, J. E. (Eds.). (1993). *Teaching for understanding: Challenges for policy and practice.* San Francisco: Jossey-Bass.

Cohen, S. (1983, Summer). The mental hygiene movement, the development of personality and the school: The medicalization of American education. *History of Education Quarterly, 23*(2), 123-149.

Coleman, J. S., Bremner, B. H., Clark, B. R., Davis, J. B., Eichorn, D. H., Grilickes, Z., Kett, J. F., Ryder, N. B., Doering, Z. B., & Mayo, J. M. (1974). *Youth: transition to adulthood: Report of the panel on youth of the president's Science Advisory Committee.* Chicago: University of Chicago Press.

Conant, J. B. (1959). *The American high school today.* New York: Signet Books.

Gardner, H. (1983). *Frames of mind: The theory of multiple intelligences.* New York: Basic Books.

Gerson, W. (2003). The networked school: Could this hybrid of home schooling and public education be the wave of the future? *Education Week, 23,* 30-31.

Glenn, C. L., Jr. (1988). *The myth of the common school.* Amherst, MA: The University of Massachusetts Press.

Goffin, S. G. (2001). Whither early childhood care and education in the next century. In L. Corno (Ed.), *Education across a century: The centennial volume: One hundredth yearbook of the National Society for the Study of Education* (pp. 76-99). Chicago: National Society for the Study of Education.

Grant, G. (1988). *The world we created at Hamilton High.* Cambridge: MA: Harvard University Press.

Jackson, P. W. (1968). *Life in classrooms.* New York: Holt, Rinehart & Winston.

Jensen, A. R. (1998). *The g factor: The science of mental ability.* Westport, CT: Praeger.

Johnson, P. (1997). *A history of the American people.* New York: HarperCollins.

Kendall, W. (1988). American conservatism and the "Prayer" decisions. In G. A. Panichas (Ed.), *Modern age: The first twenty-five years* (pp. 465-479). Indianapolis, IN: Liberty Press.

Lagemann, E. C. (2000). *An elusive science: The troubling history of education research.* Chicago: University of Chicago Press.

Levin, H. M., & Belfield, C. R. (2003). The marketplace in education. In R. E. Floden (Ed.), *Review of research in education* (pp. 183-219). Washington, DC: American Educational Research Association.

Lines, P. M. (2003). *Support for home-based education: Pioneering partnerships between public schools and families who instruct their children at home.* Eugene, OR: Clearinghouse on Educational Management.

MacDonald, H. (2000). *The burden of bad ideas: How modern intellectuals misshape our society.* Chicago: Ivan R. Dee.

McCarthy, R., D. Oppewal, Peterson, W. & Spykman, G. (1981). *Society, state & schools: A case for structural and confessional pluralism.* Grand Rapids, MI: William B. Eerdmans.

McDonald, F. (2004). *Recovering the past: A historian's memoir.* Lawrence, KA: University of Kansas Press.

Olson, M., Jr. (1971). *The logic of collective action.* Cambridge, MA: Harvard University Press.

Peshkin, A. (1986). *God's choice: The total world of a fundamentalist christian school.* Chicago: University of Chicago Press.

Ravitch, D. (2000). *Left back: A century of failed school reforms.* New York: Simon & Schuster.

Rawls, J. (1999). *A theory of justice.* Cambridge, MA: Belknap Press

Rothfeder, J. (1998, Sept). Training the 'Twitch' generation. *Executive (Supplement to Forbes) 1*, 30-36.

Rudner, L. M. (1999, March). Scholastic achievement and demographic characteristics of home school students in 1998. *Education Policy Analysis Archives, 7*, 1-31.

Somerville, S. W. (2001). Legalizing home schooling in America. *Private School Monitor, 21*, 1-11.

Stigler, J. W., & Stevenson, H. W. (1991, Spring). How asian teachers polish each lesson to perfection. *American Educator, 14*, 12-20, 43-47.

Stotsky, S. (1999). *Losing our language: How multicultural classroom instruction is undermining our children's ability to read, write and reason.* New York: Free Press.

Tyack, D. (1974). *The one best system: A history of American urban education.* Cambridge MA: Harvard University Press.

Tyack, D., & Cuban, L. (1995). *Tinkering toward utopia: A century of public school reform.* Cambridge MA: Harvard University Press.

Wells, A. S., & Oakes, J. (1996). Potential pitfalls of systemic reform: Early lessons from research on detracking. *Sociology of Education (Extra Issue)*, pp. 135-143.

West, E. G. (1965). *Education and the state: A study in political economy.* London England: The Institute of Economic Affairs.

CHAPTER 3

HOMESCHOOLING AND COMPULSORY STATE SCHOOLING

Charles L. Glenn

Homeschooling is of course and always has been the original form of education, except for those unfortunate children—now increasingly rare—who spend their childhood in institutions. Any attempt to give an account of its history must focus instead on its antithesis: compulsory state schooling. Homeschooling only becomes a phenomenon in the context of (almost) universal education in institutional settings provided by or at least regulated by the State.

THE GOAL OF STATE SCHOOLING

John Locke, the "Father" of the American Constitutional order, gives us a useful place to start a discussion of homeschooling. Locke had no great confidence in the institution of schooling, even in the elite form of English grammar schools. The priority in education, he insisted in *On Education* (1697), should be put upon "Virtue [which] is harder to be got than a knowledge of the world, and if lost in a young man is seldom

Home Schooling in Full View: A Reader, 45–68

recovered." There were more dangers than advantages to sending a boy to school, since "it is preposterous ... to sacrifice his innocency to the attaining of confidence and some little skill of bustling for himself amongst others by his conversation with ill-bred and vicious boys when the chief use of that sturdiness and standing upon his own legs is only for the preservation of his virtue." Against the argument that schools were valuable because they taught the young how to get along with peers, Locke pointed out that

> 'tis not the waggeries or cheats practiced amongst schoolboys,... that make an able man, but the principles of justice, generosity and sobriety, joined with observation and industry, qualities which I judge schoolboys do not learn much of one another.

In fact, he concluded, "it is impossible to keep a lad from the spreading contagion if you will venture him abroad in the herd and trust to chance or his own inclination for the choice of his company at school" (Locke, 1996, pp. 46-49), and it was preferable to educate him at home, with a reliable tutor. On this point Locke was in agreement with Erasmus, with Montaigne, and with Madame de Sévigné, all of whom saw education at home as clearly preferable—when possible—to formal schooling. As Montaigne had written a century before, "I don't want this boy to be imprisoned; I don't want him to be abandoned to the anger and the melancholy humor of a furious schoolteacher" (in Venard, 2003, pp. 241-242).

On the other hand, in the same essay, Locke urged that schools be set up in every parish, and that children between the ages of 3 and 14 be required to attend, expressing what would become a typical belief that obligatory schooling was a useful instrument of social discipline for the "lower orders" while unnecessary for the appropriate education of those in positions of social and political dominance.

We find the same double-mindedness in Jean-Jacques Rousseau, the eighteenth century thinker with the most profound and lasting influence. His fictional *Emile* (1762) is about the education of a youth from birth to maturity and marriage, without a day of school attendance, though it should be noted that the parents are to have no role at all; indeed, he prefers that the boy be an orphan. On the other hand, in his political writing Rousseau stresses the importance of education by and for the State to shape citizens able to will only what the State wills. In his *Discourse on Political Economy* (1755), Rousseau insisted that education had a major part to play in the maintenance of political authority, since

> that government which confines itself to mere obedience will find difficulty in getting itself obeyed. If it is good to know how to deal with men as they are, it is much better to make them what there is need that they should be.

The most absolute authority is that which penetrates a man's inmost being, and concerns itself no less with his will than with his actions. It is certain that all peoples become in the long run what the government makes them.... Make men, therefore, if you would command men.... If you would have the general will accomplished, bring all the particular wills into conformity with it;... establish the reign of virtue. (Rousseau, 1993, pp. 139-140)

Rousseau's phrase "the reign of virtue," came to have a sinister connotation during the radical phase of the French Revolution, when his name was frequently invoked as the authority for purging society of all those considered to have a corrupting influence. In his 1755 discourse, he placed great stress on education under State direction as essential to a sound political system. He continues:

To form citizens [he wrote] is not the work of a day, and to have men it is necessary to educate them when they are children ... government ought the less indiscriminately to abandon to the intelligence and patriotism and prejudices of fathers the education of their children, as that education is of still greater importance to the State than to the fathers.... Public education ... under regulations prescribed by the government, and under magistrates established by the Sovereign, is one of the fundamental rules of popular or legitimate government. (Rousseau, 1993, pp. 147-149)

Through such a system of education, Rousseau argued, the future citizen could be taught "to will nothing contrary to the will of society." So important was this instrument of government, subordinated to "the Magistrates destined to preside over such an education," that it should be considered "certainly the most important business of the State" (Rousseau, 1993, p. 149). The same emphasis on education as an instrument of government marks Rousseau's most influential political writing, *The Social Contract* (1762):

He who dares to undertake the making of a people's institutions ought to feel himself capable, so to speak, of changing human nature, of transforming each individual, who is by himself a complete and solitary whole from which he in a manner receives his life and being; of altering man's constitution for the purpose of strengthening it.... He must, in a word, take away from man his own resources and give him instead new ones alien to him, and incapable of being made use of without the help of other men... each citizen is nothing and can do nothing without the rest. (Rousseau, 1993, p. 214)

Under the "enlightened absolutism" of Austria and Prussia, the State repeatedly decreed an obligation to attend schools, though this was not effectively enforced. King Frederick William I of Prussia enacted school laws in 1713 and 1717 requiring that all children be sent to school. The *General-Land-Schul-Reglement* of 1763, the first education ordinance to apply to all of the (repeatedly enlarging) Prussian territories, included compulsory school attendance between ages 5 and 13, though pupils could be excused from the requirement earlier based on demonstrated mastery of the skills taught in elementary school, and the requirement did not apply to Catholic children, for whom a separate law was enacted in 1765. Emperor Joseph II of Austria ordered, in 1781, that all children whose parents did not provide private tutors attend school from ages 6 to 12, and that their teachers use a standard method of instruction; they were forbidden to use nonauthorized textbooks (Grimm, 1991, p. 235). Here again we can see the characteristic double-mindedness: compulsory schooling to provide a state-directed socialization to the children of the common people, while the elite could educate their children as they chose.

In his *Addresses to the German Nation* (1807), delivered during the French occupation in Berlin, philosopher Johann Fichte abandoned his earlier criticism of the state and identified it as "the means for achieving the higher purpose of educating and developing the element of pure humanity in the nation." Fichte called for a truly "national education" to fashion a "new self," a "new life," to "mold the Germans into a corporate body, which shall be stimulated and animated in all its individual members by the same interest." Only in this way, he argued, could the nation rise again from the destruction which it had suffered at the hands of Napoleon: "in the education of the nation, whose former life has died away and become nothing but a supplement to that of another [nation], to an entirely new life.... In a word, I propose a total change of the former system of education as the only means to preserve the existence of the German nation" (Fichte, 1978, p. 21).

The old education had been unable to penetrate with sufficient power to the very roots of impulse and action; the new national education must possess that power. "By this new education we want to build Germans into a single body [*Gesamtheit*], that in all its members will stimulated and animated by a single interest." Thus it must be applied to every German, so it would not be the education of a single class but that of the Nation itself, not just popular education but *national* education. This national education would possess sufficient power only if it abandoned the error of the old education, which stressed the free will of its pupils, and instead undertook to suppress freedom of the will completely and substitute for it the absolute necessity of obeying the moral imperative of duty. All true education, Fichte asserted, seeks to produce steadfastness of character; he who must be continually exhorted to do the right thing, or must exhort himself to do so, lacks such a character. "If you want to have influence over him, you must do more than talk to him; you must fashion him in such a way that he cannot will anything contrary to what you want him to will.... The new [national] education must develop this stable and unhesitating will" (Fichte, 1978, p. 22ff, p. 28f).

The radical Jacobins of the French Revolution, in the 1790s, had anticipated this vision of State-controlled schooling as an instrument of transformation of human consciousness and thus of consolidation of their regime. As Jacques-Nicolas Billaud-Varenne, an ally of Robespierre, wrote in his *Elements of Republicanism* (1793), a publication consisting "largely of paraphrases of the *Contrat social* and elaborations of Rousseau's arguments," "You will lose the younger generation by abandoning it to parents with prejudices and ignorance who give it the defective tint which they have themselves. Therefore, let the Fatherland take hold of children who are born for it alone and let it begin by plunging them into the Styx, like Achilles" (Blum, 1986, p. 183).

Robespierre himself told the National Convention, the same year, "I confess that what has been said up until now does not correspond to the idea I have formed for myself of a complete plan for education.... I am convinced of the necessity of operating a total regeneration, and, if I may express myself in this way, of creating a new people." Blum comments that "Robespierre was invoking a state that would create the citizens it desired, not one that would accommodate those it had" (Blum, 1986, p. 193, p. 242). Similarly, radical leader Danton told the National Convention that

> It is time to reestablish the grand principle, which seems too much misunderstood, that children belong to the Republic more than they do to their parents.... We must say to parents: We are not snatching them away from you, your children, but you may not withhold them from the influence of the nation. And what can the interests of an individual matter to us beside national interests?... It is in national schools that children must suck republican milk. The Republic is one and indivisible; public instruction must also be related to this center of unity. (Pierre, 1881, p. 70f)

The logic of this explicitly political use of schooling on behalf of the State, inspired in part by Plutarch's famous account of ancient Sparta as well as by Rousseau, was worked out in detail by Michel Lepeletier de Saint-Fargeau. "Never," he wrote, "in elementary schools will we be able to find other than imperfect instruction. Their radical fault is that they take hold of only a few hours and abandon all the others.... In the public institution [which he proposed], by contrast, the entire existence of the child belongs to us; the material, if I may put it this way, never comes out of the mold ... between the ages of five and twelve" (in Julia, 1981, p. 93).

Lepeletier's proposal was presented to the National Convention by Robespierre in July 1793; it would have removed all children from their families between the ages of 5 and 12 (11 for girls), placing them in common schools (*maisons d'éducation communes*) where they would receive "an education truly national, truly republican," under close supervision "every day, every moment" to ensure that they would form the correct attitudes and habits (text in Lehembre, 1989, p. 65-72). They would all, whatever the social class of their parents, wear the same clothing, eat the same food, receive the same instruction and care.

Thus, Lepeletier and Robespierre claimed, "will be formed a new race, laborious, regulated, disciplined, one which an impenetrable barrier will separate from the impure contact with our obsolete species" (in Blum, 1986, p. 186). Similarly, Robespierre's ally Saint-Just proposed, in his notes for a book on "republican institutions," that boys be educated from 5 to 16 by the State, and that "they will not return to their parents' home until age 21." "Children belong to their mother," he wrote, "until age five, if she has nursed them, and to the Republic subsequently as long as they live" (Saint-Just, 1976, pp. 265-66).

Those who sought to implement the radical program of popular education were continually frustrated both by teachers and by parents. Those teachers who were "patriots" were too often incompetent, while the more experienced teachers tended to be former members of the abolished religious orders and could not be trusted to teach pure republican morality. Parents seemed to prefer the old instruction of Catholic catechism and Bible stories, often refusing to send their children to the republican schools. They had little interest in the sort of neo-Spartan education recommended by Lepeletier, Robespierre, and Saint-Just (Furet and Ozouf, 1977, p. 99). Since teachers were almost entirely dependent on the fees paid by parents, they were under pressure to provide what the parents wanted, despite the disapproval of public authorities.

Considerable evidence shows that the condition of popular education actually worsened after the adoption of the educational program of the Revolution. In the Department of the Seine (the Paris region) by the end of 1796 there were less than 1,200 pupils in public schools against a potential enrolment of 200,000. Of 599 communes in Meuse-et-Moselle, 566 had at least one school in 1789, but only about 200 had schools a decade later. Alternative private schools flourished, often with teachers who had taught in church-sponsored schools before they were abolished. In the Seine, in 1798, there were an estimated 2,000 private schools but only 56 public primary schools (Aulard, 1903, vol. 4, p. 348; Gontard, 1959, p. 163).

As the Revolution passed out of its most radical phase and religious liberty returned, these private schools—almost all explicitly Catholic—provided serious competition for the secular public schools. A study of nine departments found that 76.7% of the schools were private in 1798. Gradually the teaching orders were allowed to re-establish themselves, welcomed not only by parents but also by local officials who had not been able to staff schools with qualified substitutes. "The spectacular development of private education, begun in 1791-1792 and accelerated starting in 1795, compensated substantially for the undeniable decline of public schools" in the revolutionary period (Grevet, 2001, pp. 145-146, 148). Where private schools were not available, many parents simply kept their children home; there was no effective obligation to attend school.

We should not confuse activity at the government level, adopting laws and regulations, with actual progress in the provision of education; there may indeed be an inverse relationship between the two phenomena. In the absence of strong social and economic demand for literacy, such top-down measures were largely futile. In Russia, where the eighteenth century tsars Peter and Catherine sought to use government-directed schooling as an instrument for modernization, prosperity, and social control, the measures taken were almost entirely without an effect on the prevailing illiteracy. Catherine's Legislative Commission (1767) "recommended obligatory education for the entire male population, and a law to that effect was adopted in 1786, under Austrian inspiration." The Commission continued:

> These reforms, though in theory representing a major break-through by spreading at least limited education in the provinces and opening the door to basic education even to free peasants, in practice remained a dead letter.... by 1801 there were twenty-two thousand pupils in all public schools ... in all of Russia. (Eklof, 1990, pp. 20-21)

More was achieved in the northern European countries where government's role was modest than in those to the south where the authority of the State was invoked in support of schooling. Nor should we assume too quickly that it was economic factors alone which made literacy a valued possession, as some neo-Marxist historians have argued; the vigor of civil society may have had more to contribute. In fact, in literate Scandinavia, education (whether in schools or in the home) was seen as essentially a religious matter, and as an expanded function of the local church (Tveit, 1991, p. 57). As Graff explained:

> Urbanization, commercialization, and industrialization had nothing to do with the process of making the Swedish people perhaps the most literate in the West before the eighteenth century.... regular personal examination by parish clergy, the church stood above a system rooted in home education....

piety, civility, orderliness, and military preparedness were the major goals. (Graff, 1991, p. 13)

Protestant Pietism gave an impulse to the achievement of general literacy in Scandinavia; it was made an official goal of the Church of Sweden in 1686 and, in large part through reliance upon home education supervised by local pastors, was largely successful within two generations. In Denmark and Norway (then a single kingdom), by contrast, much the same result was achieved through a network of elementary schools, while in Iceland literacy was nearly universal without schools (Tveit, 1991, pp. 75, 89).

In the areas of Calvinist dominance—Geneva, the Netherlands, Scotland, New England—a high degree of literacy was achieved through a combination of the requirement that communities or parishes provide schools (though not that children attend these schools) and the strong motivation of families, for religious and also for practical reasons, that their children become literate. For example, the Massachusetts colonial legislature, in 1642, required town officials "to take account from time to time of all parents and masters, and of their children, concerning their calling and employment of their children, especially of their ability to read and understand the principles of religion and the capital laws of this country." Parents and masters who neglected this duty to see to education of the children under their care were to be fined. Five years later, perhaps concluding that more institutional support was needed, the legislature required communities of appropriate sizes to maintain schools, with tuition paid either by parents "or by the inhabitants in general." But school attendance was not mandatory.

REQUIRING SCHOOL ATTENDANCE

It was not until the second half of the nineteenth century, in any country, that effective compulsion began to be exercised on parents to send their children to school. The initial proposals for compulsory attendance in the United States seem to have been associated with the concern that the children of Catholic immigrants would fail to become loyal Americans. When Catholics in New York City, in the 1840s, asked that their schools receive the same subsidies that Protestant schools enjoyed, the consequent backlash led Methodists to insist "that the control of popular elementary education belonged to the state" and even "that attendance at these state schools [should] be made compulsory" (Curran, 1954, p. 100). Catholic Bishop John Hughes charged, in turn, that the administration of the Public School Society was such that "parents or guardians of Catholic children cannot allow them to frequent such schools without doing violence to their rights of conscience." Parents should not be forced "to see their children brought up under a system of free-thinking and practical irreligion" (in Cohen, 1974, vol. II, pp. 1126-1127). Diane Ravitch points out that, in fact, "of about 12,000 Catholic children in the city in the late 1830s, only a few hundred were enrolled" in the Society's public schools. Ravitch wrote:

> The Church did not want public schools which were truly common schools, where Irish children and other Catholic children might go without fear of prejudice. Because of the Church's view of the inseparability of religion and education, the kind of nonsectarian common school which had developed in New York and in other parts of the country was wholly inimical.... The Catholics were unwilling to agree to any plan that did not recognize the distinctive character of Catholic schools, and the Society would not agree to the public funding of any distinctly sectarian school. (Ravitch, 1974, pp. 32, 56-57)

"Forced" was the operative word; "To the [Society's] assertion that the schools had the confidence of all classes, Hughes countered that the Society has been so ineffective in overcoming the reluctance of poor parents to send their children to its schools that it had applied for a 'legal enactment ... to compel an attendance'" (Katz, 1975, p. 13). This included a decision by the city council that impoverished families which did not send their children to school would be denied relief.

In 1852, Massachusetts was the first of the states to adopt a compulsory school attendance law, requiring every child aged 8 to 14 to attend a public school "during at least twelve weeks," unless he had been "otherwise furnished with the means of education for a like period of time, or has already acquired those branches of learning which are taught in common schools," or had "a bodily or mental condition" preventing school attendance. The law also made exception for cases in which "the person having the control of such child, is not able, by reason of poverty, to send such child to school, or to furnish him with the means of education" (Cohen, 1974, vol. II, pp. 1115-1116). Other states were slow to adopt such requirements; New York State, for example, made school attendance compulsory in 1874.

There was, in fact, considerable hesitation about extending government authority so far into the realm of family life. Horace Mann himself did not support compulsory attendance laws, "finding them out of harmony with the American idea of democracy" (Ensign, 1921/1969, p. 176). Wickersham wrote in his annual report for 1870 that "Pennsylvania must look in some other direction than that of a compulsory law to find the remedy we are seeking for the evil of non-attendance at school," and again that "in the spirit of our institutions, I prefer to test voluntary action fully, fairly, and patiently, before resorting to force" (Wickersham, 1870, p. xiii).

Similarly, in the Pennsylvania Constitutional Convention of 1873, former state Superintendent Charles A. Black opposed an amendment giving the legislature authority to make schooling compulsory: "I can think of no measure," he said, "that could be presented to the people of the State which would be more unpopular.... The people claim the right, and they have the right, to regulate this matter for themselves, and we have no right to interfere with their prerogative. They claim the right to send their children to school or not, and the case of monarchical Prussia is no example for them" (*Constitutional Convention*, vol. VII, p. 691). As late as 1881 the then Pennsylvania Superintendent of Public Instruction, E. E. Higbee, expressed his "very serious misgivings as to the propriety of any strictly compulsory law" (Ensign, 1969, p. 177).

As late as 1894-1895, there were 19 states without laws requiring schooling, and in those with such laws the typical period of compulsory attendance was from 8 to 14; by 1917-1918, all states had compulsory attendance laws, though in nearly half of the states pupils who had completed elementary schoolwork could be excused from further attendance. In 16 states, there were no specific requirements for issuing papers allowing school-age youth to work; in 14 others, working papers were issued to youth able to read and write, while in 5 states youth were required to complete the elementary school curriculum before receiving working papers. In several states, poverty was legally recognized as a basis for exemption from school attendance. Only 35% of children and youth in the country lived in states requiring seven years of schooling, while 38% lived in states allowing excusal of school-aged youth who had met the elementary-school standards (Robbins, 1924/1966, pp. 230-31). Obviously, the United States still had a long way to go before it achieved universal schooling at the ages now considered standard.

The same debates occurred in other countries, usually associated with an effort to render education secular and uniform. In 1869, for example, the Edinburgh municipal council passed a resolution calling for a "popular, unsectarian and undenominational system," supervised by school committees appointed by local town councils, with compulsory attendance, and with abolition of the government grants to denominational schools. The Education (Scotland) Act of 1872 made attendance compulsory from ages 5 to 13 (Anderson, 1995, p. 64f).

In England, the government-appointed Newcastle Commission reported, in 1881, that more than 90% of all children were receiving some schooling, but that the quality was very uneven. The commission found that "the Church of England had provided, through voluntary contributions, twice as much money as the State for its schools since 1833." The commission's recommendation was that schooling be supported in part by a county tax, "while leaving the voluntary system in being in so far as control by religious bodies was concerned; the latter being considered essential as the only method 'to secure the religious character of popular education.'" The way was prepared for the Education Act 1870, which would provide for "locally elected school boards to levy a rate for education, to build schools where these were lacking, provide teachers and, if they thought proper, enforce the attendance of children under thirteen" (Simon, 1960, p. 348, p. 365). Schooling became compulsory nationally in 1881 for children between five and nine inclusive, but a provision was left open for excusal of children between 10 and 13 who had reached standards set locally; efforts to make compulsory schooling more extensive were defeated.

The Austrian Imperial Primary School Law, adopted in 1869, "provided for mandatory free primary education under secular state control for boys and girls from six to fourteen," though implementation was very uneven. This extension of the period of compulsory schooling from 6 to 8 years aroused strong opposition from peasants who saw no reason for depriving them of the labor of their children for such a useless purpose; provision was finally made, in 1883, for leaving school 6 six years.

In several strongly-Catholic countries, there were unsuccessful efforts to institute compulsory school attendance as a means of limiting the influence of the Church. In Spain, in the wake of a liberal revolution, a law was enacted (1857) which would set the basic pattern of Spanish education until well into the twentieth century, "conferring on instruction at its various levels stability, juridical and administrative clarity, as well as uniformity" (Delgado, 1994, p. 18). The new law made schooling obligatory for all Spaniards aged 6 to 9, and free of charge for those whose families could not pay. It defined as public primary schools those "which are sustained entirely or in part by public funds" by local government, with supplemental assistance as needed from the State. In secondary education, the academic validity of private schools would be recognized only if their teachers had appropriate qualifications, if the curriculum was reported annually to public authorities, and if they used the same texts and followed the same programs prescribed for public schools. This new law accentuated the centralization of the educational system—"nothing escaped the authority of the Minister of Development, including the appointment of teachers," but the actual effects on expanding the provision of schooling were disappointing (Puelles, 1991, pp. 144-52; Viñao Frago, 1994).

Those who designed and implemented such centralizing measures, in Spain as elsewhere, were convinced that the authority of the State must be asserted over against that of the Catholic Church. Mandatory school attendance—lengthened in 1909—was considered necessary to ensure that schools would have the desired effect on raising the consciousness of the people (Capitán, Díaz, 2002, pp. 119, 222). "This principle of educational freedom," Liberal leader Romanones told the members of Spain's Senate in 1901, "could be fatal for those who love and defend the real liberal principles"; for "*real* freedom" to triumph, it was necessary to restrict educational freedom (García Regidor, 1994, p. 555). As the Republican leader (and novelist) in Valencia, Vicente Blasco Ibáñez, put it, "If Spain is the most backward country in Europe, the cause is four centuries of Catholic schooling" (quoted in Ruiz Rodrigo, 1994, p. 756).

With the establishment of the Second Republic in 1931, education was a primary focus of the efforts of the Left to bring about fundamental changes in Spanish society, changes which many believed required also a profound reorientation of Spanish culture. This would require reforms "from above," since insufficient awareness existed among the still largely-rural masses to press for such changes "from below;" government would have to infuse the right spirit into what occurred at the local level. "The State was the manager of the new situation, the only guarantor of an extensive and complicated educational activity. Socialism interpreted this … as part of an irreversible process, and though at times it denied the monopolizing character" of its policies, the facts did not support this denial. "On this terrain, said its most notable representatives, it could not allow rivals…. To accomplish its task, the State covered itself with the veil of neutrality and declared that instruction was secular." Inevitably, this brought the new government into conflict with private schooling, which was largely in the hands of religious orders and thus by no means available to be reshaped in secular form. "The conclusion was clear: the Republic must 'nationalize' culture, nationalizing along the way the teaching institutions" (Molero Pintado, 1977, pp. 17, 35, 55).

To accomplish its ambitious goal of fundamental cultural change, it was not enough to make the sort of superficial changes in the educational system which had been attempted in the past. The new Spanish Constitution proclaimed that "the cultural service is an essential attribution of the State, and it will provide this through educational institutions linked together by the system of the unified school. Primary instruction will be free and obligatory. The teachers and professors of public instruction are public functionaries…. Instruction will be secular, will make work the basis of its methodological activity, and will be inspired by ideals of human solidarity" (quoted in Palmero Cámara, 1990, pp. 43-44).

The national newspaper *El Socialista* wrote, "We understand by religious freedom the opportunity for man to live without being subjected to religious practices or teaching in any state institution … the immense majority of those who suffer, labor, and produce detest religious instruction and the work of priests," while the newspaper of the Republican Radical Socialist Party of Logroño province wrote that "the secular school is the torch which lights up the shadows: that's why they are so afraid of it" (in Molero Pintado, 1977, p. 71; Palmero Cámara, 1990, p. 46). There was no room, in this understanding of the function of education as an instrument of social change, for homeschooling.

The result of the inadequate development of schooling was manifest in the newly-unified Italy of the 1860s: illiteracy was 74%; half a century later it remained 32% in the north, 52% in the center, and 70% in the south of the country (Capone, 1981, p. 211). The Piedmontese and other politicians who had achieved unification were concerned that, having "made Italy," they had failed to "make Italians." The Casati Law (1859, 1861) was an expression of the intention to create uniform institutions; in 380 articles it sought to regulate every aspect of education in a top-down manner. The law made schooling obligatory from age 6 to age 12, created a centralized control by a Ministry of Public Instruction, a Council of Public Instruction—which was nominated by the government and possessed only a consultative role—and inspectors for each level of schooling. The scope and content of the curriculum was defined, and only state schools could issue valid diplomas and licenses (Pécout, 1999, p. 220). Communes were required to make provision for 2 years of primary schooling, and the larger ones for an additional 2 years

A subsequent law adopted in 1877 reduced the obligation of school attendance to only age 9. In intention, at least, "the system was coherent with liberal objectives: it ratified the supremacy of state schooling over religious schooling and codified a classic Enlightenment ideal, introducing mandatory popular instruction and at the same time seeking to reproduce and reinforce the existing social relations, providing for each class the type of instruction most appropriate to its status" (Romanelli, 1990, p. 62). Actual implementation reflected the priorities of government: to establish a small and high-quality secondary education system, designed to provide a humanistic education to middle-class youth, rather than to implement effective popular schooling. Thus the State subsidized the secondary *licei*, while leaving the expense of primary schools up to local government and parents (Capone, 1981, p. 212).

In many cases, it was only through private—often religious—initiatives that schools were created, and the government was forced to abandon any intentions which it may have had to secularize schools and instruction. It has been suggested that this resulted in part from a loss of nerve on the part of the secular elite about the possibility of popular enlightenment and laicization (Verucci, 2001, pp. 138-139). Because of the government's lack of resources and executive effectiveness, however, the Catholic

Church and its teaching orders continued to provide a large proportion of the schooling available.

Radically-anticlerical Liberals in Belgium called for a reorganization of public instruction to be secular and obligatory, and seemed to have the opportunity to carry out this program when, in the June 1878 elections, they gained a majority in both houses of the Parliament. The new government stated that "public instruction should depend exclusively upon the civil authorities," which was taken by their opponents as "a declaration of war against Catholicism; one could, from that moment, consider the hostilities as officially begun" (Verhaegen, 1905, p. 61).

Catholics saw in this a threat of a state monopoly through militantly secular schools; the bishops sent a letter addressed to Catholic parents, accusing the proposed legislation of being antireligious: "to submit the child to the regime of a school without God is to wish to destroy in his heart the Christian life from the very start." They ordered that at every Sunday mass a prayer be added, "From schools without God and teachers without faith, deliver us, Lord!" Protest meetings were held both in cities and in the countryside, with an intensity unmatched since the movement leading to independence in 1830. A petition with 317,000 signatures was submitted to Parliament, and the extensive Catholic press carried out an early example of a coordinated media campaign (Verhaegen, 1905, pp. 82, 87, 93, 99).

The Catholic reaction was rapid and successful. Of a total of 7,550 elementary school teachers, 2,253 left the public schools that had been made neutral, often at considerable sacrifice. Already in December 1879—at least according to the calculations of the Catholic Party—the free Catholic schools enrolled 379,000 pupils, the public schools 240,000. The proportion of enrollment in Catholic elementary schools rose from 13% in 1878 to 61% (more than 75% in Flanders) in 1880; by 1882 there were 622,000 pupils in Catholic elementary schools. There were 168 public schools without any pupils at all (Kossmann, 2001, p. 299; Verhaegen, 1905, pp. 136, 178). The elections in June 1884 were a victory for the Catholic party, which maintained a parliamentary majority for the next 30 years; the Liberals were out of government until 1918 (Kossman, 2001, p. 203). Most observers attributed this change—previously the Liberals had controlled the government for 13 years—to the school issue.

Similarly, in the France of the Third Republic, the institution of compulsory school attendance was part of a deliberately anticlerical strategy. A law adopted in March 1882 made elementary schooling obligatory and secular, specifically excluding from the curriculum the teaching of "obligations toward God." Henceforth, in public schools, "a day's work had to be preceded by a little lesson in morals, in place of prayers" (Zeldin, 1980, p. 178). This measure encountered resistance in some areas: in Lyon, for example, 6,000 fathers signed a petition asking that religious instruction be restored.

This resistance failing, many parents switched their children to private Catholic schools—often the same facilities and teachers which had formerly been communal schools operated by teaching congregations. "Departmental records from 1879 to 1888 suggest that many lay public schools lost about half of their enrolment to competing congregational private schools.... When their public schools were laicized in Lyon in 1879, the Soeurs de St.-Charles calculated that they had lost only 12% of their pupils" (Curtis, 2000, pp. 116, 122). It has been calculated that "the Church managed to retain about 20% of primary school children.... Many people were still willing to pay for a religious education, even when a free public one was available, and this shows the failure of the republic to create a new morality which would effectively reconcile and sum up the basic belief of the nation. There was no such thing" (Zeldin, 1980, pp. 202-203). This was especially true for girls. Twenty years after adoption of these laws, in 1901-1902, 58% of the girls and 83% of the boys in France attended public schools, and 13% of these girls in public schools were still taught by sisters. It was not until after laws were adopted forbidding members of religious congregations to teach, even in private schools, that the proportion of girls attending public schools, 75% in 1912, reached the level that the proportion of boys had reached 30 years before (Lelièvre, 1990, p. 93).

One of the most interesting examples is that of the Netherlands where, despite a high rate of literacy deriving from its Calvinist and commercial heritage, compulsory schooling was not enacted into law until 1900, and then by a 50 to 49 vote in the parliament. The Protestant leader (and future prime minister) Abraham Kuyper insisted that a requirement to attend school must not be imposed unless the schooling available respected the convictions of families, and thus included publicly-supported confessional schools (Postma, 1995, p. 34). This goal would be fully-realized in the Netherlands with the "Pacification" of 1917, and now for many decades public and private schools have stood on the same financial basis and parents have been able to choose between them without cost; some 70% of pupils attend private schools, reducing greatly the demand for home schooling.

This brief review helps to explain why, to so many Americans and Europeans, the idea of homeschooling seems so inexplicable, as a reversal of two centuries of "progress" in providing universal instruction under government supervision and, usually, in government-run institutions. This *has* been, in many respects, an enormous accomplishment, especially in countries and regions where a demand for literacy, numeracy, and more advanced skills had not already created a demand for instruction met by a variety of nongovernment schools (see West, 1975). It has been an accomplishment at a cost, however, of weakening the link between parents and the education of their children, and thus of the transmission across generations of a heritage of convictions and virtues. In effect, the State has substituted itself for parents and for communities as the privileged source of an understanding of the world and of what it means to live a decent and meaningful human life. As we have seen, that was by no means unintentional; for many of those who urged that the State undertake universal popular schooling it was the primary purpose.

We should, therefore, think about the recent astonishing revival of homeschooling, together with the strong interest in charter schools and in new faith-based schools, as signs of renewed appreciation of the primary role of the civil society of families and voluntary associations in preparing free women and men for life in a free society.

THE HOMESCHOOLING ALTERNATIVE IN OTHER COUNTRIES

In the nineteenth century the concept of "freedom of education" gave parents the right to provide their children with education at home, but this alternative fell into disuse as formal systems of schooling—both state-operated and private—became broadly available and of acceptable quality. More recently, however, there has been a revival of interest in homeschooling in a number of countries, though it has nowhere reached the scale experienced in recent years in the United States.

In most countries, it is education which is compulsory and not schooling and parents can provide that education at home, provided that they meet the achievement standards set by government. However, in most countries only a small number of children are schooled at home for academic or social reasons. The following information is taken from Glenn and De Groof (2004).

Group 1: Countries that Permit Homeschooling and Monitor the Educational Process

- In **Belgium**, compulsory education does not necessarily mean compulsory schooling. Home teaching is authorized if it meets specific requirements in order to comply with those for compulsory education.

In **Belgium**, the right of parents to educate their children at home has long been fundamental, though the availability of a variety of schools including some which are very small has made it rare for parents to do so. The 1995 education law provides a broad exemption from the requirement to attend a public school, including a specific homeschooling provision.

- In **Italy**, parents are allowed to educate their children at home, under state supervision and with the approval of the principal of the local school. The State reserves the right to verify the level of competence reached by means of examination.

- **Iceland**: the Compulsory School Act allows parents, with approval, to educate their children at home, though the implication of the language suggests that this is intended to respond to special circumstances rather than to constitute a general right to an alternative form of education.

- **Estonian** parents may ask for an exemption from the first six grades of schooling, sometimes giving as a reason the values, beliefs, and principles of the parents. The child remains on the list of the school and gets textbooks from the school, but parents are responsible for the teaching. The child may participate in some lessons (music, arts, physical education, crafts) together with other pupils.

- In **Ireland**, Article 42.2 of the 1937 Constitution provides: "Parents shall be free to provide this education in their homes or in private schools or in schools recognized or established by the State." The State has the right to supervise such education.

- In **France**, the law requires municipal supervision of children being schooled at home. While the text of the law, as drafted in 1882, requires only that the child acquire "the elementary notions of reading, writing, and calculation," an administrative judge has ruled that this should be equivalent to what the child would learn in school at the same age, and that it is the responsibility of the family to demonstrate that this requirement has been met, the progress of children being home educated is monitored at the regional level.

- In **Norway**, very few pupils are taught at home, but parents may choose homeschooling for their children for several reasons: (1) if the local population is not sufficient to maintain a school, and the child might stay at home and receive teacher guidance using different kinds of teaching aids;(2) parents have objections to the official school policy (religious and other more ideological reasons); (3) many parents were against lowering the school starting age and give their 6 year-old children homeschooling instead. Children being home educated must be registered with the local school.

- In **Portugal**, education is compulsory for children under 15, but the country accommodates home educators and has always done so. When children are recognized as being home-educated, the education that they receive is monitored so that progress can be ensured, at a very local level by the local school.
- The Education Act 1944 for **England** and **Wales** requires the parent of every child of "compulsory school age" to ensure that the child received "efficient full-time education suitable to his age, ability and aptitude," either by sending him or her to a school or by some other means, with the local education authorities monitoring the progress of children being homeschooled (of whom there are an estimated twenty thousand).
- In **Scotland**, the Education (Scotland) Act 1945 requires the parent of every child of "compulsory school age" to ensure that the child receives "efficient full-time education suitable to his age, ability and aptitude," either by sending him or her to a school or by some other means. Parents normally fulfil this duty by sending their child to school; although other means such as education at home can be used.
- In **Austria**, the compulsory education obligation may be met not only by attending a school, but also by receiving equivalent instruction such as homeschooling. The right to instruction at home is provided by the Constitution, which safeguards parents' right to teach their children who are of school age at home instead of sending them to a private or public school. The Constitutional Court ruled, in 1954, that neither the national government nor the provinces could place any kinds of limitations upon the provision of homeschooling. As a result, it may not be limited to the education of an individual child by his parents, but may extend to instruction of groups of children; such arrangements have been used as a means of starting alternative schools on a small scale. It should be noted, however, that public authorities have the right to insist that the education provided by homeschooling be equivalent to (though not identical to) that provided in the public schools. A home-schooled child's knowledge of the national curriculum is tested at the end of each academic year.
- In **Australia**, exemption from the compulsory attendance provision may be granted if parents provide an appropriate education program. District education officials are responsible for inspecting and approving home tuition programs.
- In **Canada**, the Charter of Rights and Freedoms (1982) states that every child has a right to education and that their [sic] parents have

the right to direct that education at home according to their conscientious beliefs. The right to homeschool is upheld in the education statutes of each of the ten provinces. The public school system of Edmonton (Alberta) has reached out to provide an unusual level of support to some 2,000 homeschooling families.

- In **New Zealand**, homeschooling has been legal since 1914, originally because of the remoteness of the residence of some rural families. According to the Ministry of Education, "Parents need to obtain approval from the Ministry of Education to homeschool their children during the years of compulsory schooling (6-16 years), and are given an annual grant to help with the cost of learning materials. At 1 July 1999 there were 5,451 homeschoolers recorded on the Ministry of Education's homeschooling database, which represented less than 1% of total school enrolments. These students belonged to 3,110 families. The number of homeschoolers in New Zealand has nearly doubled in the period 1993 to 1999."

- In **Russia**, parents have a right to make alternative arrangements for the education of their children, including homeschooling.

- In the **Philippines**, homeschooling is actively promoted in urban areas, both to serve pupils unable to attend school and also to relieve the overcrowding of school facilities. Students in the program are issued the same textbooks in all subjects for the school year. They are given topics to study every week and required to answer questions given by teachers at the end of each topic. Contact sessions of students and teachers are on Saturdays. These sessions are for clarification of difficult topics encountered by students during the week. The program in Quezon City addresses educational needs of working students such as factory workers, baby sitters, vendors, canteen helpers, janitors, laborers, salesladies, sickly and street children who are eager to finish secondary education.

- **Dutch** law makes provision for exemption from the mandatory schooling requirement in cases in which the conscience of the parents cannot be satisfied with the available schools and there are not enough parents locally with the same concerns to justify starting a new school. By all indications, this is an option that is used by few families and is actively discouraged.

- Since the **Chilean** Constitution affirms education freedom, homeschooling is considered legal even though there is no specific law regulating it.

Group 2:   Countries that Permit Homeschooling without Supervision

- All Finnish citizens are subject to compulsory education but compulsory education does not entail an obligation to attend school. The Constitution provides: "Instruction given at home shall not be subject to supervision by the authorities."

Group 3:   Countries that in Principle Forbid Homeschooling but make Exceptions in Individual Instances

- In **Spain**, according to the Constitution and laws, homeschooling is allowed for children who would not normally be able to attend school because of their special circumstances, but not otherwise.
- In **Greece**, in the Swiss cantons Schaffhausen and Ticino, and in the **Netherlands**, education is admissible only for children with individual educational needs.
- Although the **South African** School Act provides for the registration of a learner for education at home, there does not appear to be an express right in this regard.
- In exceptional cases home education is permitted in **Luxemburg**, and the teaching at home is required to be equivalent to that in schools.
- In most of **Switzerland** and, the basis of school attendance is not a "right to education" but an "obligation to attend school." In principle, parents may not educate their children at home even if, because of religious principles, they have good reasons for seeking this; some cantons, however, allow state-supervised home-schooling.
- In **Israel**, "requests for home education will be approved only in most exceptional cases, where it can be proven beyond any doubt that the request for home education derives from a formulated outlook which rejects institutional education of any form, or where it can be so proven that there are extraordinary circumstances, unique and most exceptional, because of which a child is unable to attend a recognized educational institute." Very few requests have been granted, and these must be renewed each year.
- Homeschooling is not expressly provided for in the **Uruguayan** educational system, but there are various accommodations, such as the possibility to take an examination at the end of the primary level of schooling which grants accreditation of competence to pro-

ceed to secondary schooling. Secondary education, in turn, permits a "free modality;" students can refrain from attending classes and receive credit for courses through taking examinations as "free" students, together with the students who attend class.

Group 4:   Countries that have Compulsory School Attendance

- **German** law, while recognizing this priority of parental responsibility, does not allow for homeschooling on the basis of the religious or pedagogical convictions of parents; it is allowed only for medical reasons.
- In **Sweden**, all children between the ages of 7 and 16 are both entitled and obliged to undergo education at a public or an approved private school.
- In **Bulgaria, Malta, El Salvador**, and other countries school attendance is compulsory.
- Schooling in **Argentina** is obligatory, which implies that pupils must attend the school chosen by their parents among the alternatives offered by those schools recognized by the State, whether state-managed or privately-managed. Although there are arrangements for cases of illness or of absence from the country, when the authorities allow parents to take charge of the education of their children, provided that the pupils are evaluated from a distance, parents or guardians responsible for the education of minors are not permitted to secede from the official education system.
- **Brazil** has a substantial problem of pupils dropping out of school after third grade, especially in the poverty-stricken Northeast, but homeschooling is not authorized or regulated by law.
- Homeschooling (and private schools) are illegal in **Cuba**.

AUTHOR'S NOTE

The historical material is drawn from Glenn (in press).

REFERENCES

Anderson, R. D. (1995). *Education and the Scottish people 1750-1918*. Oxford, United Kingdom: Clarendon Press.

Aulard, A. (Ed.) (1903). *Paris pendant la Réaction Thermidorienne et sous le Directoire: Receuil de documents*, I-IV [Paris during the Thermidorian Reaction and uder the directory: Collection of documents]. Paris, France: Maison Quantin.

Blum, C. (1986). *Rousseau and the republic of virtue: The language of politics in the French Revolution*. Ithaca, NY: Cornell University Press.

Capitán Díaz, A. (2002). *Republicanismo y educación en España (1873-1951)* [Rebublicanism and education in Spain (1873-1951)]. Madrid, Spain: Dykinson.

Capone, A. (1981). *Destra e sinistra da Cavour a Crispi (Storia d'Italia dall'Unità alla fine della Prima Republica 1)* [Right and left from Cavour to Crispi (History of Italy from unification to the end of the first republic 1)]. Milan, Italy: TEA.

Cohen, S. (1974). *Education in the United States: A documentary history* (Vols. I-V). New York: Random House.

Curran, F. X. (1954). *The churches and the schools*. Chicago: Loyola University Press.

Curtis, S. A. (2000). *Educating the faithful: Religion, schooling, and society in nineteenth-century France*. Dekalb: Northern Illinois University Press.

Delgado Criado, B. (Ed.). (1994). *Historia de la educación en España y América, volumen 3: La educación en la España contemporánea (1789-1975)* [History of education in Spain and America, Vol. 3. Education in contempary Spain (1789-1975)]. Madrid, Spain: Ediciones Morata.

Eklof, B. (1990). *Russian peasant schools*. Berkeley: University of California Press.

Ensign, F. C. (1969). *Compulsory school attendance and child labor*. New York: Arno Press and The New York Times. (Original work published 1921)

Fichte, J. G. (1978). *Reden an die deutsche Nation* [Address to the German nation]. Hamburg, Germany: Felix Meiner Verlag.

Furet, F., & Ozouf, J. (1977). *Lire et écrire: L'alphabétisation des français de Calvin à Jules Ferry* [Reading and writing: The alphabetization of the French from Calvin to Jules Ferry]. Paris: Éditions de Minuit.

García Regidor, T. (1994). Iglesia y Estado ante la educación [Church and state confronting education]. In C. B. Delgado (Ed.), *Historia de la educación en España y América, volumen 3: La educación en la España contemporánea (1789-1975)* (pp. 553-560). Madrid, Spain: Ediciones Morata.

Glenn, C. L. (in press). *The long tug-of-war: Schools between state and civil society* (Vols. I-II). Wilmington, DE: ISI Books.

Glenn, C., & Groof, J. D. (2004). *Freedom, autonomy, and accountability in education: finding the right balance* (Vols. I-III). Tilburg, The Netherlands: Wolf Legal.

Gontard, M. (1959). *L'enseignement primaire en France de la Révolution à la loi Guizot (1789-1833)* [Primary education in France from the Revolution to the Guizot Law (1789-1835)]. Paris: Les Belles Lettres.

Graff, H. J. (1991). *The legacies of literacy*. Bloomington: University of Indiana Press.

Grevet, R. (2001). *L'avènement de l'École contemporaine en France (1789-1835): Laïcisation et confessionnalisation de la culture scolaire* [The coming of the contemporary school in France (1789-1835): Secularization and confessionalization of the culture of schools)]. Villeneuve-d'Ascq, France: Presses universitaires de Septentrion.

Grimm, G. (1991). Expansion, Uniformisierung, Disziplinierung: Zur Sozialge-schichte der Schulerziehung in Österreich im Zeitalter des aufgeklärten Absolutismus [Expansion, standardization, disciplining: The social history of schooling in Austria in the period of enlightened absolutism]. In W. Schmale & N. L. Dodde (Eds.) *Revolution des Wissens? Europa und seine Schulen im Zeitalter der Aufklärung (1750-1825)* (pp. 225-254). Bochum, Germany: Verlag Dr. Dieter Winkler.

Julia, D. (1981). *Les trois couleurs du tableau noir: La Révolution* [The tricolor blackboard: The revolution]. Paris: Belin.

Katz, M. B. (1975). *Class, bureaucracy, and schools.* New York: Praeger.

Kossmann, E. H. (2001). *De lage landen 1780-1980: I (1780-1914)* [The low countries: 1780-1980: I (1780-1914)]. Amsterdam: Olympus.

Lehembre, B. (Ed.). (1989). *Naissance de l'école moderne: Les textes fondamentaux 1791-1804* [Birth of the modern school: The basic texts 1791-1804]. Paris: Nathan.

Lelièvre, C. (1990). *Histoire des institutions scolaires (depuis 1789)* [History of schools (since 1789)]. Paris: Nathan.

Locke, J. (1996). *Some thoughts concerning education and of the conduct of the understanding* (R. W. Grant & N. Tarcov, Eds.) Indianapolis, IN: Hackett.

Molero Pintado, A. (1977). *La reforma educativa de la Segunda República Española, Primer bienio* [The education reforms of the second Spanish republic: First two years]. Madrid, Spain: Santillana.

Palmero Cámara, M. de C. (1990). *Educación y sociedad en la Rioja republicana (1931-1936)* [Education and society in republican Rioja (1931-1936)]. Salamanca, Spain: Universidad Pontífica.

Pécout, G. (1999). *Il lungo Risorgimento: La nascita dell'Italia contemporanea (1770-1922)* [The long Resorgimento: The birth of contemporary Italy (1770-1922)] (R. Balzani, Trans). Milan, Italy: Bruno Mondadori.

Pierre, V. (1881). *L'école sous la Révolution française* [The school during the French Revolution]. Paris: Librairie de la Societé Bibliographique.

Postma, A. (1995). *Handboek van het Nederlandse Onderwijsrecht* [Handbook of Dutch school law]. Zwolle, The Netherlands: W.E.J. Tjeenk Willink.

Puelles Benítez, M. de (1991). *Educación e ideología en la España contemporánea* [Education and ideology in contemporary Spain]. Barcelona, Spain: Labor.

Ravitch, D. (1974). *The great school wars: New York City, 1805-1973.* New York: Basic Books.

Robbins, C. L. (1966). Elementary education. In I. L. Kandel (Ed.). *Twenty-five years of American education.* Freeport, New York: Books for Libraries. (Original work published 1924).

Romanelli, R. (1990). *L'Italia liberale, 1861-1900* [Liberal Italy, 1861-1900]. Bologna, Italy: Il Mulino.

Rousseau, J.-J. (1993). *The social contract and discourses* (G.D.H. Cole, Trans.) London: Everyman.

Ruiz Rodrigo, C. (1994). La educación en Valencia [Education in Valencia]. In C. B. Delgado (Ed.), *Historia de la educación en España y América, volumen 3: La educación en la España contemporánea (1789-1975)* (pp. 830-836). Madrid, Spain: Ediciones Morata.

Saint-Just, L. (1976). *Théorie politique* [Poltical theory] (A. Liénard, Ed.) Paris: Éditions du Seuil.

Simon, B. (1960). *The two nations and the educational structure 1780-1870*. London: Lawrence & Wishart.

Tveit, K. (1991). Schulische Erziehung in Nordeuropa 1750-1825: Dänemark, Finnland, Island, Norwegen und Schweden [Schooling in northern Europe 1750-1825: Denmark, Finland, Iceland, Norway and Sweden]. In W. Schmale & N. L. Dodde (Eds.) *Revolution des Wissens? Europa und seine Schulen im Zeitalter der Aufklärung (1750-1825)* (pp. 49-95). Bochum, Germany: Verlag Dr. Dieter Winkler.

Venard, M. (2003). L'éducation par l'école (1480-1660) [Education by schools (1480-1660)]. In F. Lebrun, M. Venard, & J. Quéniart (Eds.), *Histoire de l'enseignement et de l'éducation II. De Gutenberg aux Lumières (1480-1789)*. Paris: Perrin.

Verhaegen, P. (1905). *La lutte scolaire en Belgique* [School wars in Belgium]. Ghent, Belgium: A. Siffer.

Verucci, G. (2001). *Cattolicesimo e laicismo nell'Italia contemporanea* [Catholicism and secularism in contemporary Italy]. Milan, Italy: FrancoAngeli.

Viñao Frago, A. (1994). La ley Moyano de 1857 [The Moyano law of 1857]. In C. B. Delgado (Ed.), *Historia de la educación en España y América, volumen 3: La educación en la España contemporánea (1789-1975)* (pp. 261-265). Madrid, Spain: Ediciones Morata.

West, E. G. (1975). *Education and the industrial revolution* (2nd ed.). Indianapolis, Indiana: Liberty Fund.

Wickersham, J. P. (1870). *Report of the Superintendent of Common Schools of the Commonwealth of Pennsylvania, for the year ending June 6, 1870*. Harrisburg, PA: B. Sincerely, State Printer.

Zeldin, T. (1980). *Intellect and pride*. Oxford, England: Oxford University Press.

CHAPTER 4

HOMESCHOOLING FOR LIBERTY

Tom Smedley

INTRODUCTION

Fictional character John Galt said: "I swear by my life, and by my love of it, that I will never live for another man, or ask another man to live for me." (Rand, 1961)

Columnist Mark Steyn wrote, "The hyper-rationalism of radical individualism isn't, in the end, rational at all. You'll recall that during the Iraq war, we heard a lot of talk about ancient Mesopotamia—the land of the Sumerians, Akkadians, and Hittites—being 'the cradle of civilization.' That's the point. Without a cradle, it is hard to sustain a civilization." (Steyn, 2000).

Church Father Augustine called his deceased son Adeatus "The only man of whom I would ever say, 'I wish for you to surpass me in every way.'" (Augustine of Hippo, 2000).

If you are a father or mother, Mark Steyn sounds more convincing than John Galt. Offspring are our time machines, extending the reach of our values into centuries we will not live to see. Unless an outside agent initiates force to change the natural order of things, children normally carry forward the passions of their parents. Normal teenage rebellion is such a terrifying anomaly in the history of mankind, that Old Testament law considered it to be a capital offence.

Historical Background

When the Prussian government implemented the first truancy laws in the early 1800s, they had to march weeping kids away from their families at bayonet point. This definitely violates the zero aggression principle. Imagine a commodity of so little value that the government cannot even give it away; recipients must be forced to partake. And why the application of force? Because the state needs its docile taxpayers and cannon fodder. With characteristic thoroughness, the Prussian state decided to turn 94% of its children into those who simply followed orders. Another 4.5% went into the "talented and gifted" programs, receiving an education designed for the janissaries, the professional servitors of the state: accountants, preachers, lawyers, professors, physicians, and so forth. The children of the ruling elite, the remaining 1.5%, received a traditional education designed to impart flexibility, creativity, and rigorous thinking skills.

To the rational thinker, handing off children to paid agents of government makes as much sense as hiring the hangman as your babysitter. Yet today otherwise sane people consider it normal to frog-march a terrified 4-year-old child to the bus stop, and send him off into a penal system peopled with monsters and manipulators. "After all," the gulled parent says, "public school did me no harm!" Other than damaging your critical faculties to the point where you are unable to perceive the harm done to yourself.

Do a quick Google search for John Taylor Gatto. Public education, he affirms, succeeds at its design purpose: inducing forgetfulness, confusion, social paralysis, indifference, and emotional/intellectual dependency, under the all-seeing eye of the state and its agents.

APPLICATIONS

Homeschooling is the place where the love of liberty intersects the love of our children. This is normal, principled, child-rearing, where we take our offspring by the hand to lead them on a guided tour of the real world, the wondrous universe. It is also, in retrospect, one of the few important things I have done with my life. If you are like me, you have met too many parents in tears over how their children were alienated from them, and came to hold in contempt the defining values of their family. In stark contrast, over the course of the last 2 decades, I have met zero homeschooling parents who regretted that decision. Even parents who eventually handed their kids over to the government regarded their homeschooling years as times of unusual closeness, happiness, and adventure.

Is homeschooling hard work? Let me rephrase that: is it an ordeal to spend large blocks of time with the people you love most on earth? With personable youngsters who are alive with questions, alive with the love of learning? Who regard you as their primary expert on everything? Who are eager to try out the things you teach them? Who are avid readers, well able to engage in intelligent conversation at an early age? So where is the hardship?

Hard work, yes. Hardship, no. A few tips—No, you do not have to be omniscient to educate one's own children. This myth is promulgated by edu-crats, the folks who typically are drawn from the least intelligent members of the college population. By the time *those who know best* are done with the children entrusted to them, 80% are nonliterate. They either cannot read, or really do not like to read. They do, however, know how to respond with Pavlovian promptness to the bells.

LITERACY

The ability to read well, widely, and insightfully separates the leaders from the followers. If parents use a high-quality phonics program, such as Samuel Blumenfeld's *AlphaPhonics*, or Marie LaDoux's *Play 'n' Talk*, they can get a ready student up to speed in about 30 hours. By contrast, the typical Japanese student needs six years to become fluent in his hieroglyphic language. The typical American public school student, after years of being taught to regard words as hieroglyphics, rather than as phonic representations of sounds, is dyslexic or alexic.

If kids can read, they are already ahead of 80% of their peers. Kids also do what they see. If mom and dad's favorite form of recreation is a good book, little monkey see leads to little monkey do. Finally, block out an hour a day to read to your children. Put them to bed an hour earlier, then spend that time introducing them to Peter Rabbit and B'rer Rabbit. As novelist C. S. Lewis (2004) said, "No book is worth reading at age ten which is not equally worth reading at age fifty." There is a lot of good material out there, and you can often find incredible bargains at library sales. This regular period of concentrated attention compounds over the years to nurture hearts and minds.

SOCIALIZATION

The primary advantage of socialist education, we are told, is socialization. The ability to sniff the behinds of those around you, and ascertain your position in the pack, your place in the pecking order. In adult prisons, rapists help to put and keep "fresh meat" in its place. In kiddy penal institutions, bullies serve the same purpose. Several studies, including my own master's thesis, have measured the social maturity of home-educated children. This characteristic is normally far higher in kids who were raised in their families, than in those who were surrendered to *The Lord of the Flies* (Golding, 1959). It is easy to pick out the homeschooled kids at family reunions. They are the ones who can organize the younger cousins into games, or comfortably discuss politics with sober aunts and uncles.

If most people today could aspire to government work from high school graduation to retirement, public education might make sense. Training people to beg permission before using the bathroom makes them more dependable line workers. In terms of preparation for the real world, however, the homeschooling family links effort with reward, input with output, in a direct manner that social promotions obscure. The discipline of independent learning, imparted early, equips kids with the preparation they need to excel on the university level. The typical home-educated child can handle selected community college classes soon after he hits puberty, and hungers for adult-level challenges.

RESOURCES

Successful homeschooling families view the character of the child as a primary resource. Education is not a right, a government benefit to be given to all good children in equitable servings. Rather, education is a duty. A characteristic of good character is the desire to find, and act upon good information. Civilizations that honor "wisdom" tend to outlive and outperform any governments that happen to hold temporary power. Think of the European Jews, the Armenians, and the overseas Chinese. To the extent that parents can shape the attitudes of their children, bending them in this direction early makes the whole process work well. We do not pull our kids out of public school to recreate a classroom in the basement, with neatly regimented desks, and a blackboard at the front. Rather, learning is part of everyday life. Students spend an hour or two completing their daily work in order to keep up with their peers. Then, time invested beyond that in students' areas of passion takes them leagues ahead of their peers. Do work quickly, do it well, and time is the learner's own.

Allies also are important. America still has an astonishing number of voluntary associations that are not sponsored by the state. Although the Boy Scouts of America is under assault by the devotees of the juggernaut state, the organization has enough residual stamina to flip off their would-be masters. A good scout troop will expose a boy to a number of learning opportunities, a wide selection of mentors, and the survival skills that build a tough self-confidence.

Many homeschool families participate in, or even create, 4-H Clubs. Again, if children are involved with the troop or club, they have more opportunities to experience life with other children and families. More "teachable moments." Co-belligerents can also be helpful. God talk makes some libertarians and most Randians nervous, for example. But many of the most influential people in the homeschooling movement are Christians. You may not agree with their basic premises, but you share with them a common foe.

Typical Christian homeschooling families view it as sin to (sur)render unto Caesar that which is God's, the precious children entrusted to their care. They have staked out one zone of resistance to the state, and defend it with the passion a mother bear has for her cubs. The liberty of the family has become a third rail of American politics on every level. These people watch their legislatures with jaundiced, suspicious eyes. They often invest $100 per year in the Home School Legal Defense Association to secure the services of rabidly fanatical lawyers in case an agent of the state tries to infringe their familial liberties. Many regard with suspicion any government that demands more of them than their God does, the tithe. These fighting fundamentalists are even now throwing sand into Caesar's gears. Respect them for that.

HOPE

Lovers of classic movies recall Fritz Lang's *Metropolis*. At one point, the young protagonist's eyes are opened. The factory gate that the workers are trudging in lockstep into suddenly becomes the mouth of Moloch. The state needs a steady stream of resources to continue its work of cancerous expansion. The most valuable *resource* we can hand over is our children. Well, suppose we politely refuse to hand our children over. Suppose we raise our children to regard all the claims of the state, starting with its asserted claim to 30 hours of their lives every week, with skepticism. How likely will these children be to go along with other statist demands in the future?

The level of government that most directly affects our lives is local. More than half of the typical county's budget goes to education. As homeschooling becomes mainstream, folks begin to wonder:

IF we are pouring $200,000 a year into a classroom of 20 students, AND IF the teacher is making $40,000 a year, AND IF $10,000 a year should be gracious plenty to pay for the classroom and its utilities, THEN WHERE does the remaining $150,000 go? As Odell the Mover said, after pocketing a client's certified check and before unlocking the van, "Some damn body made a buck today." When people start asking these questions, a major societal transformation is afoot.

Let me conclude with a quote from my favorite Marxist Jesuit, the late Ivan Illich:

> Some fortuitous coincidence will render publicly obvious the structural contradictions between stated purposes and effective results in our major institutions. People will suddenly find obvious what is now evident to only a few.... Like other widely shard insights, this one will have the potential of turning public imagination inside out. Large institutions can quite suddenly lose their respectability, their legitimacy, and their reputation for serving the public good. It happened to the Roman Church in the Reformation, to royalty in the Revolution. The unthinkable became the obvious overnight: that people could and would behead their rulers. (Illich, 1980, p. 111)

REFERENCES

Augustine of Hippo. (2000). *The confessions of St. Augustine* (E. B. Pusey, Trans.) New York: Modern Library.

Blumenfeld, S. (2000). Alpha-Phonics: A primer for beginning readers. Boise, ID: Paradigm.

Golding, W. (1959). *The lord of the flies.* New York: Berkley.

Illich, I. (1980). *Tools for conviviality.* New York: Harper & Row.

LaDoux, M. (2004). *Play 'n' talk.* Oceanside, CA: Play 'n' Talk International.

Lewis, C. S. (2004). http://www.townhousebooks.com/kids.html

Rand, A. (1961). *Atlas shrugged.* New York: Signet Books.

Steyn, M. (2000). *Safe, legal and rare ... oh my!* Retrieved June, 2004, from http://www.theinterim.com/2004/june/steyn.html

CHAPTER 5

AWAY WITH ALL TEACHERS

The Cultural Politics of Homeschooling

Michael W. Apple

INTRODUCTION

If one of the marks of the growing acceptance of ideological changes is their positive presentation in the popular media, then home schooling has clearly found a place in our consciousness. It has been discussed in the national press, on television and radio, and in widely circulated magazines. Its usual presentation is that of a savior, a truly compelling alternative to a public school system that is presented as a failure. While the presentation of public schools as simply failures is deeply problematic,[1] it is the largely unqualified support of home schooling that concerns me here. I am considerably less sanguine.

Data on home schooling are not always accurate and are often difficult to compile. However, a sense of the extent of home schooling can be found in the fact that the National Home Education Research Institute has estimated that as of the 1997-1998 school year, there were 1.5 million children being home schooled in the United States. The Institute also has suggested a growth rate of 15% annually in these numbers since 1990. While these data are produced by an organization that is one of the strongest supporters of home schooling—even given the possible inflation of these figures—clearly, this is a considerable number of students.[2]

We have many issues that could be raised about the home schooling movement. I want to ask a number of critical questions about the dangers associated with it. While it is quite probable that some specific children and families will gain from home schooling, my concerns are larger. They are connected to the more extensive restructuring of this society that I believe is quite dangerous and to the manner in which our very sense of public responsibility is withering in ways that will lead to even further social inequalities. To illuminate these dangers, I shall do the following: (1) situate home schooling within the larger movement that provides much of its impetus; (2) suggest its connections with other protectionist impulses; (3) connect it to the history of and concerns about the growth of activist government; and, finally, (4) point to how it may actually hurt many other students who are not home schooled.

At the very outset of this chapter, let me state as clearly as I can that any parents who care so much about the educational experiences of their children that they actively seek to be deeply involved are to be applauded, not chastised or simply dismissed. Let me also say that it is important not to stereotype individuals who reject public schooling [3] as unthinking promoters of ideological forms that are so deeply threatening that they are, automatically, to be seen as beyond the pale of legitimate concerns. Indeed, as I have demonstrated in *Cultural Politics and Education* (Apple, 1996), complicated reasons lie behind the growth of antischool sentiments. I showed that elements of good sense, as well as bad sense, rest in such beliefs. All too many school systems *are* overly bureaucratic, are apt not to listen carefully to parents' or community concerns, or act in overly defensive ways when questions are asked about what and whose knowledge is considered official. In some ways, these kinds of criticisms are similar across the political spectrum, as both the left and right often make similar claims about the politics of recognition (see Fraser, 1997). Indeed, these very kinds of criticisms have led many progressive, activist educators to build more community-based and responsive models of curriculum and teaching in public schools (Apple & Beane, 1995, 1999).

While many home schoolers have not made their decision based on religious convictions, a large proportion have (see Detwiler, 1999; Ray, 1999). In this essay, I shall focus largely on this group, in part because it constitutes some of the most committed parents and in part because ideologically it raises a number of important issues.

Many home schoolers are guided by what they believe are biblical understandings of the family, gender relationships, legitimate knowledge, the importance of "tradition," the role of government, and the economy (Detwiler, 1999; Kintz, 1997).[4] They constitute part of what I have called the "conservative restoration" in which a tense alliance has been built among various segments of the public in favor of particular policies in education and the larger social world. Let me place this in its larger context.

Education and Conservative Modernization

Long lasting educational transformations often come not from the work of educators and researchers, but from larger social movements, which tend to push our major political, economic, and cultural institutions in specific directions. Thus, it would be impossible fully to understand educational reforms over the past decades without situating them within, say, the long struggles by multiple communities of color and women for both cultural recognition and economic redistribution (see, e.g., Fraser, 1997). Even such taken for granted things as state textbook adoption policies—among the most powerful mechanisms in the processes of defining official knowledge—are the results of widespread populist and anti-northern movements and especially the class and race struggles over culture and power that organized and re-organized the polity in the United States a century ago (Apple, 2000).

It should, then, come as no surprise that education is again witnessing the continued emergence and growing influence of powerful social movements. Some of these may lead to increased democratization and greater equality, while others are based on a fundamental shift in the very meanings of democracy and equality and are more than a little retrogressive socially and culturally. Unfortunately, the latter have emerged as the most powerful.

The rightward turn has been the result of years of well funded, creative ideological efforts by the right to form a broad-based coalition. This new alliance, what is technically called a "new hegemonic bloc", has been so successful in part because it has been able to make major inroads in the battle over common-sense.[5] That is, the alliance has creatively stitched together different social tendencies and commitments and has organized them under its own general leadership in issues dealing with welfare, culture, the economy, and as many know from personal experience, education. Its aim in educational and social policy might best be described as "conservative modernization" (Dale, 1989). In the process, democracy has been reduced to consumption practices. Citizenship has been reduced to possessive individualism; and a politics based on resentment and a fear of the "Other" has been pressed forward.

A number of major elements fall within this new alliance (see Apple, 1996, 2001 for more detailed discussion). The first group, *neo-liberals*, represent dominant economic and political elites who are intent on modernizing the economy and the institutions connected to it. They are certain that markets and consumer choice will solve all of our social problems, since *private* is necessarily good and *public* is necessarily bad—hence, their strong support of vouchers and private choice plans. While clear empirical evidence shows the very real inequalities that are created by such educational policies (Whitty, Power, & Halpin, 1998; Lauder & Hughes, 1999), this group is usually in leadership of the alliance. If we think of this new bloc as an ideological umbrella, neo-liberals are holding the umbrella's handle.

The second group, *neo-conservatives*, are economic and cultural conservatives who want a return to *high standards*, discipline, *real* knowledge, and what is in essence a form of social Darwinist competition. They are fueled by a nostalgic and quite romanticized vision of the past. It is often based on a fundamental misrecognition of the fact that what they might call the classics and real knowledge gained that status as the result of intense past conflicts and often were themselves seen as equally dangerous culturally and just as morally destabilizing as any of the new elements of the curriculum and culture they now castigate (Levine, 1996).

The third element is made up of largely white working class and middle class groups that mistrust the state and are concerned with security, the family, gender and age relations within the home, sexuality, and traditional and fundamentalist religious values and knowledge. They form an increasingly active segment of *authoritarian populists* who are powerful in education and in other areas of politics and social and cultural policy. They provide much of the support from below for neo-liberal and neo-conservative positions, since they see themselves as disenfranchised by the *secular humanism* that supposedly now pervades public schooling. They are also often among those larger numbers of people whose very economic livelihoods are most at stake in the economic restructuring and capital flight that we are now experiencing. Many home schoolers combine beliefs from all three of these tendencies; but it is the last one that seems to drive a large portion of the movement (Detwiler, 1999; Kintz, 1997).

Satan's Threat

For many on the right, one of the key enemies is public education. Secular education is turning our children into *aliens* and, by teaching them to question our ideas, is turning them against us. What are often accurate concerns about public schooling that I noted earlier—its overly bureaucratic nature, its lack of curriculum coherence, and its disconnection from the lives, hopes, and cultures of many of its communities, and more—are here often connected to more deep-seated and intimate worries, echoed in Elaine Pagels' argument that Christianity has historically defined its most fearful satanic threats not from distant enemies, but in relation to very intimate ones (Pagels, 1995). "The most dangerous characteristic of the satanic enemy is that though he will look just like us, he will nevertheless have changed completely" (quoted in Kintz, 1997, p. 73).

Some of the roots of this can be found much earlier in the conservative activist Beverly LaHaye's call for the founding of an organization to counter the rising tide of feminism. In support of Concerned Women of America, she spoke of her concern for family, nation, and religion.

> I sincerely believe that God is calling the Christian women of America to draw together in a spirit of unity and purpose to protect the rights of the family. I believe that it is time for us to set aside our doctrinal differences to work for a spiritually renewed America. Who but a woman is as deeply concerned about her children and her home? Who but women has the time, the intuition, and the drive to restore our nation?... They may call themselves feminists or humanists. The label makes little difference, because many of them are seeking the destruction of morality and human freedom. (quoted in Kintz, 1997, p. 80)

It is clear from the above quote what is seen as the satanic threat and what is at stake here. These fears about the nation, home, family, children's innocence, religious values, and traditional views of gender relations are sutured together into a more general fear of the destruction of a moral compass and personal freedom. *Our* world is disintegrating around us. Its causes are not the economically destructive policies of the globalizing economy (Greider, 1997), not the decisions of an economic elite, and not the ways in which, say, our kind of economy turns *all* things—including cherished traditions (and even our children)[6]—into commodities for sale. Rather the causes are transferred onto those institutions and people which are themselves being constantly buffeted by the same forces—public sector institutions, schooling, poor people of color, other women who have struggled for centuries to build a society that is more responsive to the hopes and dreams of many people who have been denied participation in the public sphere, and so on.[7]

As I noted at the beginning of this article, however, it is important not to stereotype individuals involved in this movement. For example, a number of men and women who are activists in rightist movements believe that some elements of feminism did improve the conditions of women overall. By focusing on equal-pay-for-equal-work and opening up job opportunities that had been traditionally denied to women who had to work for pay, women activists had benefited many people. However, for authoritarian populists, feminism and secular institutions in general still tend to break with God's law. They are much too individualistic and mis-interpret the divine relationship between families and God. In so doing, many aspects of civil rights legislation, of the public schools' curricula, and so many other parts of secular society are simply wrong.

Thus, for example, if one views the Constitution of the United States literally as divinely inspired, then it is not public institutions but the traditional family—as God's chosen association—that is the core social unit that must be protected by the Constitution (Kintz, 1997, p. 97). In a time of seeming cultural disintegration, when traditions are under threat and when the idealized family faces ever more externally-produced dangers, protecting our families and our children are key elements in returning to God's grace.[8]

Even without these religious elements, a defensive posture is clear in much of the movement. In many ways, the movement toward home schooling mirrors the growth of private consciousness in other areas of society. It is an extension of the *suburbanization* of everyday life that is so evident all around us. In essence, it is the equivalent of gated communities and of the privatization of neighborhoods, recreation, parks, and so many other things. It provides a security zone, both physically and ideologically. Linda Kintz describes it this way.

> As citizens worried about crime, taxes, poor municipal services, and poor schools abandon cities, the increasing popularity of gated communities ... fortress communities, reflects people's desire to retreat.... They want to spend more of their tax dollars on themselves instead of others.... Further, they take comfort in the social homogeneity of such communities, knowing that their neighbors act and think much as they do. (Kintz, 1997, p. 107)

This "cocooning" is not just about seeking an escape from the problems of the city (a metaphor for danger and heterogeneity). It is a rejection of the entire *idea* of the city. Cultural and intellectual diversity, complexity, ambiguity, uncertainty, and proximity to the Other— all these are to be shunned (Kintz, 1997, p. 107). In place of the city is the engineered pastoral, the neat and well-planned universe where things (and people) are in their *rightful place* and reality is safe and predictable.

Yet in so many ways such a movement mirrors something else. It is a microcosm of the increasing segmentation of American society in general. As we move to a society segregated by residence, race, economic opportunity, and income, *purity* is increasingly more apt to be found in the fact that upper classes send their children to elite private schools; where neighborliness is determined by property values; where evangelical Christians, ultraorthodox Jews, and others only interact with each other and their children are schooled in private religious schools or schooled at home (Kintz, 1997, p. 108). A world free of conflict, uncertainty, the voice and culture of the Other—in a word I used before, cocooning—is the ideal.[9]

Home schooling, thus, has many similarities with the Internet. It enables the creation of *virtual communities,* which are perfect for those with specialized interests. It gives individuals a new ability to personalize information, to choose what they want to know or what they find personally interesting. However, as many commentators are beginning to recognize, unless we are extremely cautious, customizing our lives could radically undermine the strength of local communities, many of which are already woefully weak. As Andrew Shapiro puts it,

> Shared experience is an indisputably essential ingredient [in the formation of local communities]; without it there can be no chance for mutual understanding, empathy and social cohesion. And this is precisely what personalization threatens to delete. A lack of common information would deprive individuals of a starting point for democratic dialogue. (Shapiro, 1999, p. 12)

Even with the evident shortcomings of many public schools, at the very least they provide "a kind of social glue, a common cultural reference point in our polyglot, increasingly multicultural society" (Shapiro, 1999, p. 12). Yet, whether called personalizing or cocooning, it is exactly this common reference point that is rejected by many within the home schooling movement's pursuit of freedom and choice.

This particular construction of the meaning of freedom is of considerable moment, since there is a curious contradiction within such conservatism's obsession with freedom. In many ways this emphasis on freedom is, paradoxically, based on a *fear* of freedom (Kintz, 1997, p.168). It is valued, but also loathed as a site of danger, of "a world out of control." Many home schoolers reject public schooling out of concern for equal time for their beliefs. They want "equality." Yet it is a specific vision of equality, because coupled with their fear of things out of control is a powerful anxiety that the nation's usual understanding of equality will produce uniformity (Kintz, 1997, p. 186). But this feared uniformity is not seen as the same as the religious and cultural homogeneity sponsored by the conservative project. It is a very different type of uniformity—one in which the fear that *we are all the same* actually speaks to a loss of religious particularity.

Thus, again, another paradox lies at the heart of this movement: we want everyone to be like *us* (This is a "Christian nation"; governments must bow before "a higher authority") (Smith, 1998); but we want the right to be different—a difference based on being God's elect group. Uniformity weakens our specialness. This tension—between knowing one is a member of God's elect people and is thus by definition different and also being so certain that one is correct that the world needs to be changed to fit one's image—is one of the central paradoxes behind authoritarian populist impulses. For some home schoolers, the paradox is solved by withdrawal of one's children from the public sphere to maintain their difference. And for still others, this allows them to prepare themselves and their children with an armor of Christian beliefs to go forth into the world later on to bring God's word to those who are not among the elect. Once again, let us declare our particularity, our difference, better to prepare ourselves to bring the unannointed world to our set of uniform beliefs.

Attacking the State

At the base of this fear, both of the loss of specialness and of becoming uniform in the *wrong way*, is a sense that the state is intervening in our daily lives in quite powerful ways that are causing even more losses. It is not possible to understand the growth of home schooling unless we connect it to the history of the attack on the public sphere in general and on the government (the state) in particular. To comprehend better the anti-statist impulses that lie behind a good deal of the home schooling movement, I need to place these impulses in a longer historical and social context. Some history and theory is necessary here.

One of the keys to this development is what Clarke and Newman have called the "managerial state" (Clarke & Newman, 1997) that combined bureaucratic administration and professionalism. The organization of the state centered around the application of specific rules of coordination. Routinization and predictability are among the hallmarks of such a state, coupled with a second desirable trait, that of social, political, and personal neutrality, rather than nepotism and favoritism. This bureaucratic routinization and predictability would be balanced by an emphasis on professional discretion. Here, bureaucratically regulated professionals such as teachers and administrators would still have an element of irreducible autonomy based on their training and qualifications. Their skills and judgment were to be trusted, if they acted fairly and impartially. Yet fairness and impartiality were not enough; these professionals also personalized the managerial state, making it "approachable" by not only signifying neutrality but also by acting in non-anonymous ways to foster the "public good" and to "help" individuals and families (Clarke & Newman, 1997, pp. 5-7).

Of course, such bureaucratic and professional norms were designed not only to benefit "clients." But they also acted to protect the state, by providing it with legitimacy. (The state is impartial, fair, and acts in the interests of everyone.) They also served to insulate professional judgments from critical scrutiny. (As holders of expert knowledge, we—teachers, social workers, state employees—are the ones who are to be trusted since we know best.)

Thus, from the end of World War II until approximately the mid1970s, a settlement, really a compromise, helped to legitimate an activist welfare state. Thus, bi-partisan support for the state provided and managed a larger part of social life—often putting it above a good deal of party politics. Bureaucratic administration promised to act impartially for the benefit of everyone. And professionals employed by the state, such as teachers and other educators, were there to apply expert knowledge to serve the public (Clarke & Newman, 1997, p. 8). This compromise was widely accepted and provided public schools and other public institutions with a strong measure of support since the vast majority of people continued to believe that schools, and other state agencies, did in fact act professionally and impartially in the public good.

This compromise came under severe attack, as the fiscal crisis deepened and as competition over scarce economic, political, and cultural resources grew more heated in the 1970s and beyond. The political forces of conservative movements used this crisis often in quite cynical, manipulative, and well-funded ways. The state was criticized for denying the opportunity for consumers to exercise choice. The welfare state was seen as gouging the citizen (as a taxpayer) to pay for public handouts for those who ignored personal responsibility for their actions. These *scroungers* from the underclass were seen as sexually promiscuous, immoral, and lazy as opposed to the *rest of us* who were hard-working, industrious, and moral. Poor people supposedly are a drain on all of us economically and state-sponsored support of them leads to the collapse of the family and traditional morality (Apple, 2000). These arguments may not have been totally accurate (see, for example, Fine & Weis, 1998), but they were effective.

This suturing together of neoliberal and neoconservative attacks led to a particular set of critiques against the state. For many people, the state was no longer the legitimate and neutral upholder of the public good. Instead the welfare state was an active agent of national decline, as well as an economic drain on the country's (and the family's) resources. In the words of Clarke and Newman:

> Bureaucrats were identified as actively hostile to the public—hiding behind the impersonality of regulations and "red tape" to deny choice, building bureaucratic empires at the expense of providing service, and insulated from the "real world" pressures of competition by their monopolistic position. Professionals were arraigned as motivated by self-interest, exercising power over would-be costumers, denying choice through the dubious claim that "professionals know best." Worse still ... liberalism ... was viewed as

undermining personal responsibility and family authority and as prone to trendy excesses such as egalitarianism, anti-discrimination policies, moral relativism or child-centeredness. (Clarke & Newman, 1997, p. 15)

These moral, political, and economic concerns were easily transferred to public schooling, since for many people the school was and is the public institution closest to them in their daily lives. Hence, public schooling and the teaching and curricula found within it became central targets of attack. Curricula and teachers were not impartial, but elitist. School systems were imposing the Other's morality on "us." And "real Americans" who were patriotic, religious, and moral—as opposed to everyone else— were suffering and were the new oppressed (Delfattore, 1992). While this position fits into a long history of the paranoid style of American cultural politics, often based on quite inaccurate stereotypes, it does point to a profound sense of alienation that many people feel.

Much of this anti-statism of course was fueled by the constant attention given in the media and in public pronouncements to incompetent teachers who are over-paid and have short working days and long vacations.[10] We should not minimize the effects of the conservative attacks on schools for their supposed inefficiency, wasting of financial resources, and lack of connection to the economy. After years of well-orchestrated attacks, it would be extremely odd if one did not find that the effects on popular consciousness were real. The fact that a number of these criticisms may be *partly* accurate should not be dismissed. Undoubtedly, a small group of teachers treat teaching as simply a job that gives them many holidays and free time in the summer. Administrative costs and bureaucratic requirements in schools have risen. Parents and local communities do have a justifiable right to worry about whether their daughters and sons will have decent jobs when they leave school, especially in a time when our supposedly booming economy has left millions of people behind and many of the jobs being created are anything but fulfilling and secure (Apple, 1996). (The fact that the school has very little to do with this is important.)

Yet, not only do worries about teachers fuel this movement. As I point out in my book, *Educating the "Right" Way* (Apple, 2001), public schools themselves are seen as extremely dangerous places. These schools were institutions that threatened one's very soul. Temptations and Godlessness were everywhere within them. God's truths were expunged from the curriculum and God's voice could no longer be heard. Prayers were now illegal and all of the activities that bound my life to scriptural realities were seen as deviant.

Even with the powerful negative emotions that such senses of loss and disconnection create, an additional element has entered into the emotional economy being created here with a crushing force. For an increasingly large number of parents, public schools are now seen as threatening in an even more powerful way. They are dangerous bodily; that is, they are seen as filled with physical dangers to the very lives of one's children. The spate of shootings in schools in the United States has had a major impact on the feelings of insecurity that parents have about their children. Stories of violence-ridden schools, ones that were worrisome but were seen as largely an urban problem involving the poor and children of color, were already creating an antipublic school sentiment among many conservative parents. The horrors of seeing students shoot other students, and now not in those supposedly troubled urban schools but in the suburban areas that had grown after people fled the city, exacerbated the situation. If even the schools of affluent suburbia were sites of danger, then the *only* remaining safe haven was the fortress home.[11]

Fears, no matter how powerful they are or whether they are justified or not, are not enough, however. That a person will act on her or his fears is made more or less probable by the availability of resources to support taking action. It is an almost taken for granted point, but important nonetheless, that the growth of home schooling has been stimulated by the wider accessibility to tools that make it easier for parents to engage in it. Among the most important is the Internet (see Bromley & Apple, 1998). Scores of websites are available that give advice, that provide technical and emotional support, that tell the stories of successful home schoolers, and that are more than willing to sell material at a profit. The fact that, like the conservative evangelical movement in general (Smith, 1998), a larger portion of home schoolers than before seem to have the economic resources to afford computers means that economic capital can be mobilized in antischool strategies in more flexible and dynamic ways than in earlier periods of the home schooling movement.

Since home schooling is often done using the web, it is useful to see what some of the sites say. The Teaching Home, based in Portland, Oregon, is one of the central resources for conservative Christians who wish to home school.[12] On its Website, after the following general statement on the question "Why do families home school?" a number of answers are given.

> Many Christian parents are committed to educating their children at home because of their conviction that this is God's will for their family. They are concerned for the spiritual training and character development as well as the social and academic welfare of their children.

Among the advantages listed are:

Parents can present all academic subjects from a biblical perspective and include spiritual training.

"The fear of the LORD is the beginning of wisdom, and the knowledge of the Holy One is understanding" (Prov. 9:10 NAS).

Home schooling makes quality time available to train and influence children in all areas in an integrated way.

Each child receives individual attention and has his unique needs met.

Parents can control destructive influences such as various temptations, false teachings (including secular humanism and occult influences of the New Age movement), negative peer pressure, and unsafe environments.

Children gain respect for their parents as teachers.

The family experiences unity, closeness, and mutual enjoyment of one another as they spend more time working together.

Children develop confidence and independent thinking away from the peer pressure to conform and in the security of their own home.

Children have time to explore new interests and to think.

Communication between different age groups is enhanced.

Tutorial-style education helps each child achieve his full educational potential.

Flexible scheduling can accommodate parents' work and vacation times and allow time for many activities.

This list is broader than might be allowed in some of the stereotypes of what home schooling advocates–particularly religiously conservative ones–are like, with a focus on wanting their children to explore, to achieve their full academic potential, to have "his" needs met. Yet, in this diverse list of advantages, certain themes come to the fore. At the top is biblical authority, with knowledge and understanding connected with "fear of the LORD." Real knowledge is grounded in what the Holy One has ordained. The role of the parent is largely one of training, of influencing one's children in all areas so that they are safe from the outside influences of a secular society. God/home/family is pure; the rest of the world—secular humanism, peers, popular culture—are forms of pollution, temptations, dangers. That the male pronoun is used throughout is indicative of God's wish for the man of the house to be God's chosen leader (Kintz, 1997).

Yet, saying these things must not be used as an excuse to deny the elements of concern that parents such as these express. They are *deeply* worried about the lives and futures of their children, for whom they are fully willing to sacrifice an immense amount. They do want a caring environment for their children, one in which all family members respect and care for each other, indicating powerful, positive moments in these statements. In a time when many groups of varying religious and political sentiments express the concern that children are ignored in this society, that they are simply seen as present and future consumers by people who only care whether a profit is made off of them, that our major institutions are less responsive than they should be, and that elements of popular culture are negative as well as positive—all of these sentiments are central to the concerns of home schoolers as well.

Given what I have just said, we do need to recognize elements of good sense in the critique of the state made by both the left and the right, such as the home schoolers whom I have discussed above. The government has assumed all too often that the only true holders of expertise in education, social welfare, etc. are those in positions of formal authority, leading to a situation of over-bureaucratization, to the state's being partly "colonized" by a particular fraction of the new middle class who seeks to ensure its own mobility and its own positions by employing the state for its own purposes (Bourdieu, 1996). Some schools have become sites of danger given the levels of alienation and meaningless–and the dominance of violence as an imaginary solution in the popular media. However, there is a world of difference between, say, acknowledging some historical tendencies within the state to become overly bureaucratic and not to listen carefully enough to the expressed needs of the people it is supposed to serve and a blanket rejection of public control and public institutions such as schools. This condition leads not only to cocooning, but also to threatened gains made by large groups of disadvantaged people for whom the possible destruction of public schooling is nothing short of a disaster. The final section of my analysis turns to a discussion of this.

Public and Private

We need to think *relationally* about who will be the major beneficiaries of the attack on the state and the movement toward home schooling. What if gains made by one group of people come at the expense of another, even more culturally and economically oppressed groups? As we shall see, this is not an inconsequential worry in this instance.

A distinction helpful here is that between a politics of *redistribution* and a politics of *recognition*. In the first (redistribution), the concern is for socioeconomic injustice. Here, the political-economic system of a society creates conditions that lead to exploitation (having the fruits of one's labor appropriated for the benefit of others), and/or economic marginalization (having one's paid work confined to poorly paid and undesirable jobs or having no real access to the routes to serious and better paying jobs), and/or deprivation (being constantly denied the material that would lead to an adequate standard of living). All of these socioeconomic injustices lead to arguments about whether this is a just or fair society and whether identifiable groups of people actually have equality of resources (Fraser, 1997, p. 13).

The second dynamic (recognition) is often related to redistribution in the real world, but it has its own specific history and differential power relations as well. It is related to the politics of culture and symbols. In this case, injustice is rooted in a society's social patterns of representation and interpretation. Examples of this include cultural domination (being constantly subjected to patterns of interpretation or cultural representation that are alien to one's own or even hostile to it), nonrecognition (basically being rendered invisible in the dominant cultural forms in the society), and disrespect (having oneself routinely stereotyped or maligned in public representations in the media, schools, government policies, or in everyday conduct (Fraser, 1997, p. 14). These kinds of issues surrounding the politics of recognition are central to the identities and sense of injustice of many home schoolers. Indeed, they provide the organizing framework for their critique of public schooling and their demand that they be allowed to teach their children outside of such state control.

While both forms of injustice are important, it is absolutely crucial that we recognize that an adequate response to one must not lead to the exacerbation of the other. That is, responding to the claims of injustice in recognition by one group (say religious conservatives) must not make the conditions that lead to exploitation, economic marginalization, and deprivation more likely to occur for other groups. Unfortunately, this may be the case for some of the latent effects of home schooling.

Thus, it is vitally important not to separate out the possible effects of home schooling from what we are beginning to know about the possible consequences of neo-liberal policies in general in education. As Whitty, Power, and Halpin (1998) have shown in their review of the international research on voucher and choice plans, one of the latent effects of such policies has been the reproduction of traditional hierarchies of class and race. That is, the programs clearly have differential benefits in which those who already possess economic and cultural capital reap significantly more benefits than those who do not. This pattern works very much the same ways as the stratification of economic, political, and cultural power produces inequalities in nearly every socio-economic sphere (Whitty, Power, & Halpin, 1998). One of the hidden consequences that is emerging from the expanding conservative critique of public institutions, including schools, is a growing antitax movement in which those who have chosen to place their children in privatized, marketized, and home schools do not want to pay taxes to support the schooling of the Other (Apple, 1996).

The wider results are becoming clear—a declining tax base for schooling, social services, health care, housing, and anything public for those populations (usually in the most economically depressed urban and rural areas) who suffer the most from the economic dislocations and inequalities that so deeply characterize this nation. Thus, a politics of recognition—I want to guarantee choice for my children based on my identity and special needs—has begun to have extremely negative effects on the politics of redistribution. It is absolutely crucial that we recognize that if the emergence of educational markets has consistently benefited the most advantaged parents and students and has consistently disadvantaged both economically poor parents and students and parents and students of color (Whitty, Power, & Halpin, 1998; Lauder & Hughes, 1999), then we need critically to examine the latent effects of the growth of home schooling in the same light. Will social justice lose in this equation just as it did and does in many of the other highly-publicized programs of choice?

We now have emerging evidence that social justice often does lose with the expansion of home schooling in some states. For example, the ongoing debate over the use of public money for religious purposes in education is often subverted through manipulation of loopholes that are only available to particular groups. Religiously motivated home schoolers are currently engaged in exploiting public funding in ways that are not only hidden, but ways that raise serious questions about the drain on economic resources during a time of severe budget crises in all too many school districts.

Hence, gains by some groups (say, home schoolers) can have decidedly negative effects in other spheres such as the politics of redistribution. In California, for example, charter schools have been used as a mechanism to gain public money for home schoolers. Charter school legislation in California has been employed in very interesting ways to accomplish this. In one recent study, for example, 50% of charter schools were serving home schoolers. "Independent study" charter schools (a creative pseudonym for computer-linked home schooling) have been used by both school districts and parents to gain money that otherwise might not have been available. Demonstrating the ability of school districts strategically to use charter school legislation to get money that might have been lost when parents withdraw their children to home school them, this type of charter school also signifies something else. In this and other cases, the money given to parents for enrolling in such independent study charter schools was used by the parents to purchase religious material produced and sold by Bob Jones University, one of the most conservative religious schools in the entire nation (Wells, 1999).

Thus, public money not legally available for overtly sectarian material is used to purchase religious curricula under the auspices of charter school legislation. Yet unlike all curricula used in public schools, which *must* be publicly accountable in terms of its content and costs, the material purchased for home schooling has no public accountability whatsoever. While this does give greater choice to home schoolers and does enable them to act on a politics of recognition, it not only takes money away from other students who do not have the economic resources to afford computers in the home, but it denies them a say in what the community's children will learn about the themselves and their cultures, histories, values, and so on. Since a number of textbooks used in fundamentalist religious schools expressly state such things as Islam is a false religion and embody similar claims that many citizens would find deeply offensive,[13] it does raise serious questions about whether it is appropriate for public money to be used to teach such content without any public accountability.

Thus, two things are going on here. Money is being drained from already hard-pressed school districts to support home schooling. Just as importantly, curricular materials that support the identities of religiously motivated groups are being paid for by the public *without* any accountability, even though these materials may act in such a way as to deny the claims for recognition of one of the fastest growing religions in the nation, Islam. This raises more general and quite serious issues about how the claims for recognition by religious conservatives can be financially supported when they may at times actually support discriminatory teaching.

I do not wish to be totally negative here. After all, this is a complicated issue in which there may be justfiable worries among home schoolers that their culture and values are not being listened to. But it must be openly discussed, not lost in the simple statement that we should support a politics of recognition of religiously motivated home schoolers because their culture seems to them to be not sufficiently recognized in public institutions. At the very least, the possible dangers to the public good also need to be recognized.

Conclusion

I have used this essay to raise a number of critical questions about the economic, social, and ideological tendencies that often stand behind significant parts of the home schooling movement. In the process, I have situated it within larger social movements that could have quite negative effects on our sense of community, on the health of the public sphere, and on our commitment to building a society that is less economically and racially stratified. I have suggested that issues need to be raised about the effects of its commitment to cocooning, its attack on the state, and its grow-ing use of public funding with no public accountability. Yet, I have also noted clear elements of good sense in its criticisms of the bureaucratic nature of all too many of our institutions, in its worries about the manage-rial state, and in its devotion to being active in the education of its children.

In my mind, the task is to disentangle the elements of good sense evi-dent in these concerns from the selfish and antipublic agenda that has been pushing concerned parents and community members into the arms of the conservative restoration. The task of public schools is to listen much more carefully (but still critically when necessar) to the complaints of parents such as these and to rebuild our institutions in much more responsive ways.

As I have argued in much greater detail elsewhere, all too often public schools push concerned parents who are not originally part of conserva-tive cultural and political movements into the arms of such alliances by their defensiveness and lack of responsiveness and by their silencing of democratic discussion and criticism (Apple, 1996). Of course, sometimes these criticisms are unjustified or are politically motivated by undemo-cratic agendas (Apple, 1999). However, this must not serve as an excuse for a failure to open the doors of our schools to the intense public debate that makes public education a living and vital part of our democracy.

We have models for doing exactly that, as the democratic schools movement demonstrates (Apple & Beane, 1995, 1999). While I do not want to be overly romantic here, there are models of curricula and teach-ing that are related to community sentiment, are committed to social jus-tice and fairness, and are based in schools where both teachers and students want to be. If schools fail to respond, all too many parents are pushed in the direction of an anti-school sentiment, a tragedy both for the public school system and for our already withered sense of community that is increasingly under threat. Even though state-supported schools have often served as arenas through which powerful social divisions are partly reproduced, at least in the United States such schools have also served as powerful sites for the mobilization of collective action and for the preservation of the very possibility of democratic struggle (Hogan, 1983; Reese, 1986).

As one of the few remaining institutions that *is* still public, struggles to save public education are crucial. We obviously must walk a tightrope. How do we uphold the vision of a truly public institution while at the same time rigorously criticizing its functioning? In the United States, this is one of the tasks that the critical educators involved in *Democratic Schools* and the National Coalition of Education Activists have set for themselves (Apple & Beane, 1995, 1999).[14] They have recognized that schools have contradictory impulses and pressures upon them, especially in a time of conservative modernization. It is not romantic to work actively on and through those contradictions so that the collective memory of earlier and partly successful struggles is not lost. Nor is it romantic to engage in what I have called elsewhere nonreformist reforms, whose aim is to expand the space of counter-hegemonic action in public institutions (Apple, 1995). Yet, to do this, it is necessary to defend the public nature of such public spaces.

Raymond Williams may have expressed it best when—positioning himself as an optimist without any illusions–he reminded us of the importance of the *mutual* determination of the meanings and values that should guide our social life. In expressing his commitment toward "the long revolution," his words are worth remembering. "We must speak for hope, as long as it doesn't mean suppressing the nature of the danger" (Williams, 1989, p. 322). There are identifiable dangers to identifiable groups of people in public schooling as we know it. But the privatizing alternatives, including home schooling, may be much worse.

NOTES

1. It is important that we remember that public schools were and are a victory. They constituted a gain for the majority of people who were denied access to advancement and to valued cultural capital in a stratified society. This is not to claim that the public school did not and does not have differential effects. Indeed, I have devoted many books to uncovering the connections between formal education and the recreation of inequalities (see, for example, Apple 1990, 1995). Rather, it is to say that public schooling is a site of conflict, but one that also has been a site of major victories by popular groups (Reese, 1986). Indeed, conservatives would not be so angry at schools if public schools have not had a number of progressive tendencies cemented in them.

2. For further information on the National Home Education Research Institute and on its data on home schooling, see the following website: http://www.nheri.org

3. In the United States, the term "public" schooling refers only to those schools that are organized, funded, and controlled by the state. All other schools are considered private or religious.

4. In part, the attractiveness of home schooling among religiously motivated parents is also due to a structural difference between schools in the United States and those in many other nations. Historically, although at times mythical, the separation between state-supported schooling and an officially defined state religion has been a distinctive feature of education here. Thus, the absence of religious instruction in schools has been a source of tension among many groups and has generated even more anti-school sentiment (see Nord, 1995). I have discussed some of the history of the growth of conservative evangelical movements and their relationships with anti-school sentiment in Apple (2001).

5. I have demonstrated the success of this movement both historically and empirically elsewhere. See Apple (1996) and Apple (2000). For a history of the tensions surrounding the forces of conservative modernization specifically in the United States (see Foner, 1998).

6. I am thinking here of "Channel One," the for-profit commercial television show that is in an increasingly large percentage of our middle and secondary schools. In this reform, students are sold as a captive audience to corporations intent on marketing their products to our children in schools (see Apple, 2000; Molnar, 1996).

7. Of course, the very distinction between public and private spheres has strong connections to the history of patriarchal assumptions (see Fraser, 1989).

8. This is a *particular* construction of the family. As Coontz (1992) has shown in her history of the family in the United States, it has had a very varied form, with the nuclear family that is so important to conservative formulations merely being one of many.

9. Of course, it is important to realize that there may be good reasons for some groups to engage in cocooning. Take the example of indigenous or colonized groups. Given the destruction of cultures (and bodies) of oppressed peoples, it is clear that for many of them a form of cocooning is one of the only ways in which cultures and languages can be preserved. Since dominant groups already have cultural and economic power, the relative lack of such power by oppressed peoples creates protective needs. Thus, in cases such as this, cocooning may have a more positive valance.

10. Anti-teacher discourse has a long history, especially in the United States. It was often employed to legitimate centralized and standardized curricula and centralizing decision-making about textbooks within the state. See, for example, my discussion of the growth of state textbook adoption policies in Apple (2000).

11. There have been a number of highly publicized shootings in schools in the past few years in the United States. The most well known occurred in Columbine High School in a relatively affluent community in Colorado in which two alienated students killed a teacher and 12 other students and also planted pipe bombs throughout the building. This followed upon other shootings in suburban schools. In a recent instance in a suburban but much less affluent community in Michigan, a 6-year-old boy killed a 6-year-old girl classmate after an altercation on the playground. The threat of violence is now seen as a very real possibility in schools throughout the United States.

12. This and other similar material can be found at the following website address for The Teaching Home. See http://www.teachinghome.com/qa/wy/htm.

13. See Moshe Re'em (1998) for an interesting analysis of some of this content.

14. One of the best places to turn for an understanding of the more progressive movements surrounding education and social justice in public schools in the United States is the fast-growing newspaper *Rethinking Schools*. It represents one of the most articulate outlets for critical discussions of educational policy and practice in the country and brings together multiple activist voices: teachers, community activists, parents, academics, students,

and others. It can be contacted at *Rethinking Schools*, 1001 E. Keefe Avenue, Milwaukee, Wisconsin 53212, or via email at: RSBusiness@a1.com.

REFERENCES

Apple, M. W. (1990). *Ideology and curriculum*. New York: Routledge.

Apple, M. W. (1995). *Education and power* (2nd ed.). New York: Routledge.

Apple, M. W. (1996). *Cultural politics and education*. New York: Teachers College Press.

Apple, M. W. (1999). *Power, meaning, and identity*. New York: Peter Lang.

Apple, M. W. (2000). *Official knowledge* (2nd ed.). New York: Routledge.

Apple, M. W. (2001). *Educating the "right" way: Markets, standards, god, and inequality*. New York: Routledge.

Apple, M. W., & Beane, J. A. (Eds.). (1995). *Democratic schools*. Washington, DC: Association for Supervision and Curriculum Development.

Apple, M. W., & Beane, J. A. (Eds.). (1999). *Democratic schools: Lessons from the chalk face*. Buckingham: Open University Press.

Bourdieu, P. (1996). *The state nobility*. Stanford, CA: Stanford University Press.

Bromley, H., & Apple, M. W. (Eds.). (1998). *Education/technology/power*. Albany: State University of New York Press.

Clarke, J., & Newman, J. (1997). *The managerial state*. Thousand Oaks, CA: Sage.

Coontz, S. (1992). *The way we never were: American families and the nostalgia trap*. New York: Basic Books.

Dale, R. (1989). The Thatcherite project in education. *Critical Social Policy, 9*(3), 4-19.

Delfattore, J. (1992). *What Johnny shouldn't read*. New Haven, CT: Yale University Press.

Detwiler, F. (1999). *Standing on the premises of God: The christian right's fight to redefine America's public schools*. New York: University Press.

Fine, M., & Weis, L. (1998). *The unknown city: The lives of poor and working-class young adults*. Boston: Beacon Press.

Foner, E. (1998). *The story of American freedom*. New York: W. W. Norton.

Fraser, N. (1989). *Unruly practices*. Minneapolis, MN: University of Minnesota Press.

Fraser, N. (1997). *Justice interruptus*. New York: Routledge.

Hogan, D. (1982). Education and class formation. In M. W. Apple (Ed.), Cultural and economic reproduction in education. Boston: Routledge, Keegan, and Paul.

Greider, W. (1997). *One world, ready or not*. New York: Simon & Schuster.

Kintz, L. (1997). *Between Jesus and the market*. Durham, NC: Duke University Press.

Lauder, H., & Hughes, D. (1999). *Trading in futures: Why markets in education don't work*. Philadelphia: Open University Press.

Levine, L. (1996). *The opening of the American mind*. Boston: Beacon Press.

Molnar, A. (1996). *Giving kids the business*. Boulder, CO: Westview Press.

Nord, W. (1995). *Religion and American education*. Chapel Hill, NC: University of North Carolina Press.

Pagels, E. (1995). *The origin of satan.* New York: Random House.

Ray, B. (1999). *Home schooling on the threshold: A survey of research at the dawn of the new millennium.* Salem, OR: National Home Education Research Institute.

Re'em, M. (1998). *Young minds in motion: Teaching and learning about difference in formal and non-formal settings.* Unpublished doctoral dissertation, University of Wisconsin, Madison.

Reese, W. (1986). *Power and the promise of school reform.* New York: Routledge.

Shapiro, A. (1999, June 21). The net that binds. *The Nation, 268,* 11-15.

Smith, C. (1998). *American evangelicalism.* Chicago: University of Chicago Press.

Wells, A. S. (1999). *Beyond the rhetoric of charter school reform.* Los Angeles: Graduate School of Education and Information Studies, UCLA.

Whitty, G., Power, S., & Halpin, D. (1998). *Devolution and choice in education.* Philadelphia: Open University Press.

Williams, R. (1989). *Resources of hope.* New York: Verso.

CHAPTER 6

THROUGH THE LENS OF HOMESCHOOLING

A Response to Michael Apple and Rob Reich

Nicky Hardenbergh

Michael Apple[1] and Rob Reich[2] speculate that the practice of homeschooling will have negative consequences for our society. Apple contends homeschooling contributes to the "withering" of our "very sense of public responsibility," and Reich speaks of "the civic perils of homeschooling." I wrote this response in anticipation of their participation on a panel at the 2004 Annual Meeting of the American Education Research Association (AERA).[3]

INTRODUCTION

Perhaps unwisely, I broached the topic of deregulation of home education at a recent family gathering. At the mention of the word deregulation, my sister-in-law gasped and exclaimed, "You've become a Republican!" Her comment amused me. I still consider myself a liberal, but I no longer believe that the state should have a role in the regulation of home educa-

Home Schooling in Full View: A Reader, 97–108

tion. My direct personal experience as a homeschool mom and home-school advocate,[4] coupled with my continuing explorations of the history and philosophy of education, provide me with a new lens—the home-school lens—through which to view school issues.

From my homeschooling perspective, the question of the role of the public schools in developing civic responsibility becomes a complex, mul-tidimensional topic, a topic much broader than the one-dimensional debate between politically liberal academics and politically conservative homeschool advocates, such as that staged through the AERA panel dis-cussion. In this paper I delineate three groups whose contributions would expand the discussion in other dimensions.

First, the voices of conservative academics, particularly market-based reformers, would provide a new perspective on the regulation of home education by calling into question the efficacy of compulsory attendance statutes. Second, the voices of liberal homeschoolers, both religiously and nonreligiously motivated, would paint a more accurate picture of the diversity of homeschoolers and would confirm that virtually all home-schoolers, not just religious conservatives, regard the education of their children as a family's, not the government's, responsibility. Third, the voices of educational historians would remind us that today's school con-troversies are not new but rather have been part of the political fabric of our country at least since the advent of compulsory attendance.

I then turn to a brief examination of the history of compulsory atten-dance legislation. I note that the proponents of compulsory attendance remain firmly attached to the unexamined hypothesis that public schools function as the "glue" of our society and are therefore necessary in order to promote common values. I show that such nonempirical convictions as to the necessity of public schools and compulsory attendance can be viewed as tenets of the faith of universal education. I contend that home-schoolers share this faith, with one important exception: they do not equate education with school attendance.

In conclusion, I urge academics and policymakers to focus their research efforts not on the putative deficiencies of home education, but rather on the observable outcomes of the system in which they would compel all of our children to participate. This shift of focus would benefit children in public schools, as well as children being homeschooled.

VOICES MISSING FROM THE DEBATE

The phenomenon of homeschooling today is truly multifaceted. A dia-logue about homeschooling limited only to the voices of liberal academic critics and conservative Christian advocates, however, only generates a uni-dimensional, erroneous portrait. Education professionals who seek an accurate understanding of home education need to hear other voices, including liberal homeschoolers, conservative academics, and historians of education; expanding the conversation in this way will help policymakers become aware of the diversity of the homeschool community, as well as the diversity of academic assessment of the efficacy of compulsory school attendance. As various scholars question the notion of compulsory attendance in light of the results of their empirical research findings, homeschooling parents, guided by their own experience, are reexamining the traditional assumption that compulsory school attendance is essential for the common good.

Parents who teach their children at home are affronted by the unsubstantiated assertion that their homeschooled children are somehow deficient in proper socialization for citizenship. Friends, relatives, and complete strangers who express concerns about the negative effects of homeschooling usually seek to mitigate their criticism by saying something such as, "Of course, we're not worried about *your children!* But what about the children of all those *other* parents?"

Just who are all those other parents? For Rob Reich,[5] Michael Apple, and other commentators, the parents to be concerned about are religiously motivated. While both Apple and Reich acknowledge, in passing, that there are many reasons that parents choose to homeschool, both of these critics seem most worried that the common good is at risk when religiously motivated parents are permitted to control their own children's educations. Apple (2001) explicitly singles out homeschoolers who are motivated by religious convictions because their motivations raise a number of important ideological issues (p. 173). Reich (2001) assumes that "most homeschooling parents have religious objections to placing their children in ... a school environment" (p. 7).

Those who imagine homeschoolers to be isolationists might be surprised to discover that many homeschooling parents *do* see themselves as having a stake in preserving the vitality of public schools, even though our own children do not attend. Many of us *are* ready to make what Stanford professor David Labaree (2000) terms a "substantial commitment to the education of other people's children" (p. 129). Furthermore, homeschoolers may be able to provide some fresh ideas for reform of the educational system. For example, many of us are partial to a model of noncompulsory public schools similar to public libraries, providing educational opportunities to all at public expense. By choosing to educate our children at home, we have not chosen to ignore our public responsibilities.

Homeschooling parents simply cannot be categorized in any simplistic manner, and attempting to do so results in analytical errors.[6] Virtually all homeschoolers share the conviction that the full responsibility for our children's education properly rests with the family, rather than with public officials. Beyond that one point of convergence, homeschoolers diverge to criss-cross the political, religious, socioeconomic, and pedagogical spectra.

Academic scholars, too, span the political spectrum, and conservative academics should be heard in this discussion of homeschooling. When Apple and Reich express qualms about the "consumer mentality" of homeschooling, they seem to be reacting less to the reality of homeschooling and more to their academic colleagues who support market-based reform of education. Apple (2001) calls market-based reformers "neoliberals" who, in combination with other conservative forces, pose "substantial threats to the vitality of our nation, our schools, our teachers, and our children" (p. 5). Similarly, Reich (2002) expresses the concern, surprisingly phrased, that "[c]ustomizing a child's education through homeschooling represents the victory of a consumer mentality within education, that the only purpose that education should serve is to please and satisfy the preferences of the consumer" (p. 58).

Initially, I found this criticism puzzling. I now understand that both Apple and Reich are concerned about the effect on public schools if the proposals of conservative academics for school voucher programs and other market-based reforms were to become the norm. In one important respect, Apple and Reich correctly link homeschoolers and market-based reformers: market-based reformers, as it turns out, share with homeschoolers the discovery of the ineffectiveness of compulsory attendance laws. Economists have studied the costs and benefits of compulsory attendance laws in some detail, and the results of their studies are germane to the debate over home education regulation because those statutes provide the basis for the regulation of home education.

Scholars have reached no consensus as to the effect, if any, of compulsory attendance statutes on school attendance. A landmark 1972 study (Landes & Solmon) found no observable evidence that compulsory attendance laws were responsible for levels of school attendance. In fact, the researchers concluded that the data could support the hypothesis that these statutes *followed* high enrollment, not vice versa (p. 84). Economists since that time have debated the validity of various statistical measures, but even those who discover a correlation between the statutes and school attendance find only a very modest correspondence. In a study seeking to determine the cause of soaring rates of secondary school enrollments between the years of 1910 and 1939, researchers found that less than 5% of the increase could be attributed to compulsory attendance and child labor laws combined (Goldin & Katz, 2003). There seems to be no valid reason to conclude that, without compulsory attendance laws, we would have an uneducated populace. As Milton Friedman (the original propo-

nent of school vouchers) stated over 20 years ago, "[C]ompulsory attendance laws have costs as well as benefits. [I] no longer believe the benefits
justify the costs" (1979, p. 163).

Historians provide yet a third perspective on today's debate about how
to educate our future citizens; their work shows us that today's controversies are not new. A review of the documentary evidence reveals a long
record of attempts to "restore a common culture" through a common
school curriculum (Massaro, 1993, p. 8). As David Tyack and Larry Cuban
(1995) remind us, "[r]eforming the public schools has long been a favorite
way of improving not just education but society" (p. 1). Indeed, from its
inception, compulsory school attendance has been expected to remedy
any number of intractable social problems.

EXPANDING THE ANALYSIS TO INCLUDE THE HISTORY OF COMPULSORY ATTENDANCE

The push for the passage of compulsory attendance occurred over several
decades, beginning in Massachusetts in 1852. By 1918, all states had
passed some form of compulsory attendance. These laws, however, were
not immediately embraced by all parents. As historian Richard Brown
(1996) notes, the new policy of forcing school attendance "violated widely
shared cultural and political assumptions." American traditions up to that
point had promoted "policies to encourage the institutions [such as free
schools, libraries, newspapers] that enabled citizens to become informed."
Coercion was seen to be antithetical to the development of autonomous,
informed citizens (p. 152).

The notion that compulsory attendance was not an immediately popular policy was a surprise to me. Before I began studying the history of the
topic, I supported attendance requirements because I was under the illusion that without them we would not have an educated populace. Perhaps
Reich and Apple operate under a similar illusion. A search of the historical literature convinced me, however, that the main focus of common
school reformers was upon moral education, not academic preparation.
Reformers "drew on and appealed to a pervasive Protestant-republican
ideology that held that proper education could bring about a secular millennium, could make the United States quite literally God's country"
(Tyack, 1995, p. 16). The concept that common schools would develop
responsible citizenry may have achieved general acceptance, but the
details of implementation were always a source of contention. "Neither
the form, the substance, nor the financing of public education could command unanimous agreement" (Brown, 1996, p. 86).

Unanimous agreement on these topics still eludes us. Even though common schools and compulsory attendance policies are firmly established, no reform group has achieved a lasting consensus as to the schools' curricula. Continuing disagreements affect all efforts at education reform, even those targeted at the very youngest children. Historians report, for example, that, "though preschool educators and parents have always thought preschools should help socialize young children, in the past as today they disagree as to how and to what norms" (Beatty, 1995, p. 204).

Nonetheless, a surprisingly strong consensus does exist in favor of the conviction that school socialization is a prerequisite for good citizenship. Does this proposition have empirical support? While researchers have demonstrated that both higher income and higher civic participation correlate with a higher level of education, no research results that I have seen indicate that public school attendance is a significant independent variable. On the reverse side, we have incontrovertible evidence that school attendance is no guarantee of social responsibility. Common school proponents, nevertheless, hold tenaciously to their idea that public schools are the glue of the society, without which our nation would be in serious trouble.[7] The speculative nature and the illogic of this glue argument puzzled me for years.

Specifically, I could make no sense of the contentions of reformers who champion the merits of the common school while at the same time decry the current lack of civic virtue. The advocates of schooling overlook the crucial fact that virtually all of today's adult population attended public school. If the schools were instilling the glue values, the "common values [of] decency, civility, and respect" (Reich, 2002, paragraph 19), one would expect that those qualities be widespread in our society. If the glue has not *set* despite decades of endeavors by the schools, why then do reformers continue to assert that school attendance will indeed usher in the millennium? Recently I came upon the work of sociologist John Meyer (2000). His concept of "education as transcendence" enabled me to solve this puzzle. Borrowing from Meyer, I call my analysis "education as transcendental glue."

EDUCATION AS TRANSCENDENTAL GLUE

John Meyer (2000) observes that "education is the secular religion of a modern society" and contends that the description is more than an analogy. Our modern educational system, in his view, "can usefully be conceived as a transcendental or religious institution" (p. 208). The shared transcendent values that cut across all modern educational systems can be traced to the Enlightenment, the period when Europeans began to place great faith in the instrument of reason as the tool with which to comprehend the "lawful and rationalizable Nature" as created by a "high God" (p. 209).

Achievement of the common good, according to this analysis, depends on each and every individual's being connected with this universal cosmos. In old world European countries, either a powerful monarch or an aristocracy watched over the common good. In the new American republic, however, "individual persons—not communities and states – were to be the carriers of the common good" (Meyer, 2000, p. 210). Education and educational reform became central to the promotion of the common good, since the common good was dependent on each citizen's correct understanding of the workings of this rationalized and universal cosmos. Thus the common good depended on each citizen's adherence to the faith of Universal Education.

By not attending school, homeschoolers could be seen as threatening the universality of educational participation. Simply by virtue of their education's not being regulated by an authority other than their parents, homeschooled children are a threat to the dominance of the faith of Universal Education. Put another way, they have not been properly initiated. Meyer (2000) explains the initiation concept:

> Unusual among modern social rights, education is at once an entitlement of young persons, a compulsory obligation, and the obligation of the state to provide (and parents to permit). In this, educational participation is very distinct from rights to vote, to receive welfare protections, and to be treated with due process. It is much more similar to the status of baptism in a Universal Church: a badge, initiation rite, or ceremony of compulsory personhood, linking the ordinary individual to wider truths and laws. (p. 211)

At last all those questions of "what about their socialization?" make sense. If school enrollment is analogous to an initiation rite linking my child to wider truths, naturally other members of the Universal Church are concerned that my children are excluded from its ceremonial protection. Given Meyer's analysis, it is not surprising that Apple and Reich, even while conceding the probability that individual children may benefit from it, both regard homeschooling as a practice to be discouraged, either through strict regulation or through encouraging families back to the public school system.[8]

Meyer's (2000) analysis also explains the surprising lack of empirical evidence in both Reich's and Apple's assessments. Meyer observes that "the substantive nature of the [educational] conflicts ... tend to be curiously unrelated to real social functioning and very closely related to transcendent matters" (p. 220). Certainly Reich's (2001) argument seems "unrelated to real social functioning." For example, he aims to insure, among other factors, that children develop the quality of "minimal autonomy" that is necessary for "self-governance" and "participat[ion], if he or she chooses, in political dialogue with others" (p. 21). Yet this very quality of "autonomy" cannot actually be measured or tested, as Reich himself acknowledges. Undeterred, he states that because "the empirical measurement of autonomy, especially in children," would be "an exceptionally difficult and probably quixotic quest," he wishes "to approach the question somewhat more *abstractly*" [emphasis added] (Reich, 2001, pp. 28-29). As Meyer shows, abstraction is a hallmark of many school controversies: empirical data are irrelevant if the conflict is fundamentally *not* about the concrete functioning of the school system, but instead about adherence to the faith of Universal Education.

Surprisingly, while Meyer's (2000) analysis helps me place homeschool critics in proper perspective, it also highlights my fundamental agreement with the two basic principles of this faith as Meyer outlines them: first, that "physically, biologically, socially, and psychologically" the universe functions on "coherent, lawful, universal, general principles," and, second, that individuals can comprehend these general principles (p. 217). Both tenets seem uncontroversial and would, I predict, garner broad agreement among homeschoolers.

Regrettably, Meyer (2000) makes no distinction between the system of universal education and the practice of compulsory attendance. In his analysis, "modern educational systems are built on norms … of universal participation" (p. 210) and include rules of compulsion. Meyer does, however, provide a penetrating analysis of how bizarre compulsory attendance statutes can seem when viewed from an outsider's perspective:

> Note how odd this is, given modern emphases on individual freedoms and rights. Without due process, or any demonstration of the failure or incompetence of children, we feel free and obligated to imprison them in state or public institutions for many years: a practice that, applied to any other category of persons, would be in gross violation of elementary human rights standards. The right and duty to do this to the young reflects the transcending status of education, which is constitutive of proper personhood and relates the child properly to universalized knowledge. (2000, p. 211).[9]

As we know from the experience of homeschooling, compelled school attendance and education are notions that can be uncoupled. The civic values that are of concern (and that warrant the heightened protection that the courts reserve for the government's interests in education) could be served in ways other than by requiring all children to attend school. Compulsory school attendance statutes have been in effect for over a century, yet school attendance has not been shown (and, I predict, will never *be* shown) to be either necessary or sufficient to produce future citizens who embrace their civic responsibilities. Compelled attendance, although strongly enculturated now, was once a radical new reform. It may, in the future, be superseded by new methods that better meet the needs of society.

CONCLUSION: A SHIFT IN PERSPECTIVE IS NECESSARY

When we look through the lens of homeschooling, we view compulsory common school attendance not as part of the inevitable sweep of progress, but rather as a social experiment that should be reevaluated in light of 150 years of experience.

In reevaluating the effect of school attendance on the development of citizenship, our focus of concern should be directed to the *actual functioning* of our school system. We need detailed information about the real world outcomes of various educational practices. Until replicable and reliable data exists, the responsible and ethical response, as Stephen Raudenbush (2002, paragraph 8) reminds us, "is not simply to stick to our personal beliefs on these issues, but to do the much harder work of getting the needed empirical evidence." Before the reader assumes I am suggesting that research scrutiny be focused on homeschoolers, let me hasten to explain. I am calling on academics and policymakers to focus their research efforts on evaluating and improving the quality of the system to which our children would be consigned. The goal of reformers must be to fashion remedies that respond to actual functional deficiencies. Without a finding that the common values of decency, civility, and respect are being reliably cultivated *in the school system*, there is no reason to assume that school attendance is a material variable, let alone a causal factor, in the process of developing good citizenship. Reformers need to acknowledge that school attendance and education are not equivalent expressions and that compelled attendance is not the only way, or even the best way, to produce responsible citizens.

NOTES

1. Michael Apple is professor of curriculum and instruction and educational policy studies at the University of Wisconsin. Michael Apple's contentions about homeschooling appear in his book titled, *Educating the Right Way: Markets, Standards, God, and Inequality* (2001):

    "While it is quite probable that some specific children and families will gain from homeschooling, my concerns are larger. As in my previous chapters, these concerns are connected to the more extensive restructuring of this society that I believe is quite dangerous and to the manner in which our very sense of public responsibility is withering in ways that will lead to even further social inequities" (p. 172).

2. Rob Reich is Assistant Professor of Political Science and Ethics in Society at Stanford University. Reich's article titled "The Civic Perils of Homeschooling" (2002) contains his assertion that:

    Customizing education may permit schooling to be tailored for each individual student, but total customization also threatens to insulate students from exposure to diverse ideas and people and thereby to shield them from the vibrancy of a pluralistic democracy. These risks are perhaps greatest for homeschoolers (p. 56).

3. Both men were scheduled as participants in a panel discussion held at the 2004 Annual Meeting of the American Education Research Association in San Diego. The session was titled, *Educational Choice versus Civic Responsibility: Are Home Schoolers Embracing Their Responsibilities or Fleeing from Them?* The other two panel members were Scott Somerville, an attorney with the Home School Legal Defense Association (HSLDA), and Brian Ray, founder of the National Home Education Research Institute (NHERI). Michael Apple was prevented by family illness from participating in the panel discussion.

4. My husband and I decided to homeschool our children because we recalled being bored all day in school. We began as an experiment and continued until both our children had entered college. Over the past 10 years, I have served on the boards of the Massachusetts Home Education Association (www.mhla.org) and the National Home Education Network (www.nhen.org).

5. Several times since the publication of his "Testing the Boundaries" article (2001), Rob Reich has responded graciously to questions about his views. I appreciate his willingness to do so.

6. As a 1999 U. S. Department of Education survey indicates, parents have multiple reasons for homeschooling. Respondents to the survey were asked to select all the responses that fit their situation. The most cited reason for homeschooling, 48.9%, was "can give child a better education at home," followed by "religious reasons" at 38.4%, and "poor learning environment at school," at 25.6% (Bielick, 2001, p. 10). An important fact that this survey does not record is that homeschooling motivations shift and develop over the time that a family homeschools. Many parents begin with the motivation of improving their child's learning environment and then subsequently discover immense benefit to their entire family life. Reich mistakenly divides homeschoolers into two groups: a larger group, "the Christian right [who] wish to avoid the public school at all costs," and a smaller group that "practices a different kind of homeschooling... [and seeks] partnerships with public schools" (2002, p. 57). Yet there are religiously motivated parents who wish to participate in public school programs, and nonreligiously motivated parents who vigorously object to the participation of *any* homeschoolers in public programs. Homeschoolers simply cannot be classified easily on the topic of participation in school programs, or any other topic. As Kurt J. Bauman (2002) of the United States Census Bureau indicates, "No simple division exists between reli-

giously motivated and academically motivated parents." (Bauman's online article does not contain page numbers, but his citations may be found by a text search in the document.) Bauman mentions Apple's work and observes that "home schooling may not be linked to a unified conservative agenda in quite the way he describes." Bauman correctly notes that "[t]here is a true tension between home educators and the school standards movement," Homeschoolers, in my experience, are philosophically opposed, for a variety of reasons, to national testing and nationally imposed standards. In this respect, at least, most homeschoolers are at odds with the conservative agenda as outlined by Apple. Bauman is right when he suggests that, rather than acting from any particular political or religious motivation, homeschooling parents may simply wish to "reclaim the schooling process."

7. Both Apple (2001, p. 177) and Reich (2002, p. 58) employ the "glue" metaphor in their writings.

8. While Reich specifically recommends regulation "with vigilance" of home education (2001, p. 4), Apple seems mainly concerned with stopping the trend to homeschooling by building schools where "both teachers and students want to be" (2001, p. 190).

9. I recommend Meyer's (2000) entire essay. He makes a compelling argument that the components of our educational system, which we take for granted, actually make little sense unless seen as a function of transcendent values. We assume, for example, that all children should receive an equal education. In our own experience, we are not surprised that "higher status people give personal advantages to their children or that later in life the empowered can pay the disempowered to tend their gardens, hair, and toes.... Is it not more surprising that there is a sustained worldwide effort, built on the strongest norms, to create standardized ceremonial equality?" (p. 212).

REFERENCES

Apple, M. W. (2001). *Educating the right way: Markets, standards, God, and inequality.* New York: Routledge Falmer.

Bauman, K. J. (2002, May 16). Homeschooling in the United States: Trends and characteristics. *Education Policy Analysis Archives, 10*(26). Retrieved September 18, 2004, from http://epaa.asu.edu/epaa/v10n26.html

Beatty, B. (1995). *Preschool education in America: The culture of young children from the colonial era to the present.* New Haven, CT: Yale University Press.

Bielick, S., Chandler, K., & Brougham, S. (2001, July 31). *Homeschooling in the United States: 1999* (NCES 2001-33). Washington, DC: U. S. Department of Education. Retrieved September 18, 2004, from http://nces.ed.gov/pubsearch/pubsinfo.asp?pubid=2001033

Brown, R. D. (1996). *The strength of a people: The idea of an informed citizenry in America, 1650-1870.* Chapel Hil, NC: University of North Carolina Press.

Friedman, M., & Friedman, R. (1979). *Free to choose: A personal statement.* New York: Harcourt Brace Javanovich.

Goldin, C., & Katz L. (2003). *Mass secondary schooling and the state: The role of state compulsion in the high school movement.* Retrieved September 15, 2004, from http://post.economics.harvard.edu/faculty/katz/papers/EducationState.pdf

Labaree, D. F. (2000). No exit: Public education as an inescapably public good. In L. Cuban & D. Shipps (Eds.), *Reconstructing the common good in education: Coping with intractable American dilemmas* (pp. 110-129). Stanford, CA: Stanford University Press.

Landes, W. M., & Solmon, L. C. (1972). Compulsory schooling legislation: An economic analysis of law and social change in the nineteenth century. *The Journal of Economic History, 32*(1), 54-91.

Massaro, T. M. (1993). *Constitutional literacy: A core curriculum for a multicultural nation.* Durham, NC: Duke University Press.

Meyer, J. (2000). Reflections on Education as Transcendence. In L. Cuban & D. Shipps (Eds.), *Reconstructing the common good in education: Coping with intractable American dilemmas* (pp. 206-222). Stanford, CA: Stanford University Press.

Raudenbush, S. (2002). *Scientifically based research.* Retrieved September 18, 2004, from the United States Department of Education Web site: http://www.ed.gov/nclb/methods/whatworks/research/page_pg12.html.

Reich, R. (2001, August). *Testing the boundaries of parental authority over education: The case of homeschooling.* Paper prepared for delivery at the 2001 meeting of the American Political Science Association, San Francisco. Retrieved September 18, 2004, from http://www.stanford.edu/~reich/Homeschooling2002.pdf.

Reich, R. (2002). The civic perils of homeschooling. *Educational Leadership, 57*(7), 56-59.

Tyack, D., & Cuban, L. (1995). *Tinkering toward utopia: A century of public school reform.* Cambridge, MA: Harvard University Press.

CHAPTER 7

WHY HOME SCHOOLING SHOULD BE REGULATED

Rob Reich

Everyone now knows that home schooling has gone mainstream in the United States. Once a fringe phenomenon, home schooling is legal in every one of the 50 states and is widely considered the fastest growing sector of K-12 schooling. Because education in the United States is a matter delegated to the states—the U.S. Constitution does not mention education—each state has different provisions for regulating home schooling. This patchwork regulatory environment shows a clear trend across the country, however: regulations that 30 years ago either forbade or strictly regulated home schooling have been lifted or eased. According to the Home School Legal Defense Association (HSLDA), an advocacy group for home schooling that has been instrumental in getting more permissive home school legislation passed in many states, 25 of the 50 states have no regulations governing home schooling except a requirement that parents notify a local public authority that they have set up a home school. Ten of these 25 states do not even require parental notification (Klicka, 2004).

Home schoolers are now a diverse population. No longer the preserve of left wing unschoolers and right wing religious fundamentalists, the great range of people who have chosen to home school their children make it very difficult to draw even broad generalizations about the phe-

Home Schooling in Full View: A Reader, 109–120

nomenon. Indeed, it is easy to observe a kind of internecine warfare among the two most prominent advocacy groups, the Christian-based HSLDA and the more secular and inclusive National Home Education Network (NHEN). Nevertheless, one article of faith unites all home schoolers: that home schooling should be unregulated. Home schoolers of all stripes believe that they alone should decide how their children are educated, and they join together in order to press for the absence of regulations or the most permissive regulation possible.

Home schooling should be a permissible educational option, but I believe that home schooling must be strictly regulated. In this chapter, I shall discuss and defend the need for regulating home schooling far beyond the measures taken in most states today. Regulations are necessary for a number of reasons. These reasons can be usefully classified under two separate headings: theoretical and evidentiary. I proceed by arguing for the theoretical and evidentiary basis for regulating home schooling, and I conclude with a provisional list of appropriate regulations.

THE HOME SCHOOL DEBATE

Let me begin, however, by identifying two very common pitfalls in debates about home schooling. First, arguments in favor of regulating home schooling are not hidden arguments about the virtue of public schools. Nothing I write here is a defense of public schooling in the United States. Indeed, I have argued elsewhere about the need to provide new options to children who are forced to attend failing public schools, and I have defended a version of a school voucher system that would radically reorganize the current system of public education in the U.S. (Reich, 2002, ch. 7). Moreover, my experience with home schoolers leads me to believe that the availability of high quality public schools in their neighborhood would not motivate the vast majority of them to send their children into the public school system; they home school for different reasons. Thus, to say that people need permission to home school because the public schools are woeful is a red herring.

Second, arguments about regulating home schooling ought not be a war of conflicting anecdotes about home schooling's glorious successes or horrible tragedies that so often make headlines in the United States. To promote unregulated home schooling on the basis that home schooled children often win the National Spelling Bee and annually win coveted admissions spots to Stanford and Yale is poor argumentation. It is equally poor argumentation to defend regulations on home schooling because several children each year are found starved, abused, and even killed by their home-schooling parents. These extreme and unrepresentative cases—both positive and negative—ought not to be the basis of policy-making, and they distort the public representation of and debate over home schooling. Conservative estimates place the number of home-schooled students in the United States at 1.1 million in 2003 (National Center for Educational Statistics, 2004). It is the vast middle that is worth discussing, the children who do not enroll at Stanford and who have loving, caring parents.

THEORETICAL ARGUMENTS FOR REGULATING HOME SCHOOLING

Home schooling is the education of children under the supervision of parents. In no other educational setting are parents as able to control and direct all aspects of education, for in home schools they are responsible for determining not only what children are taught, but when, how, and with whom children are taught. Home schooling therefore represents the apogee of parental authority over schooling. Unregulated home schooling is nothing less than total and complete parental authority over schooling. The theoretical arguments for regulating home schooling begin from this point, questioning whether the schooling of children should ever be under the total and complete control of parents.

Some will find this a tendentious way of framing the question. Parents, they will say, are the appropriate authority over their children. What needs defending is not parental authority over schooling but whether the state should have any authority over the upbringing of children. So let us ask two separate, but related questions: What justifies, if anything, government authority over the education of children?; and what justifies parental authority over the education of their own children?

It is important here to recognize that parents ought indeed to possess wide-ranging authority to raise their children as they see fit, including wide-ranging discretion over the education of their children. This is so for many reasons, chief among them that parents are responsible for the care of their children and that they know their children better than anyone else. Let us take it as given, therefore, that parental authority over their children is legitimate and desirable.

What reason is there, then, to think that the government ought to have any authority over the education of children, an authority that could in certain circumstances curtail the authority of parents? I think there are two answers to this question. Call the first the "citizenship argument" and call the second the "freedom argument." The citizenship argument seeks to justify providing children with a civic education and thereby avoid the development of civically disabled adults. The freedom argument seeks to justify providing children with an education that cultivates their freedom and thereby avoid the development of what I will call "ethically servile" adults. Together these arguments justify some state authority over the education of children and rule out total parental control of education.

Citizenship Argument

The citizenship argument is the most familiar reason for justifying state regulation of schooling, and for this reason I shall only provide the barest outline of it here. Versions of it can be found in a number of important Supreme Court decisions and in state laws governing education (see *Pierce v. Society of Sisters* [1925], *Brown v. Board of Education* [1954], and *Wisconsin v. Yoder* [1972] decisions). In *Yoder*, for instance, a decision that graned Amish children an exemption from 2 years of Wisconsin's compulsary attendence laws, the Court nevertheless affirmed that, "There is no doubt as to the power of a State, having a high responsibility for education of its citizens, to impose reasonable regulations for the control and duration of basic education" (*Yoder*, 1972, p 213).

Children are the youngest citizens of the state, and the state has an interest in assuring that children receive a civic education. Citizens are created, not born. And though people differ about what it means to be a citizen and can argue a long time about the catalogue of civic virtues it is proper to instill in children, the point I make here is merely that the state has a legitimate interest in trying to convey some basic ideas about citizenship through schoolhouses.

It needs to convey basic facts—the structure of government, some rudimentary history. And it needs to convey some basic procedures about political participation—that being a citizen carries certain ground rules, such as one person, one vote, that no citizen can be excluded from the political process simply because he or she has different beliefs, or differently colored skin. Finally, the state needs to ensure that basic literacy and numeracy is learned so that children can become self-sufficient, productively employed citizens, not relying on the state—that is, on the taxes of other citizens—for support. In short, the state is justified in requiring that all children—regardless of the school they attend, public, private, or home school—receive a civic education.

Freedom Argument

The freedom argument is more complicated and less evident in legal and legislative history. In this sense it is more speculative. Nevertheless, it is the heart of the moral argument that I believe is most compelling when we consider the need to regulate home schools. Begin from the first principles of a democratic state. One of the chief aims of a democracy—especially a *liberal* democracy, where liberal is understood in its classical not contemporary and partisan sense—is to protect the freedom of individuals. One of the salutary consequences of a liberal democracy that protects individual freedom is that the choices individuals make about how to lead their lives leads to social diversity, or value pluralism. It would be shocking if in a society that protected the freedom of individuals it turned out that everyone believed the same thing. Simply put, protecting the freedom of individuals is the main engine of diversity—diversity of religious belief, diversity of belief in general.

Under what circumstances should freedom be limited? The standard classical liberal response is that liberty should be restrained when the exercise of one person's liberty interferes with or harms another person. This is generally called the "harm principle" among philosophers. The liberal democratic state can legitimately pass laws that restrict your liberty to harm other people.

What is key to understand is that liberal democracies enshrine the individual, not groups or collectives. Each child is an individual, and while no liberal democrat wants children to have the same legal or political status as an adult, the fact remains that children have the same interest in freedom as adults do. That is, children are born to freedom, though are not born in the condition of being free.

The liberal democratic state therefore ought to protect the interest of children in being free, or as I have put it elsewhere, in becoming autonomous adults (Reich, 2002). The interests of children are separable from the interests of their parents, and the interests of children in becoming free or autonomous—in becoming self-governing and self-determining persons—are as important as the interests of parents in being free or autonomous. Thus, the freedom argument is at bottom about ensuring that children acquire the capacity to lead the lives they wish, to believe what they want to, and to be free, when they become adults, from the domination of other people and institutions (from their own parents as well as from the state). In other words, I seek to prevent both governmental and parental despotism over children, even a benevolent, loving despotism.

What does this have to do with home schooling? The answer is that one of the most effective and least intrusive ways the state has of discharging the obligation to protect and promote the prospective freedom of children—a freedom that they will exercise fully as adults—is to ensure that children receive an education that develops them into free or autonomous individuals, that is to say, persons who can decide for themselves how they wish to lead their lives and what sort of values they wish to endorse. Such an education, I believe, requires exposure to and engagement with value pluralism, the very social diversity that is produced in a liberal democratic state which protects individual freedom. Unregulated home schooling opens up the possibility that children will never learn about or be exposed to competing or alternative ways of life. Home-schooled children can be sheltered and isolated in a way that students in schools, even sectarian private schools, cannot be. Parents can limit opportunities for social interaction, control the curriculum, and create a learning environment in which the values of the parents are replicated and reinforced in every possible way. With little or no exposure to competing ideas or interaction with people whose convictions differ from their parents', children who are home schooled can be raised in an all-encompassing or total environment that fails to develop their capacity to think for themselves. Parents can control the socialization of their children so completely as to instill inerrant beliefs in their own worldview or unquestioning obedience to their own or others' authority. To put this in language commonly used by political theorists, the capacity of children to exit or contest their parents' way of life is undermined and they run the risk of becoming "ethically servile" (see Callan, 1997; Reich, 2002). In short, children become unfree, unable to imagine other ways of living. This is not to say, of course, that home-schooling parents are always motivated to create such total environments, though empirical evidence suggests that a large percentage of home-schooling parents are motivated by a desire to control the moral and spiritual upbringing of their children (National Center for Education Statistics, 2004, p. 3). It is just to recognize that home schooling is the only educational environment in which it is possible to do so.

Let us be honest about the implications here: protecting and promoting the prospective freedom of children by providing them an education that exposes them to and engages them intellectually with the diversity of a pluralist democracy can be threatening to parents. The social critic bell hooks has written of her own childhood, for example, "School was the place of ecstasy—pleasure and danger. To be changed by ideas was pure pleasure. But to learn ideas that ran counter to values and beliefs at home was to place oneself at risk, to enter the danger zone. Home was the place where I was forced to conform to someone else's image of who and what I should be. School was the place where I could forget that self and, through ideas, reinvent myself" (hooks, 1994, p. 3). But these are risks that must be accepted, for children have an interest in being free persons and parents cannot be entitled to ensure that their child grows up to be exactly the kind of person they want her to be.

Thus, the freedom argument leads to the conclusion that the education of children ought to be regulated in such a way as to guarantee that they learn about and engage with the diversity of ways of life in a democracy.

Receiving such an education is one very important way the state can attempt to protect and promote the future freedom and autonomy of children. It is also important, I would add, for civic reasons that go beyond what I described in the section above. The reason is that citizenship in a culturally and religiously diverse liberal democracy requires that each citizen be prepared to recognize that the values that guide his or her life will not be shared by all other citizens. Therefore, each citizen needs to learn to be able to participate democratically with citizens of diverse convictions.

The justification of state authority over the education of children is rooted in developing children into citizens (or avoiding civically disabled adults) and in developing children into free persons (or avoiding ethically servile adults). This is the structure of the theoretical argument that warrants regulation of home schooling.

Evidentiary Arguments for Regulating Home Schooling

Home schoolers and the mainstream media have publicized the idea in recent years that the academic performance of home-schooled students is better or equal to that of publicly schooled students. Advocates have used various studies to reach the conclusion that home schooling works. But contrary to popular opinion, very little if anything is known about the actual academic performance of the typical home-schooled student, the vast middle that I suggested ought to be the appropriate basis for debates about home schooling. Research on home schooling is in its infancy and what little research currently exists is either of poor quality or is capable of reaching only very limited conclusions. As a result, the very best we can say about the academic outcomes of home schooling is that we have no evidence to suggest that home schooling fails. But neither do we have any evidence that it succeeds.

One would think that the increasing number of home schoolers would attract the interest of both social scientists and policy makers. Home-schooled children, after all, are a larger population than the number of children who attend charter schools, a phenomenon that receives extraordinary attention from researchers, public policy makers, and the media. Why is it that home schooling is so little studied? A large of part of the explanation has to do with resistance from the home-school community and the unregulated nature of the enterprise.

Start with one of the biggest problems: the fact that we have no accurate data on what one would think is the truly easy question, the number of children who are home schooled. The U.S Department of Education study referenced earlier is the most scientifically rigorous and most conservative, pegging the number at 1.1 million in 2003 (NCES, 2004). Brian Ray of the National Home Education Research Institute (an advocacy organization, not an impartial research institute), however, estimates the number at 1.7 to 2.1 million (Ray, 2005). The variation in estimates here is unusually wide. How can it be that the data is so imprecise? A simple answer emerges. Because home-schooling regulations are either so minimal or so little enforced, many parents do not notify local educational officials when they decide to home school. Recall that 10 states do not even require parents to register their home schools. A great deal of home schooling occurs under the radar, so to speak, so that even if local officials wished to test or monitor the progress of home-schooled students, they would not even know how to locate them. Researchers and public officials have, quite literally, no sense of the total population of home-schooled students. This is the primary obstacle to studying home schooling.

A further concern is that an appalling amount of the research conducted on home schooling and given publicity in the media is undertaken by or sponsored by organizations whose explicit mission is to further the cause of home schooling. Even this very volume contains several chapters by advocates—Brian Ray and Scott Somerville. Of course, that research is conducted by persons whose pay comes from organizations dedicated to promoting home schooling is no reason to reject the findings out of hand. I would suggest, however, that we treat the findings of their research on home schooling in the same way that people treat the research on nicotine addiction funded by tobacco companies: with a very large dose of skepticism.

Consider one of the most widely publicized studies in the home-school research literature, the 1999 report by Lawrence Rudner titled "Scholastic Achievement and Demographic Characteristics of Home Schooled Students in 1998" (Rudner, 1999). Rudner's study was funded and sponsored by the Home School Legal Defense Association. It analyzed the test results of more than 20,000 home-schooled students using the Iowa Test of Basic Skills, and it was interpreted by many to find that the average home-schooled student outperformed his or her public school peer. But Rudner's study reaches no such conclusion, and Rudner himself issued multiple cautionary notes in the report, including the following: "Because this was not a controlled experiment, the study does not demonstrate that home schooling is superior to public or private schools and the results must be interpreted with caution" (p. 33).

Rudner used a select and unrepresentative sample, culling all of his participants from families who had purchased curricular and assessment materials from Bob Jones University. Because Bob Jones University is an evangelical Christian university (a university which gained a national reputation in the 1980s for its policy of forbidding interracial dating), the sample of participating families in Rudner's study is highly skewed toward

Christian home schoolers. Extrapolations from this data to the entire population of home schoolers are consequently highly unreliable.

Moreover, all the participants in Rudner's study had volunteered their participation. According to Rudner, more than 39,000 contracted to take the Iowa Basic Skills Test through Bob Jones, but only 20,760 agreed to participate in his study. This further biases Rudner's sample, for parents who doubt the capacity of their child to do well on the test are precisely the parents we might expect not to volunteer their participation. A careful social scientific comparison of test score data would also try to take account of the problem that public school students take the Iowa Basic Skills Test in a controlled environment; many in Rudner's study tested their own children.

Rudner himself has been frustrated by the misrepresentation of his work. In an interview with the Akron Beacon Journal, which published a pioneering week-long investigative series of articles on home schooling in 2004, Rudner claimed that his only conclusion was that if a home-schooling parent "is willing to put the time and energy and effort into it—and you have to be a rare person who is willing to do this—then in all likelihood you're going to have enormous success." Rudner also said, "I made the case in the paper that if you took the same kids and the same parents and put them in the public schools, these kids would probably do exceptionally well" (Oplinger & Willard, 2004, p. 12).

Absent rigorous, social scientific data on the outcomes of home schooling, we are left in the realm of glorified anecdote—the home schoolers who win the National Spelling Bees—and the occasional ethnographic study of small populations of home schoolers (see Stevens, 2001). But neither can give us any picture of whether home schooling works. The very best research on home schooling—the combination of random samples of large populations and ethnographic studies, yields some good information about the reasons why people home school and demographic characteristics of their households. But when we look at the academic performance of home-schooled children, the bottom line is that we know virtually nothing.

Because in the context of this volume I will be seen as a critic of home schooling, I wish to make my point very clear here. I do not suggest that home-schooled children do worse than publicly or privately schooled children. I do not accuse home-school parents of failing to teach their children well. I want to say simply that we know almost nothing about how the average home-schooled child fares academically.

Why does an absence of evidence about the academic outcomes of home schooling lead to an argument in favor of regulating home schools? Children whose parents fail to teach them to read and to write, to be capable of minimum basic skills, are suffering educational harm. In order to be sure that home-schooled children, who have no opportunity to protest or seek academic assistance elsewhere, do not suffer educational harm, home schools must be regulated.

A PROVISIONAL REGULATORY FRAMEWORK FOR HOME SCHOOLING

Recall that the purpose of these regulations is to help ensure that the state's interest in providing a civic education for children is met, and to protect the independent interest of the child in developing into a free or autonomous adult. The result is that authority over children's education will be shared between parents and the state. Or more precisely, enormous deference ought to be paid to the authority of parents in choosing and supervising the education of their children. So long as the actions of parents do not thwart the education for citizenship or the education for freedom that children ought to receive, the state need not intervene in the educational decisions and actions of parents.

I propose three minimal regulations. The results of the democratic process might yield additional regulations, which would not necessarily be inconsistent with my views, but these seem to me the bare minimum, as follows:

1. All parents who home school must register with a public official. The state needs to be able to distinguish between truants and home-schooled students, and it needs a record that specific children are being home schooled so that its other regulations can be enforced.

2. Parents must demonstrate to educational officials that their home-school curriculum meets some minimal standard. The minimal standard will include academic benchmarks as well as an assurance that children are exposed to and engaged with ideas, values, and beliefs that are different from those of the parents. For instance, every home-school curriculum should include information about a variety of religious traditions (I believe this should be the case, as well, for public and private schools.) Parents are free to teach their children that their own religious faith is the truth, but they cannot shield children from the knowledge that other people have different convictions and that these people are, from the standpoint of citizenship, their equals.

3. Parents must permit their children to be tested periodically on some kind of basic skills exam. Should home-schooled children repeatedly fail to make progress on this exam, relative to their public or private school peers, then a case could be made to compel

school attendance. Label this educational harm. (The same kind of educational harm surely exists in some public schools, of course. And this is one reason that I believe parents should have the authority to hold the state accountable for its public schools by pulling their children from failing schools and enrolling them elsewhere.)

In short, these regulations amount to the following:

- The state registers who is being home schooled.
- The state insists upon a curriculum that meets minimal academic standards and that introduces students to value pluralism.
- The state tests students periodically to ensure that minimal academic progress is being made.

Would many home schools be unable to meet these regulations? I suspect not that many, but I do not really know the answer to the question. It is worth finding out. As I have endeavored to show, it is both theoretically and practically necessary to regulate home schools. If creating and enforcing regulations would prevent even a few children from suffering educational harm or from receiving an education that stunted or disabled their freedom, the regulations would be worthwhile.

Strictly enforced regulations ensure that parents do not wield total and unchecked authority over the education of their children. What is at stake here is not a question of social utility or stability, whether home schooling could threaten democracy. What is at stake is the justice that we owe children, that they receive an education that cultivates their future citizenship, their individual freedom, and that teaches them at least basic academic skills, skills that are necessary for ably exercising both their citizenship and their freedom.

REFERENCES

Brown v. Board of Education, 347 U.S. 483 (1954).

hooks, b. (1994). *Teaching to transgress.* New York: Routledge.

Klicka, C. (2004). *Home schooling in the United States: A legal analysis.* Purcelleville, VA: HSLDA.

Oplinger, D., & Willard, D. J. (2004, November 15). Claims of academic success rely on anecdotes, flawed data analysis. *Akron Beacon Journal*, p. A1.

Meyers v. Nebraska, 262 U.S. 390 (1923).

National Center for Educational Statistics. (2004). *Issue briefs, NCES 2004-115.* Washington, DC: US Department of Education.

Pierce v. Society of Sisters, 206 U.S. 510 (1925).

Ray, B. (2005). *A quick reference worldwide: Guide to homeschooling. Facts and stats on the benefits of home school, 2002-2003.* Nashville, TN: Broadman & Holman.

Reich, R. (2002). *Bridging liberalism and multiculturalism in American education.* Chicago: University of Chicago Press.

Rudner, L. (1999). Scholastic achievement and demographic characteristics of home schooled students in 1998. *Educational Policy Analysis Archive, 7*(8), 56-74.

Stevens, M. (2001). *The kingdom of children.* Princeton, NJ: Princeton University Press.

Wisconsin v. Yoder, 406 U.S. 205 (1972).

CHAPTER 8

BEHIND THE TREND

Increases in Homeschooling among African American Families

Venus L. Taylor

An increasing number of African American families are choosing to homeschool their children. This paper examines the meaning and implications of African Americans' removal of their children from the very public schools into which the *Brown v. Board of Education* desegregation decision granted them admission five decades ago. The 50 years since the *Brown* decision have seen a persistence of the Black-White achievement gap in U.S. public school systems, and a growing number of African American parents have determined they can better educate their children at home, employing strategies that are not available in most classrooms: low pupil-teacher ratio, focused attention on academic problem areas, elimination of "tracking," and deeply committed teachers with high expectations. Higher academic achievement regardless of parental educational attainment and the flexibility to conform to a variety of family conditions and income levels make homeschooling one of the best options to prepare African American children to compete in the twenty-first century.

Home Schooling in Full View: A Reader, 121–133
Copyright © 2005 by Information Age Publishing
All rights of reproduction in any form reserved.

THE PERSISTENT ACHIEVEMENT GAP

Many African American parents have tired of waiting for traditional schooling to overcome its limitations. The persistent Black-White achievement gap is evidence of a chronic, systemic failure of the traditional school system to address the needs of African American children. One assumption held by the proponents of *Brown v. Board of Education* was that equal access would ensure equal education. However, the education of Black and White students has proven to be, persistently, less than equal. Standardized tests scores, grade retention, high school completion rates, all indicate that Black students are not faring as well as White students in America's public schools. This well-documented achievement gap has persisted over the last few decades (narrowing a bit since the 1970s, then widening again since 1992) despite numerous "school reforms" aimed to eliminate it.

The extent of the gap is lamentable:

- Grade level retention rate: "In 1999, 18% of Black students in kindergarten through 12th grade had ever repeated at least one grade. This retention rate is higher than the 9% of White students who had ever repeated a grade" (Hoffman, Llagas, & Snyder, 2003, p. 38).

- High school completion rate: "In 2000, 13% of Black 16- to 24-year-olds had not earned a high school credential. This status rate was higher than the rate for Whites (7%)" (p. 42).

- Math scores: "In 1999, 9-year-old Black students had an average NAEP mathematics scale [28 points] lower than the score for White 9-year-olds. Black 13- and 17-year-olds had average mathematics scores [more than 30 points] lower than both White ... students' scores for the same age groups" (pp. 50-51).

- Reading scores: "In 1999, average scores among Black 9-year-olds were 16% below Whites' scores (a gap of 35 points), among 13-year-olds they were 11% below Whites' scores (a gap of 29 points), and among 17-year-olds they were 10% below Whites' scores (a gap of 31 points)" (p. 48).

- Science scores: "In 1999, the gap between White and Black students ... [was] 41 points... At age 13, the gap ... [was] 39 points"(p. 52).

Nancy Kober (2001, p. 17), of the Center on Education Policy, starkly reiterates: "[T]he average 1999 reading score of Black students at age 17 was about the same as that of White students at age 13. In science, the average scores of Black and Hispanic students at age 13 were lower than the average score of White students at age 9."

Fifty years after the U.S. Supreme Court decision, the hope of *Brown v. Board of Education* has not been realized. *Brown* was successful in granting African Americans somewhat equal *access* to public education; however, the *implementation* of equal education seems beyond its reach. The cause of the achievement gap is multi-factorial, attributable in part to unequal distribution of resources between affluent and impoverished school districts, differences in parental income and education levels, and perhaps even racial bias in some schools and in the broader society. However, regardless of the gap's origins, three truths remain indisputable:

1. The gap persists despite levels of integration or similarities in parental academic attainment. Research shows that "the gap shrinks only a little when black and white (sic) children attend the same schools" (Jencks & Phillips, 1998, p. 2). Studies also reveal that Black students taught by Black teachers still consistently underachieve (Ferguson, 1998, p. 348). Additionally, a recent report of the National Center for Education Statistics (NCES) finds that the achievement gap even persists if the parents of Black and White students have the same educational attainment (Hoffman et al, 2003, pp. 48-51).

2. The current educational system is more likely to perpetuate the gap than to eradicate it. Low expectations, fixed ability tracking, and a narrowing focus on improving schools' test scores all combine to perpetuate the existing gap and make it unlikely that it will ever disappear. Knowledge of African American students' historical status as underachievers leads teachers (and others) to hold low expectations of them (pp. 29-30). Low expectations discourage teachers from exploring all possible strategies to improve student performance, and instead foster the acceptance and expectation of lower performance (Ferguson, 1998, p. 282). Tracking or ability grouping exacerbates the existing disparities by teaching lower tracks (where Blacks are overrepresented) less than higher tracks (p. 330). The problem is compounded when, motivated to improve aggregate test scores, schools are inclined to distance themselves (through restricted admissions or encouraged drop-outs) from underperforming students (Darling-Hammond, 2004, pp. 18-19). The end result is that, instead of getting the help needed to catch up to their peers, underachieving students are increasingly left behind.

3. Given an equivalent educational foundation, Blacks tend to fare as well or better than their White counterparts. A report by the NCES

indicates that, when Black and White students actually receive similar levels of prior education, Black students exhibit equal or higher rates of high school completion than their White peers. They, in turn, have equal or higher rates of post-secondary educational attainment, higher rates of college attendance, and equal or higher rates of college completion (Jacobson, Olsen, Rice, Sweetland, & Ralph, 2001, p. x). Clearly, African American students have the potential to thrive. That potential is simply being at best untapped, at worst thwarted, by the current system of public schooling.

Rather than continually subjecting our children to a failing school system, and rather than investing our hopes in yet another school reform that misses the mark, many African American parents feel obliged to seek every opportunity available to secure for our children the best chances for a bright future. Providing a strong elementary academic foundation improves children's chances of academic and financial success as adults. Therefore, an increasing number of African American parents have decided to take the reins and educate our children at home so that we may better control the quality of their education. For many of us, homeschooling is the best available option.

HOW HOMESCHOOLING ADDRESSES THE ACHIEVEMENT GAP

The nation's current sweeping school reform initiative, No Child Left Behind (NCLB), overemphasizes standardized test scores as a measure of student and school performance. The effect is that students, all of whom would benefit from lessons in fine arts and critical thinking, are instead receiving an education in test-taking strategies (Darling-Hammond, 2004, p. 18). Standardized tests are useful components of comprehensive student assessments, and offer an objective means of student comparison. However, they do not serve well as stand-alone measures of overall student achievement. And they definitely should not so dominate a school's focus as to become a substitute for curricula.

That said, homeschoolers fare better than their public school peers on numerous measures of academic achievement including standardized test scores. Without narrowing the focus of their teaching to test-score improvement (as is the tendency under NCLB) homeschooling boosts student achievement on all measures.

As proof, a 1997 study of American homeschoolers, performed by the National Home Education Research Institute (NHERI), indicated that homeschoolers score well above their traditionally schooled peers on standardized tests, averaging in the 87th percentile in reading, 80th percentile in language, 82nd percentile in math, 84th percentile in science (the national average is the 50th percentile) (Ray, YEAR, p. 18). Homeschoolers were also assessed as more socially mature, less peer dependent, less aggressive, and more engaged in their communities than their publicly or privately schooled peers (Ray, 2002, pp. 56-60).

Unlike traditional public or private schooling, homeschooling serves African Americans as well as it serves Whites. A story featured on CBN.com, Website of the Christian Broadcasting Network, reads: "The Home School Legal Defense Association is very pleased to report that African American [homeschooled] children ... do very well on standardized achievement tests. On average, they are scoring in the upper percentiles right along with white (sic) students" (Serrell, 2004). According to Brian D. Ray, of the NHERI, "Homeschoolers have been able to substantially eliminate the disparity between White and minority scores.... Math and reading scores for minority home schoolers show no significant difference when compared to Whites. In reading, both White and minority home schoolers score at the 87th percentile. Only five points separate them in math—the 82nd percentile versus the 77th percentile"(Ray, 1997).

Homeschooling outperforms public schooling in its ability to cater to the needs of all students. It is interesting to point out that the most common recommendations of school-based gap-reduction programs just happen to occur naturally in a homeschooling environment. For instance:

1. Reduction of class size. Homeschooling generally provides an average teacher-to-student ratio of 1:4 or better (Ray, 2002, p. 39). It is exceedingly rare, if not impossible, to find a public or private school with a better ratio. Working in small groups or one-on-one is highly recommended by the best educational theorists, especially for students who are lagging behind their peers.

2. Focused attention on academic problem areas for students at risk of failure. Removing struggling students from the hectic school environment, away from the distractions of student interruptions, roll call, and ringing bells, and giving them the focused attention of a loving parent or competent tutor is at least on par with any in-school intervention targeted to youth at risk. Having intimate knowledge of his/her child, a parent is best able to detect a child's confusion, use examples from the students' interests and real-life experiences to clarify lessons, match his/her teaching style to the student's learning style, and speed up or slow down the pace of instruction to meet the student's rate of knowledge assimilation.

Even the best teacher, with assistance, is not capable of providing each child with such consistent individualized instruction. Thus, at home, a child is at less risk of failure than in a traditional classroom.

3. Elimination of fixed ability grouping (tracks). Homeschooling allows flexibility to adjust to the speed and style of the learner, obviating the need to track a child or label his/her entire learning approach based on prior or unrelated performance measures. For instance, there is no inherent reason that a child who struggles with math should be taught reading in a remedial fashion. There is no reason to cover third grade material in a rudimentary fashion, simply because a child experienced prior difficulty with first grade material.

    Furthermore, most homeschooling parents resist the practice of labeling children as high- or low-achievers. Each child is taught according to his/her current ability—not locked into a learning track according to the measure of his/her past performance. In public schools, tracking tends to perpetuate the existing disparities between high and low achievers by teaching less to those in lower tracks and more to those in higher tracks; thus, since Blacks are historically overrepresented among low-achievers, tracking perpetuates the existing Black-White achievement gap (Ferguson, 1998, pp. 326-330).

4. High expectations for the success of every child. The high achievement of homeschoolers is attributable, in part, to high expectations on the part of parents. Education researcher Ronald Ferguson explains that expectations shape the interaction of teacher and student, determining how committed and to what length the teacher is willing to go to help a student succeed. A parent is naturally inclined to believe in the limitless possibility of his or her child. This belief, and the self-imposed challenge of taking full responsibility for the academic success of one's children, translates into a commitment to do whatever is necessary to ensure that success.

The positive effect of teacher expectations is illustrated by two of the few highly successful school reform programs: Great Expectations and Success for All. These programs have significantly improved the performance of struggling students not only by equipping teachers with techniques to get the best from students, but by instilling in them *the unconditioned belief that ALL children are capable of academic success.* Great Expectations was a reportedly successful 1989 school reform initiative in Oklahoma, which introduced the nurturing yet challenging teaching techniques of the famed Marva Collins (founder of Westside Preparatory School in Chicago which boasts remarkably high-achieving poor and minority students). As Ferguson describes the reform initiative:

> It aim[ed] to nurture in *all students, not only the most talented*, the expectation that they [were] destined to be important people if they [did] their best in school to prepare well for the future.... The key for teachers [was] the apparently effective program of professional development that ... helped them to *expect more and achieve more* for both themselves and their students.(emphasis added, Ferguson, 1998, pp. 303-311)

Robert Slavin, co-creator of the highly appraised Success for All program currently implemented in over 1,500 schools in 48 states, invokes this belief as one of the program's foundational principles: "[T]here is one factor we try to make consistent in all schools: a relentless focus on the success of *every child* (emphasis added, Ferguson, 1998, p. 344). The mission statement of the Success for All program reads:

> By targeting prevention and early intervention, virtually *every child can become a successful reader and student*. Never again should a single girl or boy be allowed to "fall through the cracks." (emphasis added, Slavin & Madden, 2000)

By contrast, the latest American school reform, NCLB, touts "high standards" as the remedy for failing schools and failing children. Without high expectations, the philosophy of "high standards" functions in schools much as it does in factories: once the standard is set, it is accepted that a certain percentage of product will fail to meet that standard and, thus, be discarded. Setting high standards without a fundamental shift in teacher perception and expectation, and without instilling in teachers the conviction that all children are equally capable of learning, simply widens the achievement gap by discarding a certain percentage of the student population.

Due to their historical status as underachievers, teachers tend to have lower expectations of Black students than of White students (Ferguson, 1998, pp. 29-30). This predetermined expectation limits the extent to which teachers will go to help a student succeed. As Ferguson puts it, "If they expect black (sic) children to have less potential, teachers are likely to search with less conviction for ways to help these children improve, and hence miss opportunities to reduce the black-white test score gap" (Ferguson, 1998, p. 312) He laments: "A great waste of human potential and much social injustice results from the fact that teachers are not given the incentives and support they need to set, believe in, and skillfully pursue higher goals for all students, and in particular, for African Americans and other stigmatized minorities" (Ferguson, 1998, p. 282).

Homeschooling wins, hands down, on the measure of "teacher expectation." A teacher or parent armed with the commitment to help every child in his/her charge to succeed is encouraged to try different methods and teaching styles until he/she finds what works for that child. Thus, "failure" is not an option. Success is inevitable, if not always immediate. The above measures are components of most school-based strategies aimed at reducing the achievement gap. Homeschooling outperforms traditional schooling, in part, due to its unmatchable excellence on these and other measures.

PERCEIVED BARRIERS TO HOMESCHOOLING

Homeschooling may not be accessible to everyone. However, many families have found creative ways to homeschool successfully in spite of what, on the surface, may seem like insurmountable obstacles. Some perceived barriers to homeschooling include the following:

Parental Lack of Teacher Qualification/Low Educational Attainment

As stated earlier, homeschoolers, on average, academically outperform their traditionally schooled peers. Yet, only 15% of the mothers and 6% of the fathers had ever been certified to teach (Ray, 1997, p. 30). Numerous studies have illustrated there [is] no significant relationship between student achievement and the teacher certification status of their parents (Ray, 2002, p. 77).

Additionally, although 88% of homeschooling parents have attained at least some education beyond high school, approximately one third of all homeschooling parents have acquired less than a bachelor's degree (Ray, 1997, pp. 36-37). Some studies have found no correlation (or weak correlations) between homeschooler scholastic achievement and the educational attainment of their parents (Ray, 2002, p. 78).

Other studies have found that, just as in the public school population, homeschooled "children of college graduates out-perform children whose parents do not have a college degree" (Rudner, 1998, p. 23). However, Lawrence Rudner education researcher and author of a University of Maryland homeschooler study, points out, "It is worthy to note that, at every grade level, the mean performance of home school students whose parents do not have a college degree is much higher than the mean performance of students in public schools. Their percentiles are mostly in the 65th to 69th percentile range" (Rudner, 1998, p. 23)

In practice, homeschooling parents who feel unqualified to teach certain subjects to their children often hire tutors or enlist friends or family members who possess a strength in that subject. Parents who are deeply committed to helping their children learn have been known to immerse themselves in the material and relearn subjects that they've forgotten just to teach them to their children. Often they learn new subjects along with their children. A zeal for learning and a willingness to seek assistance when necessary allow parents successfully to homeschool their children with or without higher education or teacher certification.

Challenging Family Conditions (e.g., Single-Parenting, Two-Income Families)

Single-Parents

While an overwhelming majority of homeschooling families are headed by married couples (more than 95%) (Ray, 2002, p. 39), "[r]esearch suggests that 25,000 or more single-parent families were homeschooling in the fall of 1998, and the number is increasing" (p. 37). A strong support network is crucial to success as a homeschooling single-parent ("Linda H.," 2000,). Friends or family members who assist with childcare or lessons when a single-parent needs time and space to earn an income (or just a sanity break) help provide the support necessary to homeschool. Other options, such as flexible work hours, self-employment, and cooperative living arrangements have also been employed by single-parent homeschoolers. Joyce Wardick, a homeschooling African American single-mom from Maryland, encourages single parents to take full advantage of the flexibility of homeschooling. For example, she says, "You could work during the day and home school during the night" (Appea, 2001, p. 1)

Two-Income Families

"Income is the main barrier to home schooling by blacks (sic)," explains Rudner. "Most home schoolers have one breadwinner and are fairly wealthy. Minorities don't fit that profile" (Aizenman, 2000, A01).

Homeschooling families parented by married couples typically have at least one parent at home full time. Reportedly, only 16% of home schooling mothers work outside the home (Ray, 1997, pp. 28, 30). By contrast, nationwide, in 2002, approximately 60% of married women with children worked at least part time (U.S. Department of Labor, Bureau of Labor Statistics, 2004).

Many couples, finding that the demands of dual careers prevent them from making desired lifestyle choices such as homeschooling, opt to "downsize"—decrease living expenses (smaller house, fuel-efficient car, fewer restaurant trips) making it possible to live on a lower income. The increase in family connectedness and decrease in daily stress often offset the loss of finances. Also many note that dropping a second income eradicates the extra expenses required to earn that income (childcare, auto and wardrobe maintenance, higher taxes, etc.), thus managing on one income has a less devastating effect on the bottom line than predicted. Homeschooling parent, Rebecca Kochenderfer reports:

> I quit my job in order to homeschool, and I was scared that we were going to starve. Everyone warned us that 'it takes two incomes these days just to survive,' but I have found that not to be the case. When I quit work our expenses dropped dramatically. I no longer had those sneaky work-related expenses like dry cleaning, lunches out, gas, day care, and higher taxes. By the time I subtracted the cost of working, I discovered that my $25-an-hour job was really bringing home just $7 an hour." (Kochenderfer, 1998, pp. 32-33)

However, it is possible to remain a two-income family *and* homeschool successfully. "Some families have rearranged their work hours; some have willing neighbors, relatives, or other homeschooling families who help them out; others arrange to work at home," reports Katharine Houk (1998, p. 33), cofounder of the Alliance for Parental Involvement in Education (AllPIE) in New York.

There is no one way to homeschool. It doesn't have to consist of formal classes held at certain times of the day. There are nearly as many styles of homeschooling as there are homeschoolers. That flexibility makes it adaptable to the demands of any family structure.

Perceived Expense of Homeschooling

Homeschooling is less expensive than one might expect. Cafi Cohen (1998), author of *And What About College?—How Homeschooling Leads to Admissions to the Best Colleges and Universities*, states some homeschoolers have been known to spend less than $25 per year on education. According to Dr. Ray, homeschooler surveys find, "The median amount that families spend per child per year for home education, including things such as textbooks, tuition for part-time classes, field trips, and special resources, is about $450, with the large majority spending from $375 to $525 per year, per student" (Ray, 2002, p. 38). Notably, "[r]esearch findings suggest there is little or no relationship [between the amount of money spent by homeschoolers and student achievement]" (Ray, 2002, p. 81).

American public primary schools reportedly spend around $6,582 to educate each student, placing it among the top five nations of a 30-nation comparison study performed by the National Center for Education Statistics (U.S. Department of Education, National Center for Education Statistics, 2002). Yet a 1999 report on the international achievement of eighth graders in 38 nations placed American eighth graders 18th in science achievement (Martin et al., 2002) and 19th in mathematics achievement (Martin et al., 2002). A separate comparison study placed American ninth graders ninth among 31 nations in reading achievement (Brinkley & Williams, 1996). Clearly, greater expenditure is not directly related to greater achievement.

Thanks to public and university libraries, used book stores, the internet, and homeschool support groups, inexpensive books and materials needed for successful homeschooling abound. Homeschoolers also pool resources, barter services, offer tutoring assistance, or take advantage of group rates for educational fieldtrips. Limited resources inspire dedicated homeschoolers to find creative, innovative ways to help their children learn.

The keys to overcoming obstacles to homeschooling are *creativity* and *flexibility*. Homeschooling is infinitely flexible with regard to teaching methods, curricula, scheduling, and financing. Parents are free to be as creative as necessary, accessing material and human support, to help their children learn everything they need to know. Homeschooling provides the only opportunity for a custom-tailored education. Endless flexibility and creativity make homeschooling a great fit for children and parents of any educational background, ability/disability level, or tax bracket.

CONCLUSION

Homeschooling provides the flexibility to fit a variety of parental education levels, income levels, and family situations. It can be done successfully without a large budget, a college degree, or teacher certification. Best of all, it appears to eliminate the persistent achievement gap through decreased class size, focused attention on academic problem areas, elimination of ability tracking, and high expectations for student success on the part of teacher-parents.

The legacy of the *Brown* decision is not only about access but is also about options. We African Americans owe it to our children to exercise all available opportunities to ensure their current and future success. We are not obligated to wait for schools to improve to better meet our needs; we are obligated to provide our children the best education available. Home-schoolers secure a brighter future for their children by giving them the educational foundation they deserve. Those of us who take the reins in pursuit of a sound, equal (or better) education for our children, in an effort to help them achieve their maximum potential, do so in the spirit of the proponents of *Brown v. Board of Education*.

REFERENCES

Aizenman, N. C. (2000, October 19). Prince George's joins home-school trend. *Washington Post*, p. 19.

Appea, P. (2001). *Teach your children well: African American homeschoolers.* Retreived September 1, 2004, from www.africana.com/articles/daily/index_20010

Brinkley, M., & Williams, T. (1996). *Reading literacy in the United States: Findings from the IEA Reading Study.* Washington, DC: U.S. Department of Education, National Center for Education Statistics.

Darling-Hammond, L. (2004). From "Separate but Equal" to "No Child Left Behind": The collision of new standards and old inequalities. In D. Meier & G. Wood (Eds.), *Many children left behind: How the No Child Left Behind Act is damaging our children and our schools* (pp. 18-19). Boston: Beacon Press.

Ferguson, R. F. (1998). Can schools narrow the Black-White test score gap? In C. Jencks & M. Phillips (Eds.), *The Black-White test score gap* (pp. 318-374). Washington, DC: Brookings Institution Press.

Ferguson, R. F. (1998). Teachers' perceptions and expectations and the Black-White test score gap. In C. Jencks & M. Phillips (Eds.), *The Black-White test score gap* (pp. 273-317). Washington, DC: Brookings Institution Press.

Hoffman, K., Llagas, C., & Snyder, T. D. (2003). *Status and trends in the education of Blacks.* Washington, DC: National Center for Education Statistics.

Jacobson, J., Olsen, C., Rice, J. K., Sweetland, S., & Ralph, J. (2001). *Educational Achievement and Black-White Inequality,* [NCES 2001-061], by Washington, DC: U.S. Department of Education, National Center for Education Statistics.

Jencks, C., & Phillips, M. (Eds.). (1998). The Black-White test score gap: An introduction. In *The Black-White test score gap* (pp. 1-52). Washington, DC: Brookings Institution Press.

"Linda H." (2002). Homeschooling single. In R. Barfield (Ed.), *Real-life homeschooling: The stories of 21 families who teach their children at home* (p. 158). New York: Fireside.

Kober, N. (2001). *It takes more than testing: Closing the achievement gap.* Washington, DC: Center on Education Policy

Kochenderfer, R. (1998). Homeschool may be cheaper than you think—If I homeschool, can I continue to work and earn the income we need? In L. Dobson (Ed.), *The homeschooling book of answers* (pp. 32-33). Rocklin, CA: Prima.

Martin, M. O., Mullis, I. V. S., Gonzalez, E. J., Gregory, K. D., Smith, T. A., Chrostowski, S. J., Garden, R. A., & O'Connor, K. M. (2002). *TIMSS 1999 International Science Report: Findings from IEA's Repeat of the Third International*

Mathematics and Science Study at the Eighth Grade. Chestnut Hill, MA: The International Study Center

Mullis, I. V. S., Martin, M. O., Gonzalez, E. J., Gregory, K. D., Garden, R. A., O'Connor, K. M., Chrostowski, S. J., & Smith, T. A. (2002). *TIMSS 1999 International Mathematics Report: Findings from IEA's Repeat of the Third International Mathematics and Science Study at the Eighth Grade.* Chestnut Hill, MA: The International Study Center.

Ray, B. D. (1997). *Strengths of their own: Homeschoolers across America.* Salem, OR: National Home Education Research Institute.

Ray, B. D. (2002). *Worldwide guide to homeschooling: Facts and stats on the benefits of home school.* Nashville, TN: Broadman & Holman Press.

Ray, B. D. (1997). *Home education across the United States: How do minorities fare in home education.* Retreived September 6, 2004, from www.hslda.org/docs/study/ray1997

Rudner, L. M. (1998). *Scholastic achievement and demographic characteristics of home school students in 1998.* Purcellville, VA: Homeschool Legal Defense Association. Available: www.hslda.org/docs/study/rudner1999/FullText.asp

Serrell, R. (2004). *Minority families explore homeschooling options.* Retrieved August 23, 2004, DAY, YEAR, from www.cbn.com/cbnnews/news/020220a.asp

Slavin, R. E., & Madden, N. A. (2000). *Success for All: A proven schoolwide program for the elementary grades* [Brochure]. Baltimore: Success for All Foundation.

U.S. Department of Education, National Center for Education Statistics. (2003). *Digest of Education Statistics 2002.* Retrieved August 16, 2004, from http://nces.ed.gov/programs/digest/d02/tables/dt4

U.S. Department of Labor, Bureau of Labor Statistics. (2004). *Women in the labor force: A databook.* (Report 973). Washington, DC: Author

CHAPTER 9

LEGAL RIGHTS FOR HOMESCHOOL FAMILIES

Scott W. Somerville

Hard as it is to believe, homeschooling was considered illegal in most states as late as 1975, driving families underground to hide their children at home from the public school authorities. By 1993, a political miracle had occurred: homeschooling was recognized as legal in all 50 states. This analysis focuses on the legalization of homeschooling as an example of grass-roots political activism in the best tradition of vital democracies. Proponents of homeschooling fought a four-front war: in court to argue for the rights of families to select the home; in the state legislature to get homeschooling made legal; in local communities where parents worked to build support networks for their children; and in the U.S. Congress to protect homeschoolers from laws that might force children to take tests or engage in certain programs. This chapter looks at the legal revolution as it unfolded in courts and legislatures.

CONSTITUTIONAL CHALLENGES

Twenty years ago, home education was treated as a crime in almost every state. Today, it is legal all across America, despite strong and continued

Home Schooling in Full View: A Reader, 135–149
Copyright © 2005 by Information Age Publishing
All rights of reproduction in any form reserved.

opposition from many within the educational establishment. How did this happen? This chapter traces the legal and sociological history of the modern homeschool movement, and then suggests factors that led to this movement's remarkable success.

A few states had strong leadership from above, forcing all children in the state to enroll in public or private schools. For example, the Texas Education Agency instructed local school officials that home education was not legal and that homeschoolers should be prosecuted if they would not put their children into traditional schools. Home School Legal Defense Association (HSLDA) members in Texas joined a class action suit to block this prosecution, arguing that Texas was discriminating against parents by permitting any private school to operate except a private school run by parents.

The trial court agreed that this prosecution was enough of a possibility that criminal charges against homeschoolers should be enjoined until a final determination of that question could be made (*Leeper v. Arlington*, 1987).[1] Homeschoolers in Texas were suddenly free from the threat of prosecution. The *Leeper* decision was HSLDA's first big win, and over the next few years, HSLDA filed a series of broad constitutional challenges in states where homeschoolers were under attack.

Pennsylvania and New York each had an approval law that meant that homeschoolers could not operate without individual approval by their local school superintendent. In each state, scores of HSLDA members were in court. HSLDA filed *Jeffery v. O'Donnell* (1988), in Pennsylvania and *Blackwelder v. Safnauer* (1986), in New York. The two cases made essentially identical federal claims about identical state laws on nearly identical facts. The two courts came to opposite conclusions. The *Jeffery* court struck down Pennsylvania's compulsory attendance law; the *Blackwelder* court upheld New York's.

LEGISLATIVE VICTORIES

The loss in New York did not make a big difference to homeschoolers in that state. On the same day that *Blackwelder* was decided against them, the New York Board of Regents issued regulations legalizing and regulating home education. The Pennsylvania legislature did much the same when it passed a new compulsory attendance law that permitted home education under certain conditions. By 1987, homeschoolers had achieved enough legitimacy that lawmakers were finally willing to consider permitting home education, subject to certain regulations. In general, legislators were willing to allow parents to teach their own children as long as they provided an annual notice of their intent to teach a child at home and submitted evidence of academic achievement at the end of the school year. The following states adopted home school statutes or regulations:

- 1982: Arizona, Mississippi
- 1983: Wisconsin, Montana
- 1984: Georgia, Louisiana, Rhode Island, Virginia
- 1985: Arkansas, Florida, New Mexico, Oregon, Tennessee, Washington, Wyoming
- 1986: Missouri
- 1987: Maryland, Minnesota, Vermont, West Virginia
- 1988: Colorado, New York, South Carolina, North Carolina, Pennsylvania
- 1989: North Dakota, Hawaii, Maine, Ohio
- 1990: New Hampshire, Connecticut
- 1991: Iowa

Most of the remaining states already recognized homeschooling through court decisions. By 1989 only three states remained where home education was still a crime: Iowa, North Dakota, and Michigan. The North Dakota Supreme Court ruled against homeschoolers seven times before 1989, when the "Bismarck Tea Party" persuaded the legislature to change the law. Homeschooling was still illegal in Iowa, thanks in large part to Kathy Collins, the attorney who handled home education issues for the Iowa Department of Education. In 1987, Attorney Collins wrote:

> Children are not chattel; they are not personal property. They are not "owned" by their parents, nor do they "belong" to the state. The Christian fundamentalists who want the freedom to indoctrinate their children with religious education do not understand that the law that prevents them from legally teaching their kids prevents someone else from abusing theirs. Compulsory attendance laws are protectionist in nature. Their purpose is twofold: to protect the state by ensuring a properly educated citizenry—to protect the children by ensuring that their labor is spent attaining an education. Any law that would allow Christians to teach their children without oversight or interference from the state would also allow parents with less worthy motives to lock their children in a closet, use them to baby-sit for younger siblings, or have them work twelve hours a day in the family hardware store. Opening the door for the lamb allows the lion to enter as well.
>
> It has taken nearly two centuries to enact the many legal protections existing today for children. Abrogating the state's compulsory-attendance laws, or weakening them by allowing parents to teach children at home, is no less than a giant genuflection backward. The precarious balance of parents' rights versus children's rights should never be struck in favor of the parents.

> While the Religious Right carries the Christian flag into battle, the state must steadfastly hold high the banner of the child (Collins, 1987, p. 11).

Despite Collins' very best efforts, the Iowa legislature finally passed a homeschool law in 1991. That left Michigan as the very last state to prohibit home education by anyone but a certified teacher. The DeJonge family had spent 8 years in court and had lost every single hearing before they reached the Michigan Supreme Court. By a 5-4 decision, that state high court held that the Michigan compulsory attendance law violated the rights of parents who had a sincere religious objection to using certified teachers (*People v. DeJonge*, 1993).

In a companion case, the court ruled in favor of the Clonlara School, which used certified teachers as required by law, but only for a few hours, each school year (*Clonlara, Inc. v. State Bd. of Educ.*, 1993). The rest of the instruction was provided by parents. These two cases effectively eliminated Michigan's ability to prosecute homeschoolers, but not their power to try. Two and a half years later, the legislature enacted a home education law that eliminated all notice and reporting requirements.[2] The battle for Michigan was finally over, a key victory for the state's homeschooling families.

Holding Ground

By the middle of 1993, homeschooling was finally legal in all 50 states. The challenge for the homeschooling movement shifted from making home education possible to keeping it free. This proved to be as big a task as ever.

THE NATIONAL EDUCATION ASSOCIATION

Homeschoolers have not yet won over all their opponents. The National Education Association (NEA), in particular, has voted to abolish home education every year since 1988:

> The National Education Association believes that home schooling programs cannot provide the student with a comprehensive education experience. When home schooling occurs, students enrolled must meet all state requirements. Home schooling should be limited to the children of the immediate family, with all expenses being borne by the parents/guardians. Instruction should be by persons who are licensed by the appropriate state education licensure agency, and a curriculum approved by the state department of education should be used.

NEA also believes that homeschooled students should not participate in any extracurricular activities in the public schools. NEA further believes that local public school systems should have the authority to determine grade placement and/or credits earned toward graduation for students entering or reentering the public school setting from a home-school setting (National Education Association, 2000).

U.S CONGRESS: LEGISLATING H.R. 6[3]

Given NEA's stated position and that union's influence within the Demo-cratic Party, many homeschoolers had reason to fear the election of Bill Clinton as President in 1992. The homeschool movement had abolished the last significant barrier to home education at the state level, but now they faced Democrat majorities in the House of Representatives, Senate, and White House. Would the Clinton Administration support home edu-cation? The first big test came with House Resolution 6 of 1994 (H.R. 6), a reappropriations bill for the Elementary and Secondary Education Act (ESEA). Ordinarily such bills deal with public education and would have little, if any, impact on home educators. But in 1994, a few small wording changes affected thousands upon thousands of homeschooling families, and resulted in over a million phone calls to Congress.

The Miller Amendment

Just before sending H.R. 6 back to the House floor, the Education and Labor Committee approved Congressman George Miller's amendment (Section 2124(e)) that stated:

> ASSURANCE—Each State applying for funds under this title shall provide the Secretary with the assurance that after July 1, 1998, it will require each local educational agency within the State to certify that each full time teacher in schools under the jurisdiction of the agency is certified to teach in the subject area to which he or she is assigned.

Many local school authorities believe that home and private schools are under their jurisdiction, so homeschoolers were concerned. The new defi-nition of schools in H.R. 6 made the Miller Amendment unacceptably threatening. The word nonprofit had been added to the definition of schools in H.R. 6, changing the definition for the first time since ESEA was enacted in 1965. Where the word had previously been understood to refer to public schools, it now clearly meant more.

Representative Dick Armey Offers an Amendment

Concerned by the implications of the Miller amendment and new definitions of school in H.R. 6, Representative Dick Armey (R-TX) offered his
own amendment to protect home and private schools from the certification requirement: his amendment stated that Nothing in this title shall be
construed to author or encourage Federal control over the curriculum or
practices of any private, religious, or home school. Armey's amendment
was rejected in the committee on February 14, 1994, on a straight party-
line vote in the Democratically-controlled House Education Committee.
His office called the President of HSLDA, Mike Farris, and asked him to
analyze the Miller amendment. Based upon review of Miller's amendment, the definitional language, and HSLDA's 11 years of defending
home schools against legal challenges from local education agencies, Farris felt it was imperative to add protective language to the bill.

Representative Miller Refuses to Negotiate

The HSLDA immediately contacted Representative Miller's office to
express concern and ask for clarifying language, which is the normal way
of handling such situations. Unfortunately, Miller's staff refused to consider any amendments to § 2124(e). A quick review of Representative
Miller's voting record showed that he was a staunch supporter of the
National Education Association, which had never been favorable to
homeschoolers. Triggered by the rejection of Representative Armey's
amendment, Congress's refusal to negotiate with homeschoolers, and a
vote only 9 days away, HSLDA began contacting its members.

On Tuesday, February 15, 1994, HSLDA staff began preparing for battle. President Mike Farris drafted a letter to all 435 members of Congress,
explaining the threat to homeschooling and asking them to support the
Armey amendment. Next, arrangements were made for printing, collat-
ing, and labeling an urgent alert letter from Farris to HSLDA's then
38,000 members.[4] The letter summarized the situation and outlined a
six-step plan of action for contacting Congress and spreading the alert to
friends and neighbors. Also contained in the mailing was a list of the representatives whose offices did not need to be contacted because they had
already assured HSLDA of their support for protective language.

That evening, the National Center for Home Education launched a
nationwide fax alert containing the same information to homeschool
leaders around the country. Twelve hours later, on Wednesday morning,
telephone trees across America were abuzz, thanks to the efforts of state
and support group leaders. Tens of thousands of copies of the fax alert

were photocopied and distributed. Christian television and radio shows picked up the alert.

Congressional Phone Lines Overloaded

On Thursday, February 17, 1994, more than 60 local homeschoolers volunteered to participate in an emergency Congressional Action Program lobby day. Congressional switchboards became so overloaded due to the amount of calls they were receiving that they literally shut down. Besieged by over 20,000 telephone calls to his office alone, Congressman Miller's staff finally put an answering machine on with a message claiming that he had no intent to regulate homeschoolers.

By 9:00 a.m. the following morning, the Capitol Hill switchboards were again jammed as tens of thousands of calls flooded congressional offices. Across America, homeschoolers called radio stations, faxed letters, and distributed literature on the "Home School/Private School Freedom Amendment" written by Mike Farris and sponsored by Congressman Dick Armey. When the receptionists for certain Congressmen began giving false information about H.R. 6 to callers, the National Center sent another fax broadcast to help homeschoolers respond to confusing and misleading statements about the bill.

Over the weekend, dozens of Congressmen visiting their districts for the President's Day recess were confronted at town hall meetings, in their home offices, and elsewhere by concerned parents. Congressmen were shocked by the size of the populist response to what many of them believed to be an insignificant provision in a non-controversial bill. Even the Associated Press ran a favorable nationally-syndicated story about the homeschool telephone blitz of Congress.

Little did Congress know that the battle had just begun. On Monday, February 21 (President's Day), Dr. James Dobson's *Focus on the Family* radio show featured Michael Farris and former Congressman Bob McEwen discussing the implications of H. R. 6. HSLDA's membership began receiving their urgent alert letters in the mail. Several Christian school organizations actively jumped on the H.R. 6 bandwagon, sending out their own mailings and fax alerts. Rush Limbaugh discussed H.R. 6 on his radio show. Capitol Hill switchboards again closed down as record-breaking numbers of telephone calls poured into Congress.

On Tuesday, February 22, the second wave of telephone calls hit Congress in full force. For the rest of the day, no one on Capitol Hill would get anything done. Several Congressmen could not even reach their own staff by telephone. Congressman Armey and Mike Farris continued to fight misinformation about the amendment on the Hill. HSLDA's own office received a record 10,000 incoming telephone calls. Braving an ice storm early the next morning, Mike Farris and homeschoolers from as far away as Missouri made it into Washington, D.C. to lobby Congress.

Local homeschool volunteers delivered another letter from Mike Farris to each Congressional office. Attached to this letter was a list of thousands of state and local homeschool organizations from around the country that officially supported the effort to advance the Home School/Private School Freedom Amendment. Later that day, Farris was interviewed about H.R. 6 by more national media including CNN, Pat Buchanan, and Beverly LaHaye. And, amazingly, the Democrat-controlled House Rules Committee, willing to do almost anything to stop the number of phone calls, agreed to *open rule* on the floor.

On Thursday, February 24, Armey's staff discovered that the Rules Committee inadvertently reprinted an outdated version of the Home School/Private School Amendment. HSLDA asked Massachusetts homeschool leaders Bev Somogie and Marcie Arnett to alert homeschoolers in the district of Rules Committee Chairman Joseph Moakley (D). Within the hour, Representative Moakley's office was flooded with calls and he agreed to allow Armey to revise the amendment on the floor. Senators Ford and Kildee sponsored an ineffective competing amendment and circulated letters undermining the Home School/Private School Amendment. Armey responded with his own letter, refuting Ford and Kildee's charges.

Finally, on Thursday afternoon, debate began on the two amendments. The Ford/Kildee amendment came to a vote and passed by a 424 to 1 vote. Representative Miller was the only member to vote against it. Then Armey submitted his revised amendment. Homeschoolers around the country watched C-Span with bated breath as Congressmen from both parties lined up four and five deep to state publicly their support for the cause of home educators. After an hour-and-a-half of debate, the House voted on the Armey amendment, and homeschoolers won a stunning 374-53 victory! HSLDA sent out fax number five announcing the victory to the homeschool community.

One week later, D.C. area homeschool families delivered a special 10-pound bag of apples and a note of thanks to each congressional office. Homeschoolers all over the country expressed their appreciation by sending flowers to their Congressmen. HSLDA's all-out assault on H.R. 6 had an undeniable political impact, but it did not make every homeschooler happy. Some were willing to give Representative Miller the benefit of the doubt; others felt that the Armey Amendment had the potential to federal home education instead of keeping the federal government out of it. Homeschoolers eventually founded the National Home Education

Network[5] to make sure that HSLDA was not the only group speaking for homeschoolers.

NATIONAL TESTING

Homeschoolers recognize how fragile their liberty is, and are committed to defending that liberty at all costs. Chris Klicka of HSLDA provides the following first-hand account of one of the more recent political battles for liberty:

> During the 105th Congress, I obtained a transcript of a meeting the U.S. Department of Education convened with educators from around the country to discuss the creation and implementation of a *national test* for all students. After meeting with the president of HSLDA who agreed battling this national test would be a major priority for us, I contacted Congressman Goodling's counsel [Bill Goodling was the Chairman of the House Education Committee] and told him that Mike Farris agreed we would "pull out all stops" if Goodling introduced a bill to cut off funding to Clinton's national test. The counsel said he would talk to Goodling. A week later, he explained Goodling was willing to introduce a resolution expressing the sense of the House opposing national testing.
>
> Over the next year and a half, the home schoolers had the opportunity to prove themselves again and again as we at HSLDA sent out nearly 35 nationwide fax alerts. And the home schoolers responded! Repeatedly the home schoolers flooded the House with calls and we organized our Congressional Action program volunteers to visit every office with packets exposing the dangers of the Clinton's national test. In September of 1997, we won the first round in the House; 296 to 125 to stop funding of all national testing. The home schoolers had made the ban on testing viable. A key congressional staff admitted, "Without HSLDA and the home schoolers this could not have happened!"

In October 1997, the Senate sold us out by compromising the bill allowing a national test. This was unacceptable. We told the leadership we would unleash another nationwide alert. In high stakes negotiating in conference committee, we achieved a temporary victory. We won a *one-year ban* on national testing. This meant the fight would continue in 1998. We hoped the grassroots would not become worn out.

At the beginning of the next year, our champion, Congressman Goodling, introduced H. R. 2846, a *permanent ban on national testing*. Riding on a wave of calls from the homeschoolers, the testing ban passed in a vote of 242 to 174. The fight, however, was just beginning. We still had to get the bill through the Senate. Our champion in the Senate was John

Ashcroft from Missouri. The only problem is that we did not have a vehicle to which to attach our testing amendment.

I soon received a call from Senator Lott's office, who was the majority leader, telling me there was "not a chance in _____" that our testing amendment would be successful. They had done a "whip count" earlier in the day and only found 30 senators who would support our testing ban. They urged us not to push for the amendment because we would lose big. Our lobby effort the day before, however, gave us evidence that we were very close to winning the vote. Lott's office told me it was our call. I said we wanted to go forward with the vote. I thought we could win. Besides, it might be our only chance to get a vote that year. In the meantime, the homeschoolers were delivering thousands of calls and God's people were praying.

On April 22, 1998, the vote was scheduled. It was amazing to watch. Ashcroft's amendment permanently banning national testing passed in a vote of 52-47! Far more votes than the 30 votes predicted by Lott's office. The Senate leadership was amazed. The homeschoolers had pulled it off. Later in June, we were contacted by the leadership in both the House and Senate, asking us if we would agree to have our testing amendment removed so that the A+ Education Savings Account bill could go to the president in a clean form. (The A+ bill was subsequently vetoed by the president.) We made Speaker Gingrich and Majority Leader Lott promise, in writing, that our testing amendment would be attached to another bill later in the year. In October 1998, they kept their promise in spite of intense threats from President Clinton. We finally won. A permanent ban on a national test was achieved! (C. Klicka, personal communication).

HOMESCHOOL POLITICS

In this section, we will grope for some explanation of the secrets of that success. How did this small group of ragtag radicals become the largest successful educational reform movement in America today? How did they change the laws of all 50 states and enact federal legislation over the President's objections? Three factors seem to make the difference.

Right Makes Might

Most homeschoolers believe that governments should protect the safety and integrity of the home and leave the task of childrearing to parents. When parents believe their government threatens their home instead of protecting it, families feel justified in resisting that threat. Laws fade into insignificance when parents think the government threatens the good of their children.

We need not determine whether parents actually have a right to break a law that threatens their home, although such questions have begun to reach the highest courts in our land. See, for example, *Troxel v. Granville* (2000). A mother's love is an irresistible force, and the compulsory attendance laws are hardly an immovable object. When nineteenth-century parents claimed a right to force their children to work in the potato fields instead of sending them to school, it was easy for society to insist that a child's right to an education outweighed the parent's right to the child's income.

But when twentieth-century parents claimed a right to give their children a better education at home than that in the public schools, society lost its will to resist.

Homeschoolers have gone forth on the courage of their convictions, and the opposing forces of government have melted away at their advance. Time after time, a homeschool mom with a cardboard box full of books has marched into a superintendent's office to say, "I don't care what the law says. This is what my child needs!" Time after time, the schools have found a way to work around the law, or, if the case goes to court, the judge has found the way, or, if the case is lost, the legislature finds the way, or, if the legislature refuses to act, the family moves on to another state.

Active Citizens[6]

In the 1996 National Household Education Survey (NHES), the U.S. Department of Education's National Center for Education Statistics surveyed 9,393 parents of school age children. The survey asked numerous questions about the extent of family involvement in a variety of civic activities. Some of the questions asked whether the parent had voted recently, telephoned or wrote a public official, signed a petition, attended public meetings, contributed to political campaigns, participated in community service activities, worked for a political cause, or participated in a boycott in the past 12 months. The survey differentiated public schoolers from homeschoolers and both religious and nonreligious private schoolers. Christian Smith and David Sikkink of the Department of Sociology at the University of North Carolina analyzed the data, which was published in 1999.

By comparing differences in family participation in these various forms of civic involvement, Smith and Sikkink found that homeschool families and private school families are consistently more involved in all of the civic activities examined than are families with children in public schools. In fact, by an average margin of 9.3%, the private and homeschool families are more likely than the public school families to engage in any listed forms of civic participation. Up to 13% more private and homeschoolers have given money to political causes and up to 15% more have voted in recent elections and telephoned elected officials. An amazing 26% more private and homeschool families are members of community groups and volunteer at local organizations (Smith & Sikkink, 1999, pp. 16-20).

The researchers conclude that homeschoolers and private schoolers are definitely not the isolated recluses that critics suggest they might be. It is rather the public schooling families that are clearly the least civically involved of all the schooling types (1999, p. 18). Smith and Sikkink state:

> Indeed, we have reason to believe that the organizations and practices involved in private and home schooling, in themselves, tend to foster public participation in civic affairs ... the challenges, responsibilities, and practices that private schooling and home education normally entail for their participants may actually help reinvigorate America's civic culture and the participation of our citizens in our public square.

Smith and Sikkink ponder the surprising civic lifestyle of homeschoolers. Their comments explain a great deal about the success of the home school movement:

> Most are embedded in dense relational networks of home schooling families; participate in local, state, regional, and national home schooling organizations; and engage in a variety of community activities and programs that serve the education of their children. Home schooling families meet together at playgrounds; frequent local libraries, museums, and zoos; organized drama productions, science projects, and art workshops; enroll their kids in YMCA soccer and swimming classes; organ home school association picnics and cookouts; and much more. Home schooling families also frequent home education conferences and seminars; pay close attention to education–related legislative issues; share political information with each other; and educate themselves about relevant legal concerns. Far from being private and isolated, home schooling families are typically very well networked and quite civically active. (1999, p. 20)

Even one active citizen can make a difference in his or her own community. Seventy thousand families' worth of activists can make a difference nationwide. The Home School Legal Defense Association unites these unusually effective citizen activists into a force to be reckoned with. As the United States Congress discovered during H.R. 6, a scattered but committed minority can be extraordinarily effective in this age of electronic communications.

Strength in Diversity

Kathy Collins, the attorney who used to supervise home education in Iowa, wrote homeschoolers off as Christian fundamentalists. Ms. Collins was wrong. The diversity of homeschoolers is a great strength of the homeschool movement. The increasing popularity and acceptability of home education has given it a foothold in some communities that might otherwise have never considered it. The first wave of homeschoolers was far to the left of the American political spectrum (Holt, 1981), and the second wave of evangelical homeschoolers was well to the right. The new waves of the homeschoolers are rapidly filling in the vital center of American politics. Each new wave makes it harder for politicians to remove the right to teach a child at home.

Diversity is especially useful when homeschoolers interact with legislators. There are homeschoolers who are very comfortable with the most conservative politicians, and others who are equally at home with the most liberal. When homeschool freedoms are genuinely threatened, every faction of this diverse community will quickly join together to fend off government control of home education.

Legislators must remember the diversity of home education when they consider how (or whether) to regulate it. A legislative proposal might be perfectly acceptable to most homeschoolers, yet fundamentally violate the deepest convictions of others. Dr. Mary Hood, a homeschooler herself, dealt with this issue in her doctoral dissertation:

> [I]t is important for policy-makers to recognize that no single individual, group or organization, either on a local or a national level, can possibly hope to represent the views of all home educators adequately. Whenever policy decisions are made, it is important to include representatives of the homeschool movement in the planning process in order to ensure that decisions are fair and plans are feasible. (1991, p. 3)

Diversity makes a huge difference in the way the media report on homeschooling. If home educators were uniformly conservative Republicans, many in the press would have been quick to label them part of the *vast right wing conspiracy*. But any reporter who has ever actually covered homeschoolers knows this just is not true. Homeschoolers come in too many different flavors to be stereotyped or ignored.

CONCLUSION

Homeschooling is the movement that should not have happened; yet somehow ordinary parents have overcome the combined barriers of compulsory attendance laws, social disapproval, and a hostile teacher's union. This success could never have happened if homeschoolers had all been cut from the same cloth. Any movement capable of uniting Marxist teachers and fundamentalist lawyers is probably destined to be a smashing success or a startling failure. Homeschooling managed to succeed.

Homeschoolers value this freedom and aim to keep it. In the immortal words of the preamble to the United States Constitution, we intend to "secure the blessings of Liberty to ourselves and our Posterity." Homeschoolers would not quit unless they were put in jail. As Mahatma Gandhi and Martin Luther King, Jr. knew, Western democracies lack the will to punish honest people with good motives. A totalitarian state can stamp out home education. A free people will not.

Western democracies lack the will to punish, but do not lack the will to regulate. The most remarkable thing about the modern homeschool movement is that it is still so unregulated. Almost 2% percent of America's school-aged children are now taught at home by uncertified parents, free of any day-to-day government control of content or method. As long as the National Education Association continues to resolve to abolish homeschooling, homeschoolers view *any* regulation as the first of a thousand cuts. *Any* possible restriction on homeschooling, from the ambiguous language of H.R. 6 to the development of a national test, will be met with fierce resistance from well-organized homeschoolers.

Homeschoolers still practice the politics of survival. They see themselves as a microminority, fighting to maintain a way of life in a society that may tolerate them today but could turn on them at any moment. Politicians respect groups that successfully fight for the rights of a discrete and insular minority. No candidate seeking national office would ever intentionally irritate the Jewish AntiDefamation League, for example. Homeschoolers have not earned that kind of respect—at least, not yet.

NOTES

1. The Texas Supreme Court ultimately upheld this decision in *Texas Educational Agency, et al., v. Leeper, et al.*, 893 S.W.2d 432, (Tex. 1994).

2. Michigan Compiled Laws 380.1561(3)(f) exempts a child from attendance at a public school if the child is being educated at the child's home by his or her parent or legal guardian in an organized and educational program in the subject areas of reading, spelling, mathematics, science, history, civics, literature, writing, and English grammar. There are no reporting or notification requirements.

3. The material in this section has been adapted by permission from material on the Home School Legal Defense Association Web page, at www.HSDA.org

4. HSLDA now has over 70,000 member families.
5. NHEN can be found on the Web at www.nhen.org. Its mission statement reads:

> The National Home Education Network exists to encourage and facilitate the vital grassroots work of state and local homeschooling groups and individuals by providing information, fostering networking and promoting public relations on a national level. Because we believe there is strength in a diverse network of homeschoolers, we support the freedom of all individual families to choose home education and to direct such eduation.

6. This section is taken, in large part, from Klicka (YEAR???).

REFERENCES

Blackwelder v. Safnauer, 689 F. Supp 106 (N.D.N.Y. 1986).

Clonlara, Inc. v. State Bd. of Educ., 442 Mich. 230 (1993).

Collins, K. (1987). Children are not chattel. *Free Inquiry*, 7(4), 11.

Holt, J. (1981). *Teach your own*. New York: Delacorte Press/Seymour Lawrence.

Hood, M. (1991). Contemporary philosophical influences on the homeschooling movement. *Home School Researcher*, 7(1), 1-22.

Jeffery v. O'Donnell, 702 F.Supp. 516 (M.D. PA 1988).

Klicka, C. (1999). Home-school families: Involved or isolated? *Private School Monitor*, *20*(3), 9.

Leeper v. Arlington Indep. School Dist., No. 17-88761-85 Tarrant County 17th Judicial Ct., April 13, 1987).

National Education Association. (2000). NEA 2000-2001 Resolutions, B-68. *Home Schooling*. Available at http://www.nea.org/resolutions/00/00b-68.html

People v. DeJonge, 442 Mich. 266 (1993).

Smith, C., & Sikkink, D. (1999). Is private schooling privatizing? *First Things 92*, 16-20.

Texas Educational Agency, et al., v. Leeper, et al., 893 S.W.2d 432, (Tex. 1994)

Troxel v. Granville, 530 U.S. 57, (2000).

CHAPTER 10

THE EFFECTIVENESS OF HOMESCHOOLING STUDENTS WITH SPECIAL NEEDS

Steven F. Duvall

INTRODUCTION

As homeschooling has become increasingly more common, questions persist concerning whether parents, especially when they lack teacher training, can adequately educate their children at home. These concerns are muted, at least to some degree, by reports (e.g., Ray, 1997) that, in general, homeschool students achieve above the national average. However, these reports do not typically address the achievement of homeschool students with special needs. Even so, a growing body of evidence indicates that homeschool students with special needs may outperform their similarly disabled peers who attend public schools. Additionally, this research is beginning to provide an explanation concerning how this is possible.

Compared to research that involves traditional school settings, the study of homeschooling remains in its infancy stages, particularly as it relates to students with learning problems. The purpose of this article is to familiarize readers with the homeschool research that has been conducted to date that explains why home education may be more effective

Home Schooling in Full View: A Reader, 151–166
Copyright © 2005 by Information Age Publishing

than public school instruction, even special education programs. In the following, the academic gains that were made by special needs homeschool and public school students during formal research studies will be discussed. It will be shown that the homeschool students generally outperformed their public school counterparts and an accompanying explanation of the principles that made this possible will be provided. Finally, an actual case study involving a homeschooled elementary student with learning disabilities will be reported to further demonstrate the power that is provided by a homeschool learning environment. Another purpose of discussing the case study will be to clarify how the principles discovered through research, involving both traditional schools as well as homeschools, apply to individuals who are taught at home.

FORMAL RESEARCH DISCUSSION

Estimated Number of Homeschool Students with Special Needs

Approximately 13.3% (National Center for Educational Statistics, (NCES), 2003a) of the 54 million students (NCES, 2003b) who attend traditional schools are labeled as having special needs. This includes students with disabilities such as attention deficit hyperactivity disorder, autism, behavior/ emotional disturbances, hearing impairments, learning disabilities, mental retardation, physical impairments, speech/language disorders, traumatic brain injury, and visual impairments. Assuming that disabling conditions occur at the same rate among homeschoolers as in the traditional school population, more than 250,000 children could be affected because the total number of students taught at home is now estimated to be between 1.2 (NCES, 2004) and 1.9 (National Home Education Research Institute, 2004) million. With so many children involved, it is not difficult to understand why many are concerned about whether homeschooling is a viable option for successfully educating them.

Reasons Why Parents Homeschool Their Children

Toch (1991) indicated that many parents perceived public schools as (a) having academic standards that were too low, (b) providing minimal levels of personal attention for their children, and (c) failing to promote traditional values. These ideas, coupled with parents' perceptions of schools as sometimes being unsafe environments for their children, caused some parents to forego traditional schooling in favor of home education. But regardless of parents' rationale to homeschool their children, when their children have special needs, parents can encounter opposition from local education and social agencies (T. A. Bushnell, personal communication, September 29, 2004).

Major Criticisms of Homeschooling

Most of the arguments against teaching students at home have involved issues surrounding teacher training and socialization. Regarding teacher training, parents often lack formal teacher preparation and certification and it has been suggested that this hinders their ability to teach effectively, especially when students with special needs are involved. However, children taught at home typically score higher than the national average on achievement tests (e.g., Home School Legal Defense Association, 1994; Ray, 1997). Furthermore, researchers have found that, to a large degree, parents engaged in the same teaching behaviors as certified regular and special educators in public schools (Duvall, Delquadri, & Ward, 2004; Duvall, Ward, Delquadri, & Greenwood, 1997). For example, when comparing the frequency and types of behavior that instructors exhibited in public school special education programs and homeschools (i.e., academic talking, academic questioning, academic commanding [e.g., "Tell me the first letter of the alphabet!"], reading aloud to students, talking to students about disciplinary issues, questioning students about disciplinary issues [e.g., "Are you supposed to be talking during a test?"], giving disciplinary commands, talking to students about management issues [e.g., "Let's see if you're working on the right page."], questioning students about management issues [e.g., "Is your pencil sharpened?"], making management commands [e.g., "Turn to page 55 in your math book!"], conversing about nonacademic matters [e.g., "Who won the football game last night?"], making nonacademic prompts [e.g., pointing to the letter A while waiting for the student to say A], paying attention to students, singing to students, or making no response toward any student in the classroom [e.g., silently reading a newspaper article while students work on a math assignment]), Duvall et al. (1997) found that the occurrence of any of these behaviors differed by less than 5% between the two groups.

Very similar findings occurred in another study (Duvall et al., 2004) that compared homeschool instructors' behaviors to those of regular education teachers. However, in this study it was determined that public school teachers talked somewhat more about academic and management issues. However, because it is academic talk by students instead of teachers that has been shown to be important as it relates to student achievement (e.g., Stanley & Greenwood, 1983), these marginal differences were seen as unimportant. Consequently, because both of these studies showed that parents exhibited behaviors that were very similar to public school teachers (even though the parents lacked teacher certification) during instructional times, the criticisms involving parents' lack of formal training are likely to be overstated. Such criticisms will become especially mute if future studies establish the fact that these teaching behavior similarities are typical.

The fact that the behaviors of the public school teachers and the homeschool instructors were very similar in the Duvall et al. (1997; 2004) studies was interesting, especially when considering that the educational training of the two groups differed considerably. For example, in the Duvall et al. (1997) study, all of the special education teachers had master's degrees in special education. However, of the parents involved, one had a bachelor's degree in business, one an associate's degree, and the remaining ones had not finished high school. In the Duvall et al. (2004) study, the regular education teachers possessed master's degrees in education while the homeschool instructors had only high school or general equivalency diplomas. As a result, the authors of these studies concluded that a lack of formal teacher training had not prevented the homeschool instructors from displaying the same teaching behaviors as those that were demonstrated by teaching professionals. Furthermore, because the homeschool students in these studies generally outperformed the public school students academically, they concluded that teacher training was not an important determiner of homeschool students' outcomes. In effect, it was not necessary for parents to have a teaching certificate in order to be highly effective instructors.

Concerning social development, homeschooling raises concerns because, to some degree, it limits children's interactions with others, especially as it relates to peers. However, it seems that homeschooling may only limit social interaction during the school day because Groover and Endsley (1988) showed that homeschool and traditional school students belonged to the same number of organizations (e.g., scouting and church youth groups), socialized equally as often with relatives and friends, and attended extrafamilial social activities with the same frequency as students who attended traditional schools. Consequently, homeschooling may restrict socialization, but, perhaps only during certain hours of the school day. Because the optimal level of interacting with adults and peers for social skill development is unknown, it may eventually be determined that the social interaction experienced by homeschoolers is adequate or, perhaps, even more beneficial than that to which traditional students are exposed.

The Groover and Endsley (1988) study involved regular education students but it is reasonable to assume that homeschooling would meet the social needs of students with disabilities equally as well unless, of course, it was determined that they required constant, intensive social interaction with peers during regular school hours. Even so, unless this need was established for individual students, it seems quite likely that interacting with parents and siblings (when present) would be sufficient.

Related Research

The professional literature contains many studies which suggest that parents can be effective instructors of children with disabilities when assisted by professionals (e.g., Broden, Beasley, & Hall, 1978; DuPaul & Henningson, 1993; Duvall, Elliott, Delquadri, & Hall, 1992; Gang & Pouche, 1982; Greenwood et al., 1984; Thurston & Dasta, 1990; Waldrop, 1994). For example, Broden et al. (1978) demonstrated that parents, after being trained as spelling tutors, could significantly improve their children's spelling performance. Using a tutoring procedure that required students to make multiple, correct spelling responses, the parents were able to help their children make significant gains on standardized tests and weekly test scores at school.

DuPaul and Henningson (1993) demonstrated gains in reading achievement for four elementary students with Attention Deficit Hyperactivity Disorder (ADHD) by increasing their academic engaged time (AET) via parent tutoring at home. In this study, the students experienced gains in reading at home and school as a result of the increased AET. Duvall et al. (1992) demonstrated that parents, after being trained by educators to tutor students with learning disabilities at home, could significantly increase their children's reading scores. Tutoring involved having parents work with their children less than 15 minutes a day, but the impact of tutoring was immediately evident on the daily curriculum-based measures collected at home by the parents. Furthermore, significant reading improvements were later observed in other materials at home and school, and on standardized tests.

As opposed to training parents to be academic tutors, Waldrop (1994) showed that the parents of children with ADHD were able to assist their children to achieve more in school after being trained to use behavioral techniques at home. In this study, parents were trained to provide reinforcement at home for improved student performance at school. As a result, the children's grades at school improved.

As can be seen, researchers have demonstrated that parents, when provided with training, can effectively teach their children. However, homeschooling generally involves the provision of instruction by parents who are working without the assistance of trained educators.

Academic Gains by Special Needs Students When Taught by Parents at Home and Certified Teachers in Public Schools

In their research with parents working independent of professional assistance, Duvall et al. (1997) determined that parents could effectively teach students with learning disabilities at home. In this study, the academic gains of homeschool students were compared to that of public school students who were taught in special education programs. The results of this study, the length of which spanned across two semesters, indicated that the homeschool students made more academic gains in the basic skill areas including reading, math and written language as measured by curriculum-based measures and standardized tests.

In another study that involved parents teaching their children apart from professional assistance, Duvall et al. (2004) determined that parents could effectively teach students with ADHD at home. In this study, two homeschool students with ADHD were closely matched with two similarly affected public school students. Then, over the span of one complete semester, their academic growth was measured in the areas of reading and math. As in the Duvall et al. (1997) study, the homeschool students generally made more gains as measured by curriculum-based measures and standardized tests.

Why the Homeschool Students Out-Performed Their Public School Counterparts

That the homeschool students in these two studies (i.e., Duvall et al., 1997, 2004) made more progress than the public school students appeared related to their higher levels of engagement on key instructional behaviors. These behaviors included writing, physical academic responses, reading aloud, reading silently, and academic talk, all of which have been shown to result in academic gains (e.g., Delquadri, Greenwood, Whorton, Carta & Hall, 1986; Duvall et al., 1992; Greenwood et al., 1984; Hall, Delquadri, Greenwood, & Thurston, 1982). The following discussion focuses on the importance of these behaviors because, to a large degree, they explain why the homeschool students made more gains.

Academic Engaged Time

Academic Engaged Time (AET) is an important concept for parents to understand because it is a strong determiner of academic achievement. Furthermore, the homeschool observational studies (Duvall et al, 1997; 2004) conducted to date have indicated that its high rate of occurrence during home instruction is a primary reason why students with special needs do so well when taught at home. Although it is not a direct measure of learning, it is so strongly and positively correlated with achievement that education researchers often consider increases in AET to be synonymous with increased academic outcomes (Gettinger & Seibert, 2002). The purpose of the following discussion is to introduce parents to the AET concept and its implications for educating students at home.

Brief Historical Background of AET Research

After hundreds of U.S. school districts unified during the 1950s and 1960s, educators began to realize that many students were not learning as much as expected. Researchers subsequently conducted a series of observational studies to determine the possible causes of low student achievement. In the midst of these studies, one group of behavioral researchers serendipitously discovered that students, instead of being actively engaged by their lessons, were often passive participants or, even worse, only occasionally taking part in teacher-planned activities. For example, Delquadri et al. (1986) reported that one attempt to measure generalization of a fourth grader's oral reading tutoring, from home to school, was prevented because the child was called on to read for only 10 seconds during a two week period. The child typically sat alone at his desk while the teacher worked with reading groups. Furthermore, on average, this student was actively engaged for only 8 minutes of the 60-minute reading period.

After the child was placed in a learning disabilities program in which he received 6 minutes of individualized oral reading practice each day, his correct oral reading rate increased from 15.2 words per minute to 45.7 words per minute in only two weeks while his error rate dropped from 9.8 errors per minute to 2.4 errors per minute during the same time span. Furthermore, 2 years later, instead of reading at a first grade second month level as he had as a fourth grader, this student, as a sixth grader, was reading at a fifth grade eight month level on a standardized test of reading achievement. Consequently, it became apparent that students were often failing to achieve, not because there was something inherently wrong with the students themselves but, merely because they were academically engaged at very low levels during classroom instruction.

Implications for Homeschoolers

This account illustrates an important principle (i.e., the opportunity-to-respond principle) that has been shown to explain the successes of homeschooling students with special needs. According to this principle, for students to make academic gains they must be systematically presented with opportunities to make academic responses. Academic responses include the following behaviors as they relate to a student's response to the curriculum or the teacher's lesson: (a) *writing* about a curriculum issue (for example, writing 1492 in a social studies workbook in response to a question about when Christopher Columbus discovered the Americas); (b) making a *physical academic response* (for example, typing or using a calculator to figure a problem from the math textbook); (c) *reading aloud* in, for example, the science book; (d) *reading silently* in, for example, the language textbook; and (e) *academic talk* or, for instance, talking about the location of the British Isles during a geography lesson. The amount of time during which a student is engaged in these behaviors is referred to as academic engaged time (AET). Furthermore, increasing the time that a student engages in these specific behaviors results in academic gains (e.g., Duvall et al., 1992; Greenwood et al., 1984; Greenwood et al., 1989).

In the example of the fourth grader, the student was failing due to a lack of a systematic opportunity to respond. Specifically, the child's engagement in oral reading was low, but when placed in a program for students with learning disabilities, dramatic improvement occurred as evidenced by his improvements in his reading rates. In the regular education setting, the teacher used the traditional three reading group approach that, unfortunately, often left the child working individually at his seat as other groups met with the teacher. But instead of academically engaging while other groups worked with the teacher, the fourth grader was frequently off task. When it was time for the teacher to work with the student's reading group, which was often less than the scheduled 20 minutes, the child was seldom called upon to read. Instead, the child often passively watched the teacher as she provided instruction (Delquadri et al., 1986). When placed in the special program, however, the child was required to read assigned passages orally to the teacher, individually, every day. In this class, there was much less emphasis on teacher explanations and verbal instruction, but more on verbal feedback and praise for correct student responses that maintained high levels of student academic responding.

Many studies have demonstrated that AET and academic gains covary (e.g., Broden et al., 1978; DuPaul & Henningson, 1993; Delquadri, Greenwood, Stretton, & Hall, 1983; Duvall et al., 1992; Duvall et al., 1997; Gang & Poche, 1982; Greenwood et al., 1984; Greenwood et al.,

1989; Greenwood, Dinwiddie, Terry, Wade, Stanley, Thibadeau, & Delquadri, 1984; Maheady & Harper, 1987; Thurston & Dasta, 1990). That is, when students experience low levels of AET, their progress has been slow. However, when AET is increased, academic gains are accelerated. Consequently, it is extremely important for parents to recognize that their chil.dren's achievement will be slow if the time spent making active academic responses is low, but will accelerate if academic responding time increases as it relates to the curriculum or the teacher's lessons.

Student-Teacher Ratios

One issue that can affect AET is student-teacher ratios, which are important because they can influence the level at which students become actively engaged. For example, Thurlow, Ysseldyke, Wotruba, and Algozzine (1993) demonstrated that, in general, higher levels of student AET occurred when student-teacher ratios were the lowest. In this study, 139 first through sixth graders and 54 teachers participated in a study in which students, who were receiving special education services, were served in situations involving student-teacher ratios that ranged from 1:1 to 12:1. Thurlow et al. (1993) concluded that the lowest student-teacher ratios were superior because they resulted in the highest rates of AET and achievement by students. Concerning homeschooling, this issue becomes immediately apparent because homeschools, in almost all instances, involve lower student-teacher ratios than that which is found in traditional classrooms. The implication would be that, compared to public school special education classrooms with more students, the low number of students in homeschool instructional settings would generally result in higher AET. This, in turn, would lead to greater academic gains for children with disabilities being taught at home.

Homeschool researchers (e.g., Duvall et al., 1997; Duvall et al., 2004) to date have substantiated this principle. For example, in a study of students with learning disabilities, Duvall et al. (1997) observed that homeschoolers experienced student-teacher ratios that ranged from 1:1 to 1:5 compared to public school students who, in special education programs, experienced student-teacher ratios that ranged from 1:1 to 1:15. The lower student-teacher ratios in homeschools led to AET rates that were 2.6 times as high as those observed in public school programs and higher levels of achievement as measured by curriculum based measures and standardized achievement tests.

In a study involving students with ADHD, Duvall et al. (2004) compared the academic engagement and outcomes of homeschoolers and public school students in regular education classrooms. In this study, the homeschool students experienced student-teacher ratios that averaged

2.2:1 compared to public school students who were taught in classrooms that had ratios that averaged 20.2:1. As in the Duvall et al. (1997) study, the lower homeschool student-teacher ratios led to AET rates that were more than twice as high as those observed in public school classrooms. As expected, this resulted in the homeschool students making more academic gains than the public school students.

The concept of AET that involves the key academic behaviors mentioned above is, in the author's opinion, perhaps the most important principle for homeschooling parents to understand because it explains why home education can be so effective. That is, when parents understand that specific student behaviors are critical for academic gains to occur and take steps to increase the amount of time that their children are engaged in them, then parents will ensure that their children's academic progress will be accelerated. Specifically, if parents increase the amount of time that their children spend writing, making physical academic responses, reading aloud, reading silently, and engaging in academic talk about the curriculum or the instructor's lessons, then the pace of their children's learning will quicken.

As discussed above, regardless of where (i.e., home or school) or who (e.g., parent or certified teachers) provides instruction, researchers have determined that students must have ample opportunities to make active academic responses in order to make gains. This has proven to be the case whether students have ADHD, autism, behavior/emotional disturbances, hearing impairments, learning disabilities, or mental retardation.

CASE STUDY OF A HOMESCHOOLED STUDENT WITH SEVERE LEARNING DISABILITIES

During a 21 year career as a school psychologist, the author tested over 1,500 students with learning problems. Of these, the individual who made the largest academic gains was an elementary student named Cory. Cory was diagnosed as having severe learning disabilities (LD) and the person who helped him to make extraordinary academic progress, his mother, had never graduated from high school. The purpose of this case study is to describe the progress that Cory experienced, how his mother helped him, and explain why it is possible for other homeschool children with learning problems to make better than expected gains even when their parents lack specialized teacher training.

Shortly after Cory started kindergarten in 1991, his teacher noticed that he did not learn as quickly as the other children. As the months progressed, it became obvious that Cory was falling progressively further behind his peers. By year's end, it was decided that Cory would benefit from repeating kindergarten. However, repeating a grade failed to make Cory more successful because he continued to struggle. He was subsequently evaluated by special education personnel at the end of his second year in kindergarten.

The evaluation that was conducted at Cory's neighborhood school by special education personnel indicated that he had a normal intelligence quotient (IQ) (i.e., 100). His IQ was at the 50th percentile and indicated that, intellectually, Cory functioned better than half of all similarly aged students. Consequently, the school's multidisciplinary team correctly concluded that, from an intellectual perspective, Cory had the intelligence to, at a minimum, keep up with the pace of learning that was set by his peers in the regular classroom. However, he was among the lowest achieving students in his class whether he competed with same-age peers (as he was during his first kindergarten year) or younger students (as during his second kindergarten enrollment).

Achievement testing indicated that, compared to similarly aged students around the country, Cory's skills in reading, math and written language were extremely low. So low, in fact, that his acquisition of basic skills reflected the learning of someone with an IQ of, not 100, but, below 70, or like that of a student who had mental retardation. Obviously, his IQ of 100 ruled out the possibility of mental retardation. But since he was far below his own expected level of achievement (that is, grade-level)—coupled with evidence that he was motivated to do well, had normal vision and hearing, and had not been subjected to an inconsistent educational program—provided strong evidence that he had a severe learning disability. As a result, the public school team recommended that, when Cory returned as a first grader during the fall semester, he be placed in a special education program that was designed for students with learning disabilities. Instead, Cory's mother, Mitzi, decided to educate him at home.

Mitzi reported that she felt inadequate to be Cory's teacher because both she and Cory's father had been diagnosed as having learning disabilities when they attended school years earlier. Furthermore, neither of them had gone beyond the 11th grade and Cory's father, even as an adult, could read very little. However, Mitzi was determined to help Cory learn the basic skills that he was struggling to acquire.

Two years later, after Mitzi had homeschooled Cory for the first and second grades, the author evaluated Cory with the same battery of achievement tests that the public school team had used previously. When comparing the results of the two evaluations, it was immediately evident that Cory had made outstanding progress after being homeschooled because his scores in the basic skill areas (i.e., reading, math and written language) had risen dramatically. In fact, instead of showing significant deficiencies in reading, math and written language as before, the second evaluation indicated that all of Cory's basic skills were within the normal range (i.e., between the 25th and 75th percentiles). For example, the public school team had determined that Cory scored at the 1st percentile (that is, 99 out of 100 similarly aged students would have scored higher) in reading after spending 2 years in traditional kindergarten (see Figure 10.1). However, after being homeschooled for 2 years, Cory earned a reading score at the 44th percentile. Cory's scores also went from the 5th and 1st percentiles to the 28th and 33rd percentiles in the respective areas of math and written language.

After determining that homeschooling had been very beneficial for Cory, the author visited the home on numerous occasions during the next 7 months to study how Mitzi provided instruction. Because researchers (e.g., Duvall, Delquadri, Elliott, & Hall, 1992; Duvall, Delquadri, & Ward, 2004; Duvall, Ward, Delquadri, & Greenwood, 1997; Greenwood, Delquadri, & Hall, 1984; Greenwood, Delquadri, & Hall, 1989; Hall, Delquadri, Greenwood, & Thurston, 1982; Stanley & Greenwood, 1983) had known for a long time that academic achievement was directly linked to AET, the author was interested in determining how Mitzi, who lacked teacher training in the use of procedures that increased AET, effectively met this instructional requirement.

The author conducted direct observations of Cory's homeschool environment and it soon became evident that, in a situation involving only one student, Cory spent a lot of time participating in activities that generated high levels of AET. For example, during reading instruction, Mitzi and Cory sat side-by-side every day for 30 minutes during which they

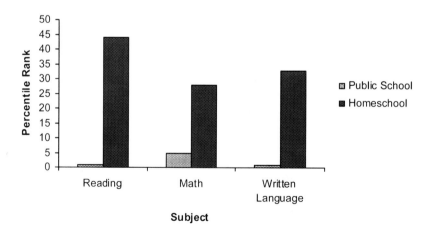

Figure 10.1.   Cory's academic performance on the Woodcock-Johnson Tests of Achievement after 2 years of public and homeschooling

would take turns reading successive paragraphs aloud to one another from the reading textbook. This obviously provided high rates of AET on Cory's part because he had to read paragraphs aloud or read along silently as his mother read to him.

In contrast, had Cory been in a classroom of 20 students, for example, it would have been difficult for a teacher to provide him with 30 minutes of daily one-on-one reading instruction like he experienced at home. In a classroom with more students, he likely would have experienced much less AET and made fewer gains as a result. In effect, it was not a particular instructional methodology (direct instruction, for example) that helped Cory make so much progress because Mitzi did not know any particular method to use when teaching him. Instead, it appeared that it had been Mitzi's approach of providing a lot of one-on-one instruction that led to many opportunities to practice reading aloud, and silently, that helped Cory to become a vastly improved reader. When observing the instructional arrangements that Mitzi established for math and written language, it was obvious that, like in reading, Cory experienced similarly high levels of one-on-one instruction and AET in those subjects, as well. Consequently, it was determined that large gains in Cory's math and written language skills had likely occurred for the same reasons as those that he had experienced in reading.

Because the author had not observed Cory when he attended public schools, one can only speculate about Cory's kindergarten experience. Even so, it seemed reasonable to assume that Cory, like the public school fourth grade student mentioned earlier, would have been engaged very little while attending a traditional classroom and, as a result, fallen well behind his peers academically. It also seems reasonable that Cory, if he had been taught in a special education program instead of at home, would have made fewer gains because he probably would have experienced less one-on-one instruction and AET. Consequently, his progress would likely have been less extraordinary.

CONCLUSION OF CASE STUDY

Cory, identified by a public school multidisciplinary team as having a severe learning disability, made extraordinary academic progress but not until he was taught at home by his mother. After studying Cory's homeschool instructional environment, it was determined that Mitzi's disciplined and persistent routine provided high amounts of AET that, in turn, enabled Cory to make large academic gains. Furthermore, it should be noted that Cory, after making enormous gains during his first 2 years of homeschooling, continued to make sizeable gains during the 7 months that the author observed him, although the gains were not as dramatic.

Much of the academic success that Cory experienced occurred because he was the only child being taught at home. Therefore, it seems possible that other parents who lacked teacher training but enjoyed low student-teacher ratios in their homeschools could also prove to be effective teachers for children with serious learning problems. Teacher training may be necessary when one must work with large groups of students, but it appears to have little bearing on student outcomes in homeschools.

Regardless of the amount of AET that a parent provided for a student, the author (who, for 21 years, had observed academic gains by many students with learning problems while working as a school psychologist) would caution parents from concluding that the extent of Cory's gains could easily be repeated. Cory's academic gains were extraordinary, so further study will be needed before researchers can predict the likelihood of how often other children could be expected to make gains as large as his. Even so, following an intensive routine like Mitzi's could help parents to accelerate their children's academic progress, even when the students had disabilities.

REFERENCES

Broden, M., Beasley, A., & Hall, R. V. (1978). In-class spelling performance: Effects of home tutoring by a parent. *Behavior Modification, 2*, 511-530.

Delquadri, J., Greenwood, C. R., Stretton, K., & Hall, R. V. (1983). The peer tutoring game: A classroom procedure for increasing opportunity to respond and spelling performance. *Education and Treatment of Children, 6*, 225-239.

Delquadri, J., Greenwood, C. R., Whorton, D., Carta, J. J., & Hall, R. V. (1986). Classwide peer tutoring. *Exceptional Children, 52*, 535-542.

DuPaul, G. J., & Henningson, P. N. (1993). Peer tutoring effects on the classroom performance of children with attention deficit hyperactivity disorder. *School Psychology Review. 22*, 134-143.

Duvall, S. F., Delquadri, J. C., Elliott, M., & Hall, R. V. (1992). Parent-tutoring procedures: Experimental analysis and validation of generalization in oral reading across passages, settings, and time. *Journal of Behavioral Education, 2*(3), 281-303.

Duvall, S. F., Delquadri, J. C., & Ward, D. L. (2004). A preliminary investigation of the effectiveness of homeschool instructional environments for students with attention deficit hyperactivity disorder. *School Psychology Review, 33*(1), 140-158.

Duvall, S. F., Delquadri, J. C., Ward, D. L., & Greenwood, C. R. (1997). An exploratory study of homeschool instructional environments and their effects on the basic skills of students with learning disabilities. *Education and Treatment of Children, 20*, 150-172.

Gang, D., & Pouche, C. E. (1982). An effective program to train parents as reading tutors for their children. *Education and Treatment of Children, 5*, 211-232.

Gettinger, M., & Seibert, J. K. (2002). Best practices in increasing academic learning time. In A. Thomas & J. Grimes (Eds.), *Best practices in school psychology IV* (pp. 773-787). Bethesda, MD: The National Association of School Psychologists.

Greenwood, C. R., Delquadri, J. C., & Hall, R. V. (1984). Opportunity to respond and student academic performance. In W. L. Heward, T. E. Heron, J. D. Hill, & J. Trap-Porter (Eds.), *Behavior analysis in education* (pp. 58-88). Columbus, OH: Charles Merrill.

Greenwood, C. R., Delquadri, J., & Hall, R. V. (1989). Longitudinal effects of classwide peer tutoring. *Journal of Educational psychology, 81*(3), 371-383.

Greenwood, C. R., Dinwiddie, G., Terry, B., Wade, L., Stanley, S., Thibadeau, S., & Delquadri, J. (1984). Teacher- versus peer-mediated instruction: An eco-behavioral analysis of achievement outcomes. *Journal of Applied Behavior Analysis, 17*, 521-538.

Groover, S. V., & Endsley, R. C. (1988). *Family environment and attitudes of homeschoolers and nonhomeschoolers*. (Report No. PS-019-040). Athens, GA: University of Georgia, Department of Child and Family Development. (ERIC Document Reproduction Service No. ED 323 027).

Hall, R. V., Delquadri, J. C., Greenwood, C. R., & Thurston, L. (1982). The importance of opportunity to respond in children's academic success. In E. Edgar, N. Haring, J. Jenkins, & C. Pious (Eds.), *Serving young handicapped children: Issues and research* (pp. 107-149). Austin, TX: Pro-Ed.

Home School Legal Defense Association. (1994). *A nationwide study of home education in Canada*. Paeonian Springs, VA.

Maheady, L., & Harper, G. F. (1987). A classwide peer-tutoring program to improve the spelling performance of low-income third and fourth grade students. *Education and Treatment of Children, 10*, 120-133.

National Center for Educational Statistics. (2004, July). *1.1 million homeschooled students in the United States in 2003*. Retrieved October 12, 2004, from http://nces.ed.gov/nhes/homeschool/

National Center for Educational Statistics. (2003a). *Table 52. Children 3 to 21 years old served in federally supported programs for the disabled by type of disability: 1976-77 to 2000-01*. Retrieved October 12, 2004, from http://nces.ed.gov/programs/digest/d03/tables/dt052.asp

National Center for Educational Statistics. (2003b). *Projections of education statistics to 2013*. Retrieved October 12, 2004, from http://nces.ed.gov//programs/projections/tables/table_01.asp

National Home Education Research Institute. (2004). Retrieved October 12, 2004, from http://www.nheri.org.

Ray, B. (1997). *Strengths of their own—Homeschoolers across America: Academic achievement, family characteristics, and longitudinal traits*. Salem, OR: National Home Education Research Institute.

Stanley, S. O., & Greenwood, C. R. (1983). Assessing opportunity to respond in classroom environments: How much opportunity to respond does the minority, disadvantaged student receive in school? *Exceptional Children, 49*, 370-373.

Thurlow, M. L., Ysseldyke, J. E., Wotruba, J. W., & Algozzine, B. (1993). Instruction in special education under varying student-teacher ratios. *Elementary School Journal, 3*, 305-320.

Thurston, L. P., & Dasta, K. (1990). An analysis of in-home parent tutoring procedures: Effects on children's academic behavior at home and at school and on parents' tutoring behaviors. *Remedial and Special Education, 11*, 41-52.

Toch, T. (1991, December). The exodus. *U.S. News & World Report*, pp. 66-77.

Waldrop, R. D. (1994). Selection of patients for management of attention deficit hyperactivity disorder in a private practice setting. *Clinical Pediatrics, 33*, 83-87.

CHAPTER 11

HOME-SCHOOLERS

How Well Do They Perform on the SAT for College Admissions?

Clive R. Belfield

INTRODUCTION

Home-schooling is the ultimate in educational privatization: the education of children who home-school is typically privately funded, privately provided, and (almost fully) privately regulated. Of the 55 million school-aged children in the U.S. in 2002, approximately 800,000 to 1.2 million (1.6-1.9%) are being schooled at home (National Center for Educational Statistics, NCES, 2001). This figure—albeit imprecise—is considerably higher than the numbers of students in charter schools and voucher programs, reforms, which have attracted considerably more academic attention. On average, it is about 10% of the numbers in private schools, although in Arizona the home-school to private school ratio is 46%, in Montana 45%, in Kansas 35%, in West Virginia 34%, in New Mexico 34%, and in Nevada 30%. Within the public sphere, also, home-schooling seems to be garnering broad-based support: whereas in 1985, only 16% of

Home Schooling in Full View: A Reader, 167–177
Copyright © 2005 by Information Age Publishing
All rights of reproduction in any form reserved.

families thought home-schooling a good thing, by 2001 this figure had risen to 41% (Rose & Gallup, 2001, p. 46).

This development and increasing acceptance of home-schooling prompts many fundamental questions in relation to the organization of the U.S. school system. As an alternative to public schooling, home-schooling may satisfy families with particular educational preferences (typically religious) or those who are disaffected by publicly-funded choices (see Stevens, 2001). Its growth may cast doubt on the efficiency of a schoolhouse operation, in that home provision is regarded as more effective.

Moreover, some are concerned about the public goods produced by home-schooling and the welfare of the children involved. Finally, home-schooling may have a strong economic impact on family expenditure patterns, time allocations, labor force participation, housing prices (near good schools), and preferences for public services. Our focus here is modest, looking at the educational achievements of home-schoolers. Even this modest task, however, is harder than it sounds.

WOULD WE EXPECT HOME-SCHOOLERS TO DO WELL ON ACADEMIC TESTS?

To predict and explain the academic performance of home-schoolers, it is first necessary to identify its features: What is it about home-schooling that promotes or impairs achievement? This is a tough question because home-schooling is not easy to describe.

The Practice of Home-Schooling

As an educational practice, home-schooling is diverse. It is not a discrete and determinate form of education provision, particularly when contrasted with enrollment at a public school which has a formal governance structure and offers a definite pedagogy and standard curriculum, taught by a teacher as part of a regular instructional program fitted into the academic calendar.

Indeed, home-schooling is sometimes lauded for not being four-walls education, with some families explicitly motivated by a desire to unschool their children (Stevens, 2001). Other families may follow the formal approach of a school (e.g., with timetables or lesson plans). Complete home-schooling means no interaction between the student and a school (although community resources may be used). With home-based education, the student draws on school resources (e.g., for specialist courses) or participates in a school distance-learning program (e.g., an umbrella school). This approach is reasonably common: one fifth of home-school families send their children to school for part of the day (NCES, 2001). Furthermore, many home-schoolers attend school over their childhood, perhaps spending only 2 years home-schooling (Lines, 2002; Isenberg, 2002).

Finally, home-school families face diverse regulations and laws across the states (Buss, 2000). Whereas nine states (including Texas) have little-to-no regulation, 11 states impose regulations, which may include assessments and inspections. Also, home-schools may be classified either as not a private school, a private school, or even a public school (Lambert, 2001). These differences will mean differences in how home-schools operate.

The theoretical evidence is limited. Advocates contend that small classes, flexible instruction (without age-tracking), and dedicated parent-teachers should make home-schooling more effective than other forms of education (but, Cai Y., Reeve, J, & Robinson, D. T. (2002) find home-school teachers use more controlling teaching styles). Yet, educational outcomes may be skewed toward those on which the family has competence, and educational progress may be slow if there is no formative assessment or peer pressure to learn (although home-school parents may exert more pressure or have higher expectations).

In short, it is very difficult to identify what it is about the provision of home-schooling that should lead to better or worse academic performance.

The Families Who Home-School

Looking at the families who home-school gives some insight into what to expect when home-schoolers take academic tests. Early adopters of home-schooling have been described as either ideologues or pedagogues (Nemer, 2002): either they did not agree with what was taught in public schools or felt they could do a better job of educating their children themselves. As the population of home-schoolers grows, other characteristics can be identified: unlike public school families, home-schooling families are more religious, more conservative, white, somewhat more affluent, and headed by parents with somewhat more years of education (Lines, 2002). These characteristics can help in forming expectations of test scores.

First, overwhelming evidence shows that the main determinants of academic achievement is family background. Thus, *if home-schoolers are from somewhat more affluent families, they will do well on tests, regardless of the relative pedagogic efficacy of home-schooling provision*. Indeed, to make any statement about the effectiveness of a home-school educational program, family background characteristics must be accounted for.

Other inferences must be more cautious. On the one hand, the religiosity of home-schoolers may mean that test scores are less of a priority; other values (such as piety) may be more important from education. On the other hand, we have evidence that home-school families are responsive to the quality of public schools: in areas where public schools report poor academic results, home-schooling is more common (Houston & Toma, 2003). This suggests home-schoolers are motivated by a desire for high academic achievement. Finally, applying choice models to the enrollment decision, home-schoolers appear to have characteristics that are intermediate between the public and private school sectors, e.g., on religion, maternal education, ethnicity, and maternal employment (Belfield, 2004). In other words, it makes a difference whom home-schoolers are compared against.

HOW WELL DO HOME-SCHOOLERS DO ON ACADEMIC TESTS?

Practical difficulties arise in obtaining data to identify the impact of home-schooling. The ideal source would be state or district-level data in states where test information is required. However, review of the data available across nine states with high regulation of home-schooling yields very limited information. In five such states (Washinton, Utah, West Virginia, Pennsylvania, New York), home-school students are not required to take state assessments or their results are not recorded. This situation arises because: test assessment is often voluntary for these students; tests are administered at district level and not available from state data; and test results may be returned to parents without being recorded. Also, where data are available the samples are often very small.

Even with data, a number of empirical challenges remain. The first is the common concern over the endogeneity of school choice, that is different types of families that choose the type of school that their children attend, and little can be inferred about the effects of schools for students who do not attend them. The second is the need to distinguish the absolute performance of home-schoolers from the treatment effect of home-schooling. Given the above-median resources of many home-schooling families, academic performance should be high even if home-schooling itself is not differentially effective.

Full controls for family background are needed, however, to identify a treatment effect. Finally, home-schoolers can often choose which tests to take and when to take them (and have parents administer them), introducing other biases. So, although Ray (2000, pp. 74-75) and Rudner (1999) review mean home-schooling achievement levels and find relatively high scores, they apply neither school choice endogeneity controls nor family background controls (and in some cases the test was applied in the home).

Recently, achievement data of home-schoolers on the SAT has become available. The SAT may be useful: in reflecting final outcomes of schooling; in being applied in a standard manner under test conditions; and in that it is a high-stakes test, well correlated with future college completion and earnings. Reasonably large samples of home-schoolers take the SAT to compare against public or private students. However, it only captures the academic achievement of college-aspirant home-schoolers.

The characteristics of the 2001 cohort of SAT test-takers by school type are reported in Table 11.1. The home-school cohort is 6,033. As found elsewhere, home-schoolers tend to be white, with a first language that is English, and without a disability. However, whereas around half of all public students and two-thirds of religious school students profess a religious faith, the figure for home-schoolers is just above two-fifths. Yet, a high

Table 11.1. Characteristics of SAT-Takers by School Type (%)

	Home School	Public School	Private-Independent School	Private-Religious School
Student characteristics:				
African American	2.70%	10.10%	3.84%	5.69%
Hispanic	2.45	7.95	3.05	8.17
1st lang. not English	1.33	6.52	3.40	3.68
Disabled	4.36	6.47	7.73	6.50
Male	46.88	45.24	52.66	49.70
Religious faith	41.80	52.51	36.79	66.69
Religion: Baptist	17.70	11.08	5.08	6.52
Religion: Catholic	5.77	18.39	9.32	45.22
Mother's education:				
High school	0.01	5.97	1.28	2.49
BA/Graduate degree	32.94	30.86	38.65	38.31
Family income:				
$80K-$100K	8	11	11	19
>$100K	11	16	45	12
Observations	6,033	975,117	54,682	137,671

Source: ETS data, 2001.

proportion of these home-schoolers are Baptists: their adherence rate is 17.7%, compared to 11.1% within the public schools. Home-schoolers are very unlikely to have a mother who reports a high school education, but they are not strongly represented in the upper tail of the education distribution. Similarly, many home-schooling families are in the middle of the distribution of household incomes. The wealthiest families send their children to private schools.

Table 11.2 indicates the SAT scores of students according to school type. The first row shows the raw test score, unadjusted for selection effects and family background controls. Crucially, the need for endogeneity correction is evident from the bottom rows of Table 11.3: home-schoolers make up only 0.5% of all SAT test-takers, a proportion considerably below their representation in the student population and lower than any other school type. Thus, observed home-schoolers' scores are likely to be inflated: the negative correlation between test-taking proportions and test

Table 11.2.   SAT Test Scores by School Type

	Home School	Public School	Private - Independent School	Private-Religious School
SAT Total				
Test score raw	1,093.1	1,012.6	1,123.8	1,055.6
Predicted score	1,054.5	1,021.1	1,064.4	1,050.5
SAT Math				
Test score raw	526.5	510.1	566.9	523.3
Predicted score	527.7	513.4	534.8	528.0
SAT Verbal				
Test score raw	566.6	502.6	556.9	532.3
Predicted score	526.7	507.8	529.6	522.6
% of test-takers	0.5%	83.1%	4.7%	11.7%
% of students[a]	1.5%	89.4%	1.1%	8.0%
Observations[b]	6,033	975,117	54,682	137,671

Source: ETS data (2001).
[a]Predicted test scores based on OLS estimation with SAT test score dependent variables and independent variables of: mother's education (6); father's education (6); gender; grade level; disability; first language not English (1); ethnicity (4); U.S. citizen (1); religion (10); Higher Education Carnegie class in state; state-level fees; state requires tests; state-level SAT participation rate; state-level participation rate squared; county-level poverty rate; county-level household income; district-level public school percent local funding; district-level per-pupil expenditures in public school; district-level ratio of at-risk students; district-level ratio of instructional expenditures; county-level public school teacher-student ratios. Full specification available from author. [b]NCES Digest of Education and Private School Survey (www.nces.ed.gov).

**Table 11.3. SAT Test-score Gradients by
Socioeconomic Status by School Type**

	Home School	Public School	Private-Independent School	Private-Religious School
	Effect Size Premium Relative to SES Q1 (Lowest Quintile)			
SAT Total				
SES Q2	0.32	0.16	0.21	0.14
SES Q3	0.38	0.26	0.36	0.24
SES Q4	0.60	0.47	0.62	0.45
SES Q5	0.63	0.52	0.70	0.47
SAT Math				
SES Q2	0.12	0.08	0.09	0.07
SES Q3	0.14	0.12	0.16	0.11
SES Q4	0.25	0.22	0.29	0.22
SES Q5	0.27	0.24	0.31	0.22
SAT Verbal				
SES Q2	0.20	0.09	0.12	0.07
SES Q3	0.24	0.14	0.20	0.13
SES Q4	0.35	0.25	0.33	0.23
SES Q5	0.36	0.28	0.38	0.25
Observations	6,033	975,117	54,682	137,671

Source: ETS data, 2001; population of test-takers, with exclusion of foreign nationals, missing income, ages 14-24. OLS estimation as per Table 11.2. All effects are statistically significant at $p < 0.05$.

scores on the SAT has long been noted. For raw scores, home-schoolers obtain high SAT-total scores, with a mean of 1093; this is 0.4 (0.2) standard deviations above the public school (private religious school) scores, but 0.15 standard deviations below those in private-independent schools. However, the strength of the selection effect means that absolute scores are unlikely to be useful indicators.

Nevertheless, it is possible to make some conclusions in relative terms. Notably, most of the home-schooling premium comes from higher SAT-verbal scores and not the SAT-math scores. (This distinction between verbal/reading and math scores is also found in Rudner's (1999) data). Accounting for a treatment effect of indeterminate size from home-schooling, it appears to be much greater for verbal than math. This discrepancy may reflect greater parental competence across the subject disciplines.

Table 11.2 also reports scores with controls for family background (and a stable array of other covariates listed in the table notes, including the state level SAT test-taking participation rate). After controlling for these covariants, the predicted SAT-total scores for home-schoolers and private-independent school students converge toward the mean: the home-school premium over private-religious school students falls almost to zero. Also, home-schoolers actually perform worse than would be predicted on SAT-math. The differences between raw and predicted scores give some indication of the strength of covarying characteristics in explaining test-score differences. Ultimately, there is not a large gap between the scores across school types.

With a large caveat about family backgrounds driving test scores, the SAT data can also be used to look at differences across socioeconomic status. Perhaps home-schoolers show steeper socioeconomic status (SES) gradients on test scores. Using the SAT data, these gradients are reported in Table 11.43. Splitting the cohort by school type, ordinary least squares (OLS) estimation is applied to the SAT outcome measures. The effect size coefficients on socioeconomic status by quintile are reported, relative to those test takers in the lowest quintile. In all cases, being in a higher SES quintile is associated with a higher test score. SAT scores increase as SES increases, with evidence of stronger family background effects for home-schoolers.

Those students in the second quintile score 0.32 standard deviations higher than those in the bottom quintile, the largest of the differentials according to school type. Across the four quintiles, both home-schoolers and private-independent school students show strong family background effects, relative to public and private-religious school students. The effects are evident across math and verbal scores, but the verbal gradients for home-school are steeper. Family background matters for all students, but especially for home-schoolers.

Those drawing conclusions from these test score comparisons must be cautious—even though with this analysis we are still unable to address the differential selection into test taking by home-schoolers. So far at least, the results do not indicate home-schoolers are at a disadvantage.

A FRAMEWORK FOR EVALUATING HOME SCHOOLING

The evidence on home school test scores presented here is equivocal: the home-schoolers who take the SAT do well enough, but that does not necessarily mean that 'home-schooling' is an effective educational mode *per se*. More importantly, other considerations may be more important than test scores in the debate over home-schooling.

Freedom of Choice

Clearly, home-schooling and home-based education represent an expansion of educational options in terms of the technology of schooling. Indeed, parts of educational process—including access, administration, use of teacher and physical resources, and assessment—may be chosen openly by the family, such that the education market is greatly liberalized. Such opportunities will be attractive to some parents, even for a short duration, especially where families are able to negotiate with their public school for tailored home-based education. Also, if the broader purpose of education is to create a diverse society, then an array of choices may be socially desirable. Given that home-schooling families do not receive public funds (or receive fewer funds than with full-time enrollment), this independent choice has considerable persuasive power.

Efficiency

Where home-schoolers are eligible for public funds, the criterion of efficiency becomes important. From a state's perspective, a higher proportion of home-schoolers should result in savings where home-schoolers do not receive public funds. However, this saving will be offset where these conditions apply: (a) home-schoolers draw on public resources as part of a home-based education plan; (b) home-school families can claim tax credits, tax deductions, and funding through cyber/virtual charter schools; and (c) additional regulatory costs are incurred by the state. Unfortunately, limited information is available on these other associated costs.

Social Cohesion

Home-schooling should be evaluated in terms of the public benefits that are generated. Critics of home-schooling argue that it reduces the socially beneficial outcomes from schooling, both for home-schooler and society at large (see Reich, 2002). It separates children from their peers, impairing identity formation/choice and the appreciation of social values and norms (e.g., if it elides into 'indoctrination'; see Buss, 2000). In rebuttal, home-schooling needs not be an isolating experience: home-schoolers do attend school and may have strong ties to their local (religious) community (Medlin, 2000). It need not be incompatible with public values: some home-schooling parents would like public schools to teach communitarian values more intensely. Also, where education is intended to create a diverse society, then a plurality of educational options should be promoted. So far, the general public is ambivalent: being asked whether home-schooling promotes good citizenship, equal numbers agree as disagree (Rose & Gallup, 2001, p. 46).

Equity

Home-schooling should also be evaluated in terms of equity, an important motivation for state intervention in the education system. Here, the main issue relates to the complete transfer of responsibility for a child's education from the state to the individual family.

First, home-schooling clearly weakens the opportunity for a community to guarantee or verify that children obtain a reasonable level of education or personal well-being. From society's perspective these parental preferences cannot be taken as given. Moreover, although family resources are the main determinant of all children's education, for home-schoolers they become almost the only determinant. Home-schooling may therefore entrench intergenerational attributes, such that highly educated or wealthy families transfer resources to their children most effectively. Educational inequalities and perhaps inequities may be perpetuated.

HOME-SCHOOLING IN THE FUTURE

The debate over home-schooling will grow more intense if home-schooling grows. Such growth will depend on several factors. First, home-schooling epitomizes freedom of choice as to how education is provided; although full home-schooling is limited to families with substantial home resources, short-term or part-time home-schooling is an option for many. Families may appreciate such freedom. Second, the growth of home-schooling may depend on social acceptance, which thus far appears to be increasing (albeit in somewhat of an evidentiary vacuum). Finally, where home-schooling appears to be effective for the individual in terms of academic achievement, then other families will adopt the practice. On this last issue, however, much more high quality evidence needs to brought to bear as home-schoolers take the SAT, state tests, and other standardized assessments that allow rigorous comparisons.

REFERENCES

Belfield, C. R. (2004). Modeling school choice: Comparing public, private, and home-schooling enrollment options. *Educational Policy Analysis Archives, 12*(30).

Buss, E. (2000). The adolescent's stake in the allocation of educational control between parent and state. *University of Chicago Law Review, 67,* 1233-1289.

Cai, Y., Reeve, J, & Robinson, D. T. (2002). Home schooling and teaching style: Comparing the motivating styles of home school and public school teachers. *Journal of Educational Psychology, 94,* 372-380.

Houston, R. G., & Toma, E. F. (2003). Home-schooling: An alternative school choice. *Southern Economic Journal, 69,* 920-935.

Isenberg, E. (2002). *Home schooling: School choice and women's time use.* Working paper., Washington University, St. Louis, MO.

Lambert, S. A. (2001). Finding the way back home: Funding for home school children under the individuals with disabilities education act. *Columbia Law Review, 101,* 1709-1729.

Lines, P. (2002). Support for home-based study. *ERIC Clearinghouse on Educational Management,* Eugene, OR: University of Oregon.

National Center for Educational Statistics. (2001). *Home-schooling in the United States, 1999.* http://nces.ed.gov

Nember, K. M. (2002). *Understudied education: Toward building a homeschooling research agenda.* NCSPE Occasional paper. www.ncspe.org

Medlin, R. G. (2000). Home schooling and the question of socialization. *Peabody Journal of Education, 75,* 107-123.

Ray, B. D. (2000). Home schooling: The ameliorator of negative influences on learning? *Peabody Journal of Education, 75,* 71-106.

Reich, R. (2002). The civic perils of homeschooling. *Educational Leadership, 59,* 56-59.

Rose, L. C., & Gallup, A. M. (2001). *33rd poll of the public's attitudes toward the public schools.* Available at www.pdkintl.org/kappan/kimages/kpoll83.pdf

Rudner, L. M. (1999). Scholastic achievement and demographic characteristics of home-school students in 1998. *Education Policy Analysis Archives, 7,* 8.

Stevens, M. L. (2001). *Kingdom of children: Culture and controversy in the home-schooling movement.* Princeton, NJ: Princeton University Press.

CHAPTER 12

HOMESCHOOLED STUDENTS AND THE IVY LEAGUE

Gaining Admission to Highly Selective Universities in the United States

Joy A. Marean, Marc F. Ott, and Matthew J. Rush

INTRODUCTION

Based on a 1994 survey (Lines, 1997), young people who were home-schooled are enrolling in American colleges and universities in increasing numbers. Since the educational experience of homeschooled students differs markedly from the educational background of most American high school seniors, it is interesting to learn how homeschooled students fare in the college application process. As most homeschooled students present themselves to prospective colleges and universities in a dissimilar manner (i.e., with regard to transcripts), admission officers consider the applications of homeschooled students differently than most applications they receive.

Given the variety and sheer number of colleges and universities in the United States that might accept and enroll homeschooled students, the

Home Schooling in Full View: A Reader, 179–197

focus of this particular study is on the Ivy League institutions (alphabetically): Brown, Cornell, Columbia, Dartmouth, Harvard, Pennsylvania, Princeton, and Yale. From conversations with admissions offices of all of the Ivy League universities, the researchers sought to learn the answer to the following question: *What criteria do the admission officers of Ivy League universities use to consider and offer admission to students who have been home-schooled?*

RESEARCH METHODOLOGY

To answer this question, the researchers employed three data-gathering methods. First, the research team conducted a literature review, which included an assessment of the application forms of the Ivy League universities. Second, the researchers asked admission offices for data on the number of applications, acceptances, and enrollments for the 2002-2003 academic year for both the entire incoming class and for the home-schooled population. Third, a questionnaire was used to interview the admissions directors with the following questions:

- What criteria, in particular, would you base your decision on accepting a homeschooled applicant, such as requiring an interview?
- Do your homeschooled applicants typically submit transcripts? What do they submit as an indication of their achievements? How do you evaluate it?
- Are SAT results weighed more for homeschoolers?
- Do you require subject-based standard tests, such as the SAT II?
- Do you assess their social maturity? If so, how?
- Who generally writes the letters of recommendation?
- Do you require interviews? If yes, what types of questions do you ask?
- How has your perception changed towards homeschooled applications over the years?
- Do you feel homeschoolers adapt well at your college? What kinds of challenges do they face upon starting college?
- Do you foresee accepting more homeschoolers in the future? Do you foresee the application to acceptance rate will increase for homeschoolers?
- Will the fact that a student is homeschooled give him/her a greater chance of being accepted, if you have two candidates equal academically and from an extra-curricular standpoint?

LITERATURE REVIEW

Given the relatively small number of students being homeschooled in the United States today, it is understandable that few books are available about college admissions for homeschoolers. Moreover, not surprisingly, all of these books were written by individuals who homeschooled their own children through high school and assisted them in the college application process. These particular individuals—Cafi Cohen, Jeanne Gowen Dennis, Loretta Heuer, and Mary and Michael Leppert—are well-known in the homeschooling community.

The information presented in these books both describes the experience of each author's homeschooling family with college admissions and shares feedback from other homeschooling families and admissions directors. All of the authors strive to offer advice and encouragement to parents contemplating homeschooling their children through high school. They provide specific tips on how to help prepare them for the college admissions process. While none of the books specifically focuses on Ivy League admissions, all of them include information about highly selective colleges.

The importance of record keeping and proper documentation is stressed by all of the authors to be best prepared for the college application process. Homeschooling parents and their children should do the following: (1) keep work samples on hand; (2) create lists of books read and curricular materials used; (3) file the grade reports and transcripts issued by any homeschooling umbrella organization, local school and community college; (4) note all extracurricular activities pursued, part-time jobs held, and internships completed; (5) record the results of all standardized tests taken; and (6) log the amount of time spent on each academic subject at home. This information can then be used to create a "home-brewed" (i.e., homemade: term used by Cafi Cohen, 2000a, p. 52) transcript, a portfolio, or a narrative report, which is submitted with a homeschooled student's application materials.

Cafi Cohen and Loretta Heuer also emphasize the quality of the documentation submitted to admissions officers. Cohen (2000a) writes that "selective colleges [especially] need written proof … of [the] educational achievements of homeschooling, [which] allows admissions officers to rank [homeschooled] students with other applicants and determine if a [homeschooled] student will do well at their school" (p. 50). Heuer (2000) notes "as a homeschooler, your transcript will definitely mark you as unique, but the clearer your transcript is, the more effectively it helps distinguish you from the rest of the applicant pool" (p. 144).

Since the issue of socialization is a typical concern to those outside the homeschooling community—including most college admissions officers—the authors comment on how this might be addressed in both the homeschooling high school and the college application process. Dennis (2000) writes that since Ivy League universities "attract the nation's best students, they can afford to be extremely particular about those they admit. To increase their chances of acceptance, homeschooled students should get involved in community institutions such as church, scouts, volunteer work, or whatever can amplify their extracurricular profiles" (p. 157). Cohen (2000a) also note that colleges "like to see evidence of group activities on homeschoolers' applications" (p. 15). In addition to enhancing their application materials, participation in extracurricular activities indicates that the homeschoolers have socialized with others, outside of their family.

Participation in extracurricular activities also allows homeschoolers to acquire letters of recommendation written by individuals other than their parents. Dennis (2000) suggests "involvement in a 'normal' academic situation like a community college course so that [homeschoolers] can submit letters of recommendation from academic teachers outside the family" (p. 157). Cohen (2000a) advise that "homeschooled students ... request letters of recommendation from any adult with whom they work for any length of time—4-H Club and scout leaders, church leaders and choir directors, volunteer program directors, employers, coaches, music and dance teachers, homeschool support group leaders, tutors, [etc.]" (p. 59). Cohen (2000a) describes the "three essential components of [these] letters of recommendation: a statement describing the adult's experience with the student; a description of the student's skills, accomplishments, and character traits; and the actual recommendation" (pp. 59-60).

Standard testing is also addressed in the literature. Cohen (2000a) states that admissions officers "put more weight on SAT and ACT test scores" (p. 175) and that the most competitive colleges "request that applicants submit scores from one to three [SAT II] subject tests" (p. 221). In *And What About College?* Cohen (2000b) writes that "homeschooled applicants to Ivy League schools will want to follow-up and take [Advanced Placement] tests" (p. 114). Cohen (2000b) adds that the "Pennsylvania Homeschoolers' Association has ... made Advanced Placement courses available to homeschoolers nationwide" (p. 115).

Dennis notes that for "homeschool students, because so little weight can be given to the transcript in terms of what the GPA means or how the student has competed among a group of peers, a lot more weight is given to standardized test scores, either the SAT or ACT" (p. 17). Dennis also includes the Home School Legal Defense Association's recommendation that homeschoolers "take an achievement test every year at the high school level, even if the state law doesn't require it" (p. 93). Finally, in *The Homeschooling Almanac*, Leppert and Leppert (2001) write that "homeschoolers are accepted on an equal basis at private, high-standard institu-tions with their school-educated counterparts (who characteristically represent the upper 10 to 15 percent of their graduating classes) assum-ing their SAT scores are high" (p. 167).

All authors also recommend student-initiated contact and interviews with admissions officers when applying to competitive colleges. Dennis writes that "at any highly selective college, homeschooled students should establish contact within the admissions office and have an interview where they review their coursework and what they have accomplished in school and in the community and to explain their objectives for this next stage of their education" (p. 206). Dennis adds that as much as [admissions offic-ers] want to hear from parents as well, the students [should] be the ones to arrange the interview and explain their accomplishments, goals, and objectives—not the parent/teacher" (p. 206). Cohen (2000b) states that "interviews are marketing opportunities, a time for homeschooler[s] to sell themselves and make homeschooling like a normal educational alter-native" (p. 240). Leppert and Leppert also note that "homeschoolers are accepted at private, high-standard institutions assuming their personal interviews are favorable (p. 167).

Several of the authors encourage homeschooling high school students and their parents to be flexible and positive and to comply with the admissions process to increase the chances of acceptance. Cohen (2000a) suggests that homeschooling parents "contact [the] colleges of interest and work with their suggested [academic] preparation" (p. 40). Dennis states that "the willingness to cooperate with admissions departments is essential. Homeschoolers who refuse to cooperate are asking for special privileges. It is unreasonable to expect colleges to guess their educational background and academic abilities" (p. 35). Heuer (2000) adds "whether you want to go to an Ivy League university or an art schoolthe rule is the same: Give them what they need so they can say yes" (p. 10).

Finally, all of the authors offer words of praise and encouragement regarding homeschoolers and the college admissions process. Cohen (2000a) states that "when admissions officers examine a homeschooled student's application, they see more than just another teenager with good test scores, decent grades, and the standard list of high school activities; their atypical activities ... get the attention of admissions officers" (p. 13). Cohen (2000a) adds that the "college admissions officers can see the applicant's learning experience and the time spent on these activities; this is one area where a homeschooler can really stand out from traditional applicants" (p. 105). Dennis writes that "most colleges are finding home-school graduates to be strong students who are desirable additions to their academic communities, [and that] many of them are endeavoring to find new ways to market their colleges to homeschooled students" (p.

134). Heuer writes that "admissions office[s] [are] bound to take note of you just for being a homeschooler, and if you're a capable homeschooling student; most colleges would probably like to admit you" (p. 185). Finally, Leppert and Leppert add that "all universities and colleges have come to accept homeschoolers, including the Ivy League; all colleges and universities have similar admissions attitudes in that they are looking for well-trained minds to educate further and recognize that homeschoolers' minds are as well-trained as any" (p. 168).

The cover story article of the Brown University alumni magazine published in January/February 2002 also provides information about homeschooled students who have been accepted by Ivy League universities. Sutton (2002) shares with the reader several interviews done with both Brown alumni and current Brown students who were homeschooled. Associate Dean Joyce Reed, a Brown graduate, homeschooled her five children while living in a remote area of Hawaii; two of them were accepted and enrolled at Brown University. Reed believes that homeschooled students "are the epitome of Brown students—they've learned to be self-directed, they take risks, they face challenges with total fervor, and they don't back off" (p. 49). Attracted by Brown University's "tradition of independence and self-direction," writes Sutton that "a new generation of homeschoolers is arriving—and thriving—on campus" (p. 47).

With regard to the college admissions process, Sutton notes that "Brown is considered receptive to homeschoolers because it does not require them to supply any more information than traditional applicants" (p. 52). Sutton adds that "when Brown admission officers come across a homeschooler's application, they look for evidence of good writing skills and some sort of 'outside assessment,' such as courses taken at a community college or standardized test scores" (p. 52).

Sutton also quotes Brown University admission officer Michael Goldberger, who states that the "evaluation process for homeschoolers is not much different from that of other applicants; in a homeschool situation, our approach is, let's see what they give us and go from there" (p. 52). Tibet Sprague '04, for example, tells that the transcript he gave Brown "included no grades (except for those he earned at the University of Massachusetts); instead, it detailed the books he had read, the musical instruments he played, the science projects he completed, and even the cultural events attended" (p. 52). Sprague believes that he had an advantage over college applicants with typical high school backgrounds: "Their acceptance was based almost on grades and scores, but I could present everything I had done during the last four years, show every aspect of my intelligence and creativity, without lingering on my shortcomings" (pp. 52-53).

In reviewing the application forms of the eight Ivy League universities, a few homeschooler-friendly components were found. On the Secondary School Report form, space is provided to explain a school's grading system and if a class rank is not available (Princeton, Brown, Cornell, Harvard, and Penn). All of the universities also request on this form that the secondary school representative submit a "school profile" (i.e., a description or summary appraisal of the school), allowing a homeschooling family to provide information about their educational philosophy, academic program, and other components of their education.

While the essay portion of the application form allows students to share information about themselves, their views on a subject, and so forth, several universities offer additional options to applicants beyond the required or suggested essay topics. For example, Princeton has a "Hodge-Podge" form, which asks the applicants to indicate their favorite book, favorite recording, favorite movie, and so on. Cornell has an optional essay, which allows applicants to "tell … anything else about [themselves] that [they] want us to know." Harvard, too, offers additional essays, which give applicants the opportunity "to convey important information about themselves or their accomplishments." As stated above in the literature, homeschoolers are encouraged to write an essay about their homeschooling experience so that admissions officers understand more clearly their educational background.

Letters of reference forms are an especially important component of a homeschooler's admissions packet. In addition to the standard "Teacher Letter of Reference" forms, several of the Ivies offer additional reference forms. Dartmouth, for example, has a "Peer Evaluation" form, which asks a friend of the applicant to write "a statement … based on his/her knowledge and observation of [the] candidate" that describes the applicant's "maturity, ability to work with others, his/her interest, special talents, and experiences." Princeton has an "Optional Reference" form, which allows the applicant to "have an additional person who knows [him/her] well write on [his/her] behalf; that person may be, for instance, a brother or sister, a parent, a coach, a music instructor, and employer, or a friend."

In asking students to identify which secondary school they attend, only Dartmouth and Harvard use the "Common Application" form, limiting the educational options choices to public, private, and parochial schools. The other universities provide a blank space in which the secondary school name may be written. Additionally, the University of Pennsylvania is currently the only Ivy League university to offer "Home School" as a choice for secondary school type on its application form.

Finally, on all of the Ivy League application forms, homeschooled applicants have the opportunity to indicate the extracurricular activities in which they have participated, leadership positions which they have held, and work-related experiences that they have completed. All authors encourage homeschool students to take advantage of writing about their experiences.

SURVEY RESEARCH INSTRUMENT

Questionnaires served as the instrument to gather data from the various admissions offices. The first asked for numbers of applications, acceptances, and enrollments for homeschoolers and their total figures. It also included a general question on how the college or university processes homeschooled applicants. Team members emailed the first questionnaire to the admissions offices prior to the formal telephone or in-person interviews. Unfortunately, only a few people responded. The second questionnaire contained detailed questions on the application process with regard to homeschooled students. Team members sent it shortly before the interviews, allowing time for data gathering by the individual school's admissions personnel.

Each interview, except for the one at Columbia University, was conducted by telephone. The second questionnaire provided direction to the interview process as the researchers collected both qualitative and quantitative data.

RESEARCH FINDINGS

Table 12.1 includes the names and titles of the people interviewed. The researchers were unable to obtain information from Princeton and Harvard Universities. The data gathered from Columbia University excludes the School of Engineering, and for Cornell University, the information is only from the College of Agriculture & Life Sciences, one of its seven undergraduate colleges.

Table 12.2 contains a summary of relevant information transcribed from the interviews.

Additional quotes from the interviews:

- Gavin Bradley: "Since Columbia offers a more traditional Western curriculum, we also attract and admit students that are less 'off beat,' and we are less open to a 'progressive' educational background. As a result, we are more skeptical to homeschooling as a concept."

Table 12.1. Names and Titles of People Interviewed in Each Institution

University	Name	Title
Brown University	Elisha Anderson	Assistant Director of Admissions
Columbia University (excluding School of Engineering)	Gavin Bradley	Associate Director of Admissions
Cornell University (College of Agriculture & Life Sciences)	Rob Springall	Director of Admissions
Dartmouth College	Chris Bradt	Assistant Director of Admissions
University of Pennsylvania	Bruce Chamberlain	Regional Director of Admissions
Yale University	Richard Shaw	Dean of Admissions

- Rob Springall: His responses to all families with kids applying at a very young age: "Let them be an adolescent. Enjoy childhood. Slow down."
- Bruce Chamberlain: "We would not want to hold a homeschooled student to a higher standard, but we do attempt to get as much information as possible from all perspective students. We have a rule in the admissions office, 'keep your eye on the applicant.'"

Note: While Cornell did supply us with data, it represented only that from one of the seven colleges on campus. Yale did not provide any data at all. Tables 12.3 and 12.4 include 2001-2002 admissions data for Columbia University and Dartmouth College, University of Pennsylvania and Brown University, and Table 12.5 summarizes the findings for the four universities.

Each university varied in its acceptance rate for homeschoolers as compared to the total rate of acceptance for its freshman class. However, it is not clear if those variations are statistically different. In the last table, the calculation of the percentages of acceptances and yield are taken from each university and not from the same table (denoted by the asterisk). For instance, the average yield (equal to the percentage of accepted students who enroll) of homeschoolers is 52%, which is the average of 25% (Columbia), 67% (Dartmouth), 67% (Pennsylvania), and 50% (Brown).

In summary, it is not obvious that homeschoolers are dealt with differently than those who are not homeschooled. Without both the statistical test to prove this and all of the data from the eight Ivy League universities, the results cannot be generalized to make a broad statement on homeschoolers' acceptance rate, even among highly selective colleges.

Table 12.2. Summary of the Interview Transcriptions

	Brown University	Columbia University	Cornell University	Dartmouth College	University of Pennsylvania	Yale University
1. Transcript evaluation	Transcripts include a variety of educational courses: their own, distance learning, community colleges, etc. Problems: difficult to understand, gaps, too brief and not substantiated.	Not weighed strongly. Often clearer and more comprehensive than regular school transcripts.	"While we are not trying to challenge the parents, we ask for textbooks used, topics covered, and related experiences."	See "Other Information Required."	Receive a wide variety of portfolios, materials, and assessments. "We suggest they write one paragraph synopsis of each course." "We are hoping to create guidelines as to the exposure of the five major academic areas."	Viewed with "great trepidation," since they typically get straight A's. Some students, however, take courses at community colleges.
2. SAT I weighed	It helps that the scores are high and/or the student has taken more tests than necessary.	Weighed more heavily.	Receive more scrutiny. "We try to put them in context with students nationally and internationally."	Not necessarily weighed more, especially if the transcript information is comprehensive.	Not weighed more.	Weighed much more heavily. Their test scores are usually very strong.
3. SAT II policy	All students need to submit at least three SAT II scores. Homeschoolers are advised to take more than three tests.	All students need to submit at least three SAT II scores (one must be writing). No penalties for extended testing time. Homeschoolers need to take two additional tests.	SAT II are not required. 60-70% of the students submit two or three SAT II scores.	All students must take the SAT I or ACT and any three SAT II exam. Same comments as above.	Not required. Homeschoolers are encouraged to submit two SAT II scores (one English and one Math- especially if they want to major in business).	All students must submit SAT II scores. "For homeschoolers, the more the better."

4. Letters of recommendation	Two letters are required Homeschoolers should submit three to five letters. Letters by parents, other family members, hired tutors present conflict of interest. College professors offer more objectivity.	All students must submit recommendations from two teachers and one counselor. For homeschoolers, the more the better, especially outside the immediate family.	Two recommendations are required other than from parents. Homeschoolers typically do more experiential learning, so we also receive more information about personal characteristics.	All students must submit four recommendations: one counselor; two teachers, one peer. For homeschoolers, the more outside of the family, the better.	Would like an objective academic person, like a tutor or community leader. "We encourage that they get recommendations from community college or local high school instructors (if possible)."	The more the better, without being flooded with information.
5. Interview policy	Not required, but recommended 70% of applicants are interviewed.	Not required. Admissions may follow-up by telephone.	Not required, but alumni attempt to interview every applicant. Feedback offered provides information from a neutral party.	Not required. It can be helpful to back up information or provide new information. Homeschoolers are not specifically encouraged to be interviewed.	Not required. 75% of the applicant pool is interviewed by the alumni.	Interviews are not required. Homeschoolers are highly encouraged to interview.
6. Other information required	n/a	Program of Study created for the student and written by the person in charge is required.	n/a	Require a detailed profile of the program, incl. coursework and educational philosophy.	n/a	n/a

(table continues)

Table 12.2. Continued

	Brown University	Columbia University	Cornell University	Dartmouth College	University of Pennsylvania	Yale University
7. Home-schooled applicants have an advantage	It has not been decided if homeschoolers as a subset are considered a diversity factor.	Skeptical towards homeschooled students. Transition to live in NYC may be too challenging, especially when they are so young. Columbia offers a traditional curriculum for more conventional students.	n/a	Homeschooling is a diversity factor that is considered positively and can help in the admissions process.	If the spark is within the candidate (not the parent), they'll bring an edge, different experiences, and perspectives that are very interesting. "We like to have the whole mixture of students here."	No affirmative action toward homeschoolers. It is an open-ended process where the entire picture is looked at: Can the student succeed academically? How can the student contribute to the university?
8. Future Outlook	More homeschoolers are applying. Their acceptance rate is pretty consistent with the all-college admit rate.	Foresee accepting more homeschooled students, since the applications are raising strongly. Homeschooled acceptance rate will remain similar to regular applicants.	Haven't really seen a trend.	Acceptance rate for homeschoolers will probably drop as it will for regular applicants.	"If the quality is there, I feel like our student body will mirror that of the society. On the whole, I feel as if we are as 'home-school friendly' as any college can be."	Receiving more applicants and gaining experience. Their documents are usually excellent.

9. On-campus adaptation	n/a	The interviewed admissions officer did not know. He suggested consulting the Brown Alumni Magazine article that highlights homeschoolers on campus.	Overall they blend in well. Students are not "unsocialized." Concerned about young students enrolling at 15-16 years of age, whether homeschooled or not.	Do not follow-up in particular; since the numbers are small. They seem to transition in fine.	If there are concerns, they are flagged. Students are denied admissions more for academic reasons than social reasons. Summer "bridge" is offered to 1st generation college students, athletes, and home-schoolers.	Seem to have some difficulties adapting: 1. Often first time away from home. 2. They often come at a very young age. No specific support system is in place.

**Table 12.3. Homeschoolers' Admissions Data for
Columbia University and Dartmouth University**

| | Columbia | | Dartmouth | |
	Total	Homeschoolers	Total	Homeschoolers
Applications	14,094	22	10,193	25
Acceptances	1,721	4	2,900	6
Enrollments	1,009	1	1,068	4
% of acceptances	12%	18%	28%	24%
% yield	59%	25%	37%	67%

**Table 12.4. Admissions Data for
University of Pennsylvania and Brown University**

| | Penn | | Brown | |
	Total	Homeschoolers	Total	Homeschoolers
Applications	18,784	47	14,612	50
Acceptances	3,951	6	2,490	8
Enrollments	2,451	4	1,485	4
% of acceptances	21%	13%	17%	16%
% Yield	62%	67%	60%	50%

Table 12.5. Admissions Data Summary

| | Averages | |
	Total	Homeschoolers
Applications	14,421	36
Acceptances	2,766	6
Enrollments	1,503	3
% of acceptances	20%	18%
Yield	54%	52%*

AN ANALYSIS OF THE FINDINGS

What criteria do the admissions officers of Ivy League universities use to consider and offer admissions to students who have been homeschooled? Based on the information in Table 12.2, each category is analyzed as followed:

- *Transcripts:*   They include a variety of educational resources, such as distance learning, community college and high school courses, and their own coursework. Admissions officers view transcripts with trepidation and do not weigh them strongly in the admissions process. In providing information, homeschooling families have been very innovative. According to Lines (1997), they were among the first to try portfolio assessments.

- *SAT I:*   Standardized tests are a useful and objective tool to assess applicants. Since the validity of grades issued by homeschool applicants can be questioned, admissions offices typically weigh test results more heavily in the application process. Advanced Placement (AP) course results are also looked upon favorably since exams are monitored externally.

- *SAT II:*   Most colleges now require SAT II test results. Admissions officers typically encourage homeschooled students to submit more of these subject-based test scores than non-homeschooled applicants.

- *Letters of recommendations:*   Admissions officers are looking for objective recommendations and, therefore, would like to receive letters from outside the family. Recommendations written by college professors, high school teachers, and community leaders are suggested.

- *Interview policy:* Interestingly, interviews are not required for homeschooled applicants. Some universities attempt to interview as many candidates as possible. Homeschooled students are often strongly encouraged to interview.

- *Other required information:*   Columbia and Dartmouth specifically require a curricular overview, written by the person in charge of the student's education.

- *Homeschool advantage:*   With the exception of Dartmouth and Columbia, universities do not consider homeschooling as a form of diversity that will affect the admissions decision.

- *Future outlook:*   All universities have seen a boost in the number of applicants from homeschooled students within the past decade. Only Brown was able to provide us with numbers of homeschooled applicants from previous years. Colleges are becoming more comfortable with considering those applications. Admissions officers foresee a continued increase of applications; however, some predict that the acceptance rate of homeschoolers will remain congruent with the general applicant pool.

- *On-campus adaptation:*   At least one institution suggested that some homeschoolers apply to college at a younger age than most high school students. Not necessarily the consensus of Ivy League admissions offices, some colleges were concerned about the ability of homeschooled students to adapt to campus life, especially for students who enroll at a young age. Universities typically offer a nonmandatory support system (i.e., Summer Bridge Program at the University of Pennsylvania). Admissions offices do not specifically track students who have been homeschooled. Moreover, they do not have much information concerning on-campus adaptation.

Ivy League universities do not have any specific procedures in place for homeschooled applicants; the entire profile of each applicant is reviewed. Homeschooled students typically do not receive any preferential treatment or have to meet higher standards for acceptance. Admissions officers focus more on their academic abilities than social skills. The reasons to either deny or accept any applicant appear to be similar for homeschooled students.

Columbia is the only university skeptical to homeschooling as a concept, according to Gavin Bradley, Associate Director of Admissions (C. Bradley, personal communication, November 19, 2002). He notes that New York City is a more challenging place to live for a young adult and does not offer the same strong sense of community. Moreover, since the city offers numerous activities, Columbia students are faced with more distractions than those of a traditional campus setting. Dartmouth, on the other hand, considers homeschooling to be a component of diversity that could be viewed favorably in admissions decisions. The University of Pennsylvania mentioned they feel that they are as homeschool friendly as any college can be.

It is almost equally challenging for homeschooled applicants to be accepted (18%) as it is for nonhomeschooled applicants (20%). The difference of 2% is so small that it can be considered insignificant. The yield is also almost identical: 54% for all students and 52% for homeschooled students. Most of the information compiled in the literature review is congruent with the findings from the interviews with the admissions officers.

STUDY LIMITATIONS

The research of homeschool applications to Ivy League institutions has several limitations: from statistical verification to unknown demographics of those who were accepted. The first limitation involved communication with the admissions offices. Establishing exactly what constitutes a homeschooled experience was the first task in the research. The research team used the National Center of Educational Statistics (1997) definition of homeschoolers which reads, Students were considered to be home-schooled if their parents reported them being schooled at home instead of public or private schools, if their enrollment in public or private schools did not exceed 25 hours a week, and if they were not being home schooled solely because of a temporary illness (p. 2). While this particular definition was used in formulating interview questions, each university's admissions office may have its own understanding of what defines a homeschooled student, which could affect the numbers of homeschooled applicants, numbers of acceptances, and subsequent enrollments. Consequently, the percentages addressed in the findings section would be inaccurate.

The second limitation is also related to the data. The research team only asked for data from the 2002-03 academic year. While limiting the questions to a 1-year sample of admission numbers makes data analysis easier, it also makes it impossible to assess any time trends. The sample size of eight Ivy League colleges and universities may limit the detection of differences that actually exist. It is also important to note that the nature of the admissions process is subjective. Regardless of previous educational background, all files are evaluated subjectively. While focusing on a group of schools is more manageable, the ideal study might gather similar information from a large number of schools with similar enrollments and/or academic rigor and then compare the data to make more generalizable inferences.

A more comprehensive study would be possible. By looking more specifically at homeschoolers in each of the schools, further research might address socialization issues. In an ideal setting, the research team would have had both the time and opportunity to visit each campus, meet with a group of homeschooled students and a group of nonhomeschooled students, and then compare the groups in their social adjustment, involvement in extracurricular activities, and academic progress. This evaluation of *in college* performance could then be compared to the cohort of non-homeschooled students attending the same university under equal admittance requirements.

RECOMMENDATIONS

Because homeschooling is a rapidly growing educational choice among American families, we would suggest several recommendations for admissions offices to improve assessments of the ways with which homeschooled applicants are treated and reviewed. The researchers recommend that institutions of higher education reconstruct their application forms so that homeschooling is an option that prospective students can check.

Only one of the institutions within the Ivy League (University of Pennsylvania) had such a check box.

To establish more credible data, it may benefit admissions offices, in conjunction with the dean of academic studies and the student's advisor, to track homeschoolers upon their arrival on campus. Grades are easy to follow and assess, but also consider questions of academic adjustment. For example, has greater structure provided by the college environment interfered with the homeschooled student's ability to learn? On the other hand, has the more structured environment and prescribed curriculum allowed the homeschooler to focus intently and to achieve high marks in their classes?

Detractors of homeschooling raise some concerns about these students' lack of social integration and adjustment. However, both the literature reviewed and the interviews conducted suggest that socialization is not a negative factor in a homeschooler's collegiate experience. In fact, most believe that homeschooled students are better adjusted, better prepared, and more likely to succeed. As Dennis (2000) states "More often, homeschoolers are more mature than traditional students are because they are used to interacting with adults" (p. 33). The homeschooling movement could gain more credibility if universities were willing to track their progress as a separate group of students. Such information about homeschoolers could be gathered from deans of residential life, deans of student life, residential hall advisors, faculty, or even by their peers.

CONCLUSION

Homeschooled students have much to offer to highly selective colleges and universities in the United States: a breadth of knowledge and experience; confidence and ease in working with adults; a clear sense of their academic strengths and weaknesses; and a self-directed, purposeful approach toward learning. This research study has demonstrated that through proper documentation of their academic program of study, outside letters of recommendation, participation in extracurricular activities, interviews with admissions directors, and standardized test scores, their rather unique educational background has allowed them to gain entry to the Ivy League.

ACKNOWLEDGEMENTS

This research project was conducted in the fall of 2002 as a component of our academic program at Teachers College, Columbia University and submitted as a joint requirement for courses about school choice and research methodologies.

REFERENCES

Cohen, C. (2000a). *And what about college? How homeschooling can lead to admissions to the best colleges and universities*. Cambridge, MA: Holt Associates.

Cohen, C. (2000b). *Homeschoolers' college admissions handbook: Preparing your 12-to-18-year-old for a smooth transition*. Roseville, CA: Prima.

Dennis, J. G. (2000). *Homeschooling high school: Planning ahead for college admission*. Lynnwood, WA: Emerald Books.

Heuer, L. (2000). *The homeschooler's guide to portfolios and transcripts*. New York: Arco.

Leppert, M., & Leppert, M. (2001). *Homeschooling almanac, 2002-2003*. Roseville, CA: Prima.

Lines, P. (1997). *Homeschooling: An overview for education policymakers*. Washington, DC: U.S. Department of Education.

National Center for Education Statistics. (1997). *Homeschooling in the United States*. Washington DC: U.S. Department of Educational Research and Improvement.

Sutton, J. (2002, January/February). Homeschooling comes to age. *Brown Alumni Magazine*, pp. 47-53.

CHAPTER 13

HOME SCHOOLING

A British Perspective

Sean Gabb

HISTORICAL BACKGROUND

Home schooling can be loosely defined as any education provided otherwise than by formal schooling outside the home. Such education may be provided by parents or guardians, or by tutors engaged by parents or guardians. So defined, home schooling has a long history in England. Most notably, it was the custom of the kings and queens to have their children educated at home. Indeed, the children of the present queen are the first in the Royal Family to have attended any school. She was herself educated at home by private tutors. The education of Queen Victoria was supervised by Baroness Lehtzen, a German governess. That of George III was supervised by the Marquis of Bute, who after the king's accession in 1760, became one of the country's less effective prime ministers. Certainly, he was one of the less fortunate.

It was the custom of the wealthier classes to send their sons to one of the various public or grammar schools set up since the middle ages—the oldest, King's School in Canterbury, dating back apparently to 597. But this was by no means a universal custom. Though the education provided

Home Schooling in Full View: A Reader, 199–227
Copyright © 2005 by Information Age Publishing
All rights of reproduction in any form reserved.

was usually excellent, if rather narrowly focused on the classical languages, it was often attended by severe disadvantages. Teachers frequently maintained discipline with the most savage violence. Take, for example, Nicholas Udall (1504-1556). An admired scholar and translator and a friend of royalty, he was the author of *Ralph Roister Doister*, the first comic play in English and the obvious model for later works by Marlowe and Shakespeare. He was also headmaster of Eton College. In 1541, he was dismissed for theft of school property and sexual abuse of the boys. His great partiality for flogging was noted, but not held against him. Nor was his general behavior thought that scandalous: in 1555, the year before his death, he was appointed headmaster of Westminister School, and a street near the school is now named after him. Nearly 2 centuries later, in 1809, Dr. Keate was appointed headmaster of Eton, and remains famous for the violent beatings he inflicted on the poet Shelley and on a generation of Victorian notables.

The teachers aside, there were the boys. Collective bullying, generally ignored by the teachers, was the norm, and could result in serious maiming or even death. The fagging system allowed older boys to treat the younger as their personal servants, and was an opportunity for gross cruelty. According to one man who had been a fag at Eton in 1824,

> [t]he practice of fagging had become an organized system of brutality, and cruelty. I was frequently kept up until one or two o'clock in the morning, waiting on my masters at upper and indulging every sort of bullying at their hands. I have been beaten on my palms with the back of a brush, or struck on both sides of my face because I had not closed the shutter near my master's bed tight enough or because in making his bed I had left the seam of the lower sheet uppermost. (quoted in Gathorne-Hardy, 1977)

Not surprisingly, many parents chose to have their sons educated at home, either wholly or partially. John Stuart Mill was educated entirely by this father, and the account of that education forms a notorious part of his *Autobiography*. Edward Gibbon and Thomas Babbington Macaulay received part of their education at home and part at local day schools. Such was the case with many other notable figures in English history.

For girls, formal schooling was at least a rarity before the nineteeth century. Although academies allowed girls to study a basic curriculum, nothing for girls was equivalent to the public and grammar schools available to boys. The general custom among the wealthier classes was to educate girls at home, or to give them to an unmarried female relative for teaching, and then perhaps to send them in their later teens to a finishing college where they acquired the accomplishments suitable to a young lady. Jane Austin, for example, had only 1 year of formal schooling around the age of 10.

The poorer classes had, before the beginning of compulsory state education, a wide range of semiformal schooling as described at length in the
writings of the educational historian E.G. West, who also shows that the
absence of state funding and compulsion before 1870 did not prevent
most people in England from learning to read (see West, 1965, 1974).

With the great improvements in the quality of the independent schools
and the establishment of compulsory state education for the poorer
classes, attendance at school had become for all classes and both sexes the
general custom by the end of the nineteenth century. Before then, however, it can be said that formal schooling was one educational option
among many. Even by the twentieth century, it was by no means universal.
Noel Coward, for example, was educated almost wholly at home, briefly
attending the Chapel Royal Choir School (Kenrick, n.d.). Agatha Christie
had no formal schooling before the age of 16.[1] She later wrote that her
mother "the best way to bring up girls was to let them run wild as much as
possible; to give them food, fresh air and not to force their minds in any
way" (quoted in Kingsley, 1998). C.S. Lewis had only 2 years of formal
schooling as a child—part of this at Wynyard School in Watford—a place
he later called "Belsen" (C.S. Lewis Foundation, n.d.).

Basic education organized by the State came later to England later
than in almost every other civilized country. Legislation to allow local
authorities to maintain elementary schools was passed only in 1870. It
took a further 30 years of cautious advance to make education compulsory and then free in the state schools, and then for local authorities to be
allowed to set up secondary schools. The reasons for this late start and
slow advance were an ideological dislike of state activity that remained
strong among all classes well into the twentieth century, and a bitter dispute between the Christian sects and the State over the continuing viability of the religious schools in an environment of free state education, and
between the sects over the nature of religious instruction in the state
schools (see West, 1965, for more on these debates). While these disputes
have largely faded into history, their former importance has left clear
traces in the English law of education.

THE LAW ON HOME SCHOOLING IN ENGLAND

The law of education in England can be summarized in the statement that
while parents have a legal duty to educate their children, families have no
requirement to send them to school. The British Government openly
accepts this summary, declaring on one of its Websites: "Parents are
allowed to educate their children at home instead of school if they choose

to do so. Under English law, it is education that is compulsory, not school-ing"(Parents Centre, n.d.)

This is echoed by the current secretary of state for education: "My department recognizes and respects the right to choose to home educate" ("A Matter," 2004). The relevant legal wording was settled in section 36 of the Education Act 1944: "The parent of every child of compulsory school age shall cause him to receive efficient full-time education suitable:

(a) to his age, ability and aptitude, and
(b) to any special education needs he may have, either by regular atten-dance at school *or otherwise*" (emphasis added)

This wording was carried unchanged into section 7 of the Education Act 1996.[2]

The legal meaning of the words "suitable education" was clarified in the case of *Harrison & Harrison v. Stevenson* on an appeal brought in 1981 in the Worcester Crown Court. In this case, the judge defined a "suitable education" as one such as (1) "To prepare the children in life for modern civilized society, and (2) To enable them to achieve their full potential."[3]

In the subsequent judicial review case of *R vs. Secretary of State for Edu-cation, ex parte Talmud Torah Machzikei Hadass School Trust* (1985), Mr. Jus-tice Woolf held that: "Education is 'suitable' if it primarily equips a child for life within the community of which he is a member, rather than the way of life in the wider country as a whole, as long as it does not foreclose the child's options in later years to adopt some other form of life if he wishes to do so."[4] As it currently stands—in September 2004—the law does not require parents to register their children with any school; and, within the defined meaning of "suitable" they can provide their children with whatever education they please. Parents who wish to teach their chil-dren at home are not legally required:

- To seek permission from the Local Education Authority to educate "otherwise";
- To inform the Local Education Authority that they have children of school age;
- To have regular contact with the Local Education Authority;
- To have premises equipped to any specified standard;
- To have any teaching or other educational qualifications of their own;
- To cover any specific syllabus;
- To have any fixed timetable;
- To prepare lesson plans of any kind;

- To observe normal school hours or terms;
- To give formal lessons;
- To allow their children to mix with others.

Sections 437-443 of the Education Act 1996 oblige Local Education Authorities within England and Wales to take action if it appears that a child is not receiving a "suitable" education. If it established that a child is not receiving a "suitable" education, the Local Education Authority may serve a notice on parents requiring them to establish that such an education is being provided.[5] However, in the case of *R v. Gwent County Council ex parte Perry* (1985), the courts held that the Local Education Authority should give parents "a fair and reasonable opportunity to satisfy it that proper education is being provided, having first allowed a sufficient time to set in motion arrangements for home education."[6]

But failure eventually to comply with this notice may be followed by a school attendance order. This may be challenged in the courts, which will dismiss the notice if shown—on the balance of probabilities—that the child is indeed receiving an education that a reasonable person would consider to be "suitable."

This legal duty placed on Local Education Authorities applies only where children appear not to be receiving a "suitable" education. Where no evidence is available that they are not receiving such an education, they have no legal right to seek information from parents. This is not an absolute bar on making enquiries. In the case of *Philips v. Brown* (1980), the courts held that the Local Education Authority is entitled to ask parents for information as a basis for making the decision as to whether the education they are providing is efficient. If the parent fails to provide information, it could be concluded that *prima facie* the parents are in breach of their duty.[7]

But the Local Education Authority is not allowed to specify the nature and presentation of such information. Nor can they carry into their enquiry assumptions and expectations based on their experience of formal schooling. On the Parent Centre Website, maintained by the Department for Education and Skills, the authorities confirm that:

LEAs have no automatic right of access to parents' home. Parents may wish to offer an alternative way of demonstrating that they are providing suitable education, for example through showing examples of work and agreeing to a meeting at another venue. (Parents Centre, n.d.)

A formal procedure is to be followed when a child is registered with a school, but the parents wish to withdraw him for teaching at home, there is a formal procedure to be followed. The Education (Pupil Registration)

Regulation 9(c), 1995 sets out the conditions under which a child may be removed from the admission register of a school. His name must be removed if: "He has ceased to attend the school and the proprietor has received written notification from the parent that the pupil is receiving education otherwise than at school."[8]

Again, parents do not need to seek permission from the Local Education Authority of their intention to educate a child at home. Nor are they obliged to inform the Local Education Authority—though the proprietor of the school must report the removal of the child within ten school days. An exception to this rule is in the case of children registered at a school providing for special needs. Here, consent must be obtained from the Local Education Authority before removing a child—see the Education (Pupil Registration) Regulation 9(2), 1995. The purpose of this exception, though, is simply to ensure that the Local Education Authority can maintain continuity in its provision for special educational needs. It is not intended to be used to prevent education at home.

The law also provides for those parents who wish to educate their children partly at home and partly at school. In such cases, children are registered at a school for full-time education—and the school collects funding from the authorities on that basis—but the child is granted leave of absence from the school. The law insists that children of school age who are registered at a school must attend regularly. However, such leave of absence does not constitute irregular attendance. During such absences, the child is officially present, though is in fact being educated elsewhere. It seems reasonable that, in such cases, the consent of the school at which the child is registered must first be obtained. Again, it is not a matter in which the Local Education Authority has any right to intervene.[9]

THE LAW ON HOME SCHOOLING IN SCOTLAND

England and Scotland have been united under a single Crown since 1603, and under a common central government since 1707—though this latter fact is somewhat altered by the recent establishment of a Scottish Assembly with limited powers. The Union of 1707 provided for a single country, but with two systems of law and administration. This continues to be the case with education. The law on home schooling in Scotland is broadly similar to that in England, so far as parents are not required to register their children at any school, and can educate them at home without supervision.[10]

This being said, there are significant differences with regard to withdrawing children from school. According to section 35(1) of the Education (Scotland) Act 1980:

Where a child of school age who has attended a public school on one or more occasions fails without reasonable excuse to attend regularly at the said school, then, unless the education authority have consented to the withdrawal of the child from the school (which consent shall not be unreasonably withheld), his parent shall be guilty of an offence against this section.

The meaning of this is that parents who wish to withdraw their children from school must obtain the consent of the local Director of Education. The authorities will then investigate to see whether the proposed course of study is "suitable," and may give or withhold consent for the withdrawal.

The Scottish Executive has refused to give any detailed guidance on how the right to withdrawal is to be exercised, and there is a shortage of Scottish case law on the matter. However, it is generally assumed that the English case law generally applies; and this would be taken into account by the Scottish courts in the event of any legal proceedings.

THE LAW ON HOME SCHOOLING IN NORTHERN IRELAND

The northern six counties of Ireland are part of the United Kingdom, and are governed—depending on political circumstances—either directly from London or by a local executive body. As with Scotland, Northern Ireland has its own legal and administrative system. The wording of the relevant legislation is copied directly from the English Act. Section 45(1) of the Education and Libraries Northern Ireland Order 1986 states that: "The parent of every child of compulsory school age shall cause him to receive efficient full-time education suitable to his age, ability and aptitude and to any special educational needs he may have, either by regular attendance at school or otherwise."[11] Parents have an unquestioned legal right to educate their children at home, and may withdraw their children if already registered at a school in the same way as in England. As with Scotland, there is a shortage of local case law on the interpretation of the legislation. Again, though, it is assumed that the English case law would be taken into account in any legal proceedings.

THE NUMBER OF CHILDREN IN HOME SCHOOLING

Because parents are not required by law to inform anyone of their decision, we have no reliable way of knowing how many children in the United Kingdom are educated at home. All numbers given in the literature are estimates based on extrapolations, and are much disputed concerning the reliability of their underlying methodologies. According to Roland Meighan, now retired but formerly the special professor of education at Nottingham University, England could have as many as 84,000 children educated at home. That is about 1% of the English school population.[12]

However, Brenda Holloway, a trustee of the Home Education Advisory Service,[13] says that his methodology is flawed. He takes the 7,000 families registered with the various home education organizations, multiples this by three on the assumption that there are three children per family, and then further multiplies by four on the assumption that only one in four families bothers to register (Cook, 2002b). These multipliers are no more than guesses, and so the figure of 84,000 cannot be accepted as an accurate measurement of the numbers.

With this in mind, it is worth noting other alleged numbers, without necessarily accepting their reliability. According to Eileen Wilson, "informal spokesperson' for Education, as of May 2000, 25,000 British families are educating their own children (Freely, 2000)[14] According to Leslie Safran, founder of The Otherwise Club, as of May 2004, as many as 150,000 children were being educated at home in the United Kingdom (Redwood, 2004).[15] According to Alison Preuss, of the Schoolhouse Home Education Association, as of August 2004, 6,000 children were being educated at home in Scotland (Grant, 2004). According to the journalist Morag Lindsay, as of February 2002, 50,000 children being educated at home in Scotland (Lindsay, 2002).

Radically different figures are thrown around in reporting and in debates. They are copied from statement to statement and often garbled in the process. Most of the time, their provenance is unknown, and their underlying methodology cannot even be guessed. No one knows what the numbers are. No one can know unless the British Government will include some relevant questions in the 2011 census. Even then, no one will probably know the truth, as many people involved in home schooling are too suspicious of the authorities to risk revealing themselves.[17]

A further difficulty in measuring or even estimating the number of children educated at home is the loose definition of home schooling. It can cover those children who never go to school, those who attend but with leaves of absence, and those who go to school for several years of their education, but only before or after being taught at home. Doubtless, other subcategories can be imagined. We do not know the overall numbers. We do not know the numbers in any of these subcategories. We therefore cannot know what proportion each subcategory is to the whole.

Nevertheless, we can be reasonably sure about two facts about the numbers. First, we know that home schooling is not confined to any one social or religious group. It is not the case that all—or perhaps even the majority—of parents who choose to educate their children at home are religious fundamentalists or well-educated middle class dissenters from the mainstream. In 2002, Paula Rothermel of the University of Durham published her research *Home-Education: Rationales, Practices and Outcomes.* In this, she explored the aims and practices of families involved in home schooling. Her methodology involved a questionnaire survey completed by 419 families and 196 assessments evaluating the psychosocial and academic development of home-educated children aged eleven years and under.

She found that at least 14% of the parents in the sample were employed in manual and unskilled occupations; and that at least 38% of parents in the study had been educated at comprehensive schools and at least 21% had no postschool qualifications. While 47.5% of parents had attended university, at least 27.7% of parents in the study had not. The families studied included travelers, those on low incomes, those whose children had been in care, religious believers, ethnic minorities, single parents, and gay couples. In short, the study showed that parents from just about every group in society choose to educate their children at home (Rothermel, 2002).

Second, it is uncontested that the numbers of children being educated at home has risen considerably during the past generation. We do not need to accept the claim by Professor Meighan that the number of families involved rose from 10 in 1977 to 10,000 in 1997 (Hartley-Brewer, 1997). But the weight of anecdotal evidence, and the fact that home schooling is increasingly discussed in the media, and the increasing perception of—and perhaps just the increase in—the reasons why parents choose to educate their children at home, indicates a substantial rise in numbers.

THE REASONS FOR HOME SCHOOLING

The reasons why parents choose to educate their children at home or all or part of the time are perhaps as many as the parents involved. This being so, we can divide the reasons under several broad headings. There is dissatisfaction with discipline or safety at school. There is dissatisfaction with the quality of the curriculum offered by the schools. There are religious or ideological objections to the whole experience of education as provided by the state sector. It is not possible to know which of these is the main reason. In many cases, it is a combination of many reasons that has led to the decision to educate at home. But the reasons are worth separating so far as possible, and discussing in the order given.

Discipline and Safety

In its antibullying pack, *Bullying: Don't Suffer in Silence*, the Department for Education and Skills adopts a wide definition of the word. Bullying is defined as:

- Physical: hitting, kicking, taking belongings
- Verbal: name calling, insulting, making offensive remarks
- Indirect: spreading nasty stories about someone, exclusion from social groups, being made the subject of malicious rumours (Department for Education and Skills, 2004, p. 9).[18]

The information pack uses information gathered from a survey of five primary schools and 14 secondary schools across England in 1997, taking evidence from 2,308 pupils aged 10 to 14 years. It showed that bullying then, as defined, was widespread: 32.3% of children reported that they had been bullied once or twice, and 4.1% that they were bullied several times a week (Department for Education and Skills, 2004, p. 10). The risks of bullying were stated to be:

> Victims may be reluctant to attend school and are often absent. They may be more anxious and insecure than others, having fewer friends and often feeling unhappy and lonely. Victims can suffer from low self-esteem and negative self-image, looking upon themselves as failures—feeling stupid, ashamed and unattractive.
>
> Victims may present a variety of symptoms to health professionals, including fits, faints, vomiting, limb pains, paralysis, hyperventilation, visual symptoms, headaches, stomach aches, bed wetting, sleeping difficulties and sadness. Being bullied may lead to depression or, in the most serious cases, attempted suicide. It may lead to anxiety, depression, loneliness and lack of trust in adult life. (Department for Education and Skills, 2004, p. 12)

In 2002, it was reported that more than 20 children every year in Britain were committing suicide because of bullying and other pressures at school (Turner, 2002). In the summer term of 2003, 12,800 children in England were suspended from school for attacking other pupils and a further 336 were expelled, presumably for more vicious attacks; 4,000 others were suspended and 280 excluded permanently for assaulting adults.[19]

Though schools are required to take the matter seriously, it is in practice very hard to police bullying. Teachers cannot be present at all times in the class and playground—and certainly cannot control what happens on the way to and from school. And even reporting a bully can make things worse for a child. Not surprisingly, experience or just fear of bullying has prompted many parents to educate their children at home.

According to Belinda Harris Reed of Education Otherwise: "We are getting 100 new families a month. I don't think that people take on home educating lightly. Now most people take their children out of school because of bullying, not like me for a philosophical viewpoint" ("More Parents," 2004).

Take the case of Edward Lupton. In 1993, when he was 13, he decided to leave school because of persistent bullying. He explains: "I was picked on at school, and by one boy in particular. Whenever I walked past he'd say "Jelly belly' or 'You're so fat'" (Mcauley, 1995). The bully made his life miserable. He had lost his father in a car crash at the age of 3. He was bullied about not having a father as well as about being overweight. Eventually, he took himself out of school and studied at home with his mother.

Take the case of Christianna, who:

> was twelve when her parents reluctantly withdrew her from school in March 1996. Christianna is a very bright girl and her parents had been pleased initially when their daughter gained a place at a prestigious girl's grammar school.
>
> Christianna's father was a further education lecturer and her mother a primary teacher; Christianna has a brother a few years younger. Family circumstances were not easy. Mr. K was suffering from cancer and had been unable to work full-time for several years. Mrs. K also worked as a supply teacher as the burden of caring for two children and a sick husband had made full-time work impossible. The family had very little money and lived in a somewhat derelict house situated in the middle of woods close to an otherwise densely populated urban centre.
>
> Christianna was badly bullied at school; she did not fit in. Although the school was selective Christianna was called a "Buff ", as she was keen to learn and possibly envied for her exceptional ability and the ease with which she learned. The other girls all seemed to have plenty of money for fashionable clothes and were more interested in pop music and boys than their studies. This at least was Christianna's perception. (Alpress & Turnbull, 2000)

It is unlikely that the problem of bullying has diminished in recent years. It has now been joined by ethnic gang fights in areas of high immigration, extortion rackets, drug abuse, sexual predation, and a general mirroring within school of the social problems that now take up so much of the political debate in Britain.

Curriculum and Quality of Instruction

Though the claim is hotly denied by the government and other interested bodies, it is widely believed that standards of education have been steadily falling in the state sector. Every year, the examination results suggest steady improvement, with more passes than ever before and higher grades. This is increasingly dismissed as a statistical illusion brought about by making the papers easier and by lowering the marking standards. According to Peter Oborne (2004), writing in *The Spectator*,

> An important series of articles in the *Economist* has shown how a growing number of universities now regard A-levels as such a worthless measure of achievement that they are searching for other methods of assessing potential students. In medical and veterinary science, six of the top faculties in Britain now select through a special biomedical admissions test. Eight law schools are now following suit, with a legal aptitude test. Other universities have simply given up on A-levels as a method of sorting out bright students. Leeds Metropolitan and Huddersfield universities, which have 20 applicants for each physiotherapy place, just choose successful applicants randomly from those with the right grades.

In 2003, Channel Four screened a series called *That'll Teach 'Em*. In this, a class was assembled of 16-year-old students who had achieved high grades in the General Certificate of Secondary Education examinations. These were given 4 weeks of the sort of education a grammar school had provided in the 1950s and then set examinations based on the old O Level papers. Most did badly in English language and English literature. Most failed mathematics and about half history. "Most people failed maths" said Thomas Jewell, normally a pupil at Churchill community school in north Somerset. "It was quite hard. We weren't able to use a calculator and we had a lot of arithmetic to do" (Newell & Lock, 2003).

Commenting on the series, Chris Woodhead, the former chief inspector of schools, said comparing GSCEs and O Levels was a valid exercise. "The fact is today's students do not have the ability to write an essay" he said "and they do not have the body of knowledge that was needed to do well in a O-level. GCSEs have been dumbed down" (Newell & Lock, 2003).

Added to declining education standards is the growth of bureaucratic control over the whole system. The National Curriculum was introduced in 1988 as a means of raising standards across England. It has become an inflexible burden on schools, effectively centralizing control over education. It determines the content of what will be taught, and sets attainment targets for learning. It also determines how performance will be assessed and reported. Naturally, it constrains all effort at innovation, and prevents the tailoring of curriculum to the actual or perceived needs of children.

Mary Rose is a former schoolteacher living in Gloucestershire. She started educating her five children at home after the introduction of the national Curriculum in 1988. She voices the growing belief that the state sector is now so rigid that it cannot accommodate the needs of individual children: "In the old days teachers had time to build up a rapport with children.... But now, immediately after the register it's on with the numeracy and literacy hour and everything is scripted. There's been a sea change in the approach to education" (Cookb, 2002).

Radical disenchantment with the state education system, and with those parts of the independent sector that follow the National Curriculum, has determined many parents to educate their children at home. Some parents choose home schooling as a first alternative. Others choose it only because they cannot afford the preferred alternative of a special school in the independent sector.

Take the case of Molly, age 9, reported by Mike Alpress and Eileen Turnbull:

> She lives on a run down council estate, close to drug dealers and addicts, on the outskirts of a large Essex Town. Neither of her parents work, her Father has been unemployed for many years. Her older siblings, both articulate and intelligent, were home educated for some years but now attend school.
>
> Molly is a gifted child, with a flare for mathematics in particular. She is currently studying for G.C.S.E. Maths with a view to taking the exam next summer. It has come to the stage that she is now better than her parents at maths and they are at a loss as to how to meet her needs. Contact has been made with the National Association for Gifted Children, and Molly's Father has tried to "tap-in" to some of the current government innovations for clever children, but has, thus far, been frustrated due to many of them only taking place in the larger cities. The family does not own a car and the cost and paucity of public transport makes it difficult for them to travel outside the immediate locality.
>
> Molly's parents are reluctant to send her to a local school as they feel she will be "different" and not get the teaching she requires. To send her to a "good" state school outside the local area would mean having to pay fares, which they cannot afford. They obviously are not in a position to pay for a place at an independent school for Molly, and do not have any guarantees that she would get the teaching she needs even if they were to afford it.
>
> Molly studies all areas of the curriculum. Her work rate is colossal with reams of recorded work. Comparatively little practical work is done, probably because of the cost of materials. She does have books, but the vast majority of them are "hand-me downs" from when her elder siblings were educated at home. Expensive visits out are few and far between. However, Molly is a talented all rounder. She plays several musical instruments, including piano (for which she has lessons) and guitar. She swims for the local Swimming club, plays hockey and is a member of the local St John's Ambulance Brigade. (Alpress and Eileen Turnbull, 2000)

Religious and Ideological Dissent

The curriculum provided within the great majority of British schools is secular in tone. It is also neutral or even liberal on matters of sexual conduct. This is so in the state sector, and also in much of the independent sector—not excepting even the religious schools. There are deeply religious families who find this unacceptable, who cannot afford or otherwise gain access to alternative schooling, and who therefore choose home schooling. They choose this for the negative reason, just stated, that the schools available are said to be agents of secular humanist indoctrination, and for the positive reason that their faith requires learning to be integrated into home life.

Take the example of Stuart McKay, a Pentecostal preacher, and his wife Diane, the manager of a charity shop. Interviewed in 2002, they said they were motivated by their strong Christian faith to educate their six older children at home, and that they would educate their youngest child at home as soon as she was able to understand the instruction. Mrs. McKay adds:

> We do it partly because the Bible says it is the parents' duty to teach their children. But also when Reuben [their eldest child] was about to start school 10 years ago, there was a big thing about bullying.... We wanted to teach him ourselves. It worked so well, we carried on with the rest of our children. (quoted in Garavelli, 2002)

Take Jane Villalobos, a Roman Catholic mother of four from Birmingham. She was concerned that her children would lose their faith if they attended school. She says: "I looked at Catholic schools and felt that the chances of my children still practicing their faith at the age of 18 would be very slim.... I felt that the most important thing for all of them was to keep their faith."

She decided to educate her children at home, wondering "if I would be undermining the system by taking them out.... But ultimately, as a parent your responsibility is for your own children" (quoted in Holmes, 2003).

It is not only Christians who educate their children at home. Rubana Akhgar is a Muslim living in Ilford. She belongs to a radical group that believes in turning Britain into an Islamic state. She does not trust the education that her children would receive in even the most firmly Islamic independent school. So she educates them at home. She says: "I want to protect my children from this society and bring them up in a strict Islamic environment so that it becomes a complete way of life for them. I don't think they will reject it but if they did I would be devastated because they would end up in hellfire for the hereafter" (quoted in Duguid, 2003).

Nor is it only the strongly religious who have a principled objection to school. Take Roland Meighan, the retired academic already mentioned. He is a radical liberal in his politics. He quotes Bertrand Russell in nearly all his writings. He is an advocate of the look-say method of learning to read, and despises the phonic system so loved by educational conservatives. For him, the great benefit of home schooling is not that it serves to bring a child up within a minority tradition, but that it liberates the mind and creates true individuality. Children do not need to be sent to school to learn, he says. Instead;

> Parents soon find out that young children are natural learners. They are like explorers or research scientists busily gathering information and making meaning out of the world. Most of this learning is not the result of teaching, but rather a constant and universal learning activity as natural as breathing. Our brains are programmed to learn unless discouraged. A healthy brain stimulates itself by interacting with what it finds interesting or challenging in the world around it. It learns from any mistakes and operates a self-correcting process. (Meighan, n.d.)

Intellectually, he is an heir of Jean-Jacques Rousseau (n.d.), who, in his *Emile, ou l'éducation*, argued for a form of private education that preserved the inherent goodness of an alleged natural state while also providing the instruction needed to become a successful, and therefore a moral, person. It is the duty of parents to support this natural process—encouraging, supporting, tolerating, above all understanding that it is through their own efforts that children learn to make sense of their world, and also "acquire the attitudes and skills necessary for successful learning throughout their lives." The process can be slowed and even wholly prevented by "insensitive adult interference." "Sadly, the schools available to us, whether state or private, are often based on an impositional model which, sooner or later, causes children to lose confidence in their natural learning and its self-correcting features, and instead, learn to be dependent on others to 'school' their minds" (Rousseau, n.d.) He says elsewhere: "It's a fascist doctrine which says you've got to force people to learn, that they won't do it without compulsion"(quoted in Cook, 2002a)

For Professor Meighan and those who agree with him, home schooling is the ultimate in progressive education. Indeed, many such people dislike the term home schooling. They are happier with unschooling. Their objection to school is not necessarily the content of education, but the process of its delivery. Like Professor Meighan, they believe that there should be no artificial boundaries between playing and learning and working or between ages. For them, education is a process that begins at birth, and is best achieved by encouraging individuals to learn by themselves.[20]

Among many other reasons for home schooling, one of the strangest is the lack of provision by local authorities. In 2002, Anthony Dixon was among 80 children in the London Borough of Hackney who, because of a failure of planning by the Local Education Authority, were left without any school at all and had to be taught at home (Cohen, 2002). This kind of home schooling by default comes into a separate category. However, what mostly connects parents who choose to educate their children at home is a dislike of the formal school curriculum and its delivery as these have emerged in recent years.

METHODS OF HOME SCHOOLING

For obvious reasons, it is not possible to describe—except at immense length—the methods that parents use for teaching their children at home. Some parents follow the National Curriculum at home, believing that they can do better than the state schools. So far as possible, they duplicate schools at home, complete with fixed hours, textbooks, report cards, and field trips. Others reject the National Curriculum, preferring to concentrate on music or Latin, or whatever they themselves think a suitable education for their children. This may involve some duplication of school. It may also involve a much less conventional style of education. As said, the devoutly religious prefer to integrate instruction into normal family life. Those who share the views of Professor Meighan will use methods many regard as at least eccentric.[21]

Take the case of Mika and Naomi van Hees:

It's nearly noon on a damp Thursday in term time, and two 7-year-old sisters are bouncing and laughing on a big trampoline behind their house in deepest Wales. Their mother is looking on with a fond smile, their father watches as he walks past with a bucket to feed the ducks. Why aren't they at school?

They are, in a sense. Mika and Naomi are home-educated, and, except for some formal lessons with their father on Mondays and outside lessons in gymnastics and piano, they do pretty much what they want. That might be using the computer, playing chess and backgammon or helping to bake bread for the 15 members of this 160-acre "eco-community" a few miles from the wild Pembrokeshire coast.

"We give them the space not to do something until they're ready for it," says their mother, Anja van Hees. "They have such perseverance when they're interested, like when they helped to cut down an ash tree. Sometimes they might draw all day long, or they might do nothing and just go to bed—they're very in tune with their physical needs."

The girls are identical twins, but with different interests: Naomi loves horses and has learnt to read—her favorite book is Hansel and Gretel. Mika

doesn't read yet and prefers numbers and learning tables. "I've been building Lego and doing jigsaws this morning," she says.

But they share a wary attitude towards formal schooling, even though
they have friends at the local primary in Newport. "School's not very nice
because you have to stay inside all the time," says Naomi. "But I might go to
college when I'm more grown up." Mika adds: "You're locked inside a building and you have to do what they say. The only time you can go out is at
playtime. Here we can go out and see the animals when we want." (quoted
in Cook, 2002b)

What cannot be doubted is the wealth of resources available to parents
who choose to educate their children at home. Until the 1980s, the main
resource other than the knowledge of parents themselves was books
bought or borrowed form libraries. This was then supplemented by videos and floppy disks of material, mostly acquired form the United States.
Nowadays, a Google search using the terms "home schooling" or "homeschooling" and "resources" will turn up tens of thousands of pages cater-
ing to every possible religious and philosophical and other point of view.
There are lesson plans, and software packages, and advice to parents on
teaching methods and dealing with special needs, and whole scanned
texts. Much of this, inevitably, is American. But this is no problem for
British home schoolers. Given the ubiquity of Internet access—either in
the home or in public libraries—no one can claim that children educated
at home are necessarily deprived of suitable learning materials.

In his specific praise of home schooling, Professor Meighan speaks for
himself and for only a section of the whole movement. But in his claims
about its modern feasibility, he speaks for all

Schools were established in an information-poor society, but we're in
an information-rich society now: there's radio, TV, video, the Internet,
books, and specialist magazines. Of course people can do it at home
(Cook 2002b).

THE EFFECTS OF HOME SCHOOLING

The effects, however defined and measured, of educating children at
home are generally claimed to be at least satisfactory. This may be
because they are. But, as repeatedly said, we do not know how many children are being educated at home. The large home schooling movement
in Britain, and the much larger movement in the United States both lay
stress on the benefits of educating children at home. So do most academic
researchers. But home schooling is only likely to be reported when it is
successful. There may be many—even many more—failures, which are not
reported. In estimating the effects of home schooling, we may be in the

position of a man who studies gambling by only looking at those come forward and talk about their winnings.

This skeptical point being made—and it must be kept in mind—it is worth looking at the conclusions reached by Dr. Rothermel, which are the largest and most rigorous available for the United Kingdom. She reports that:

> The results show that 64% of the home-educated Reception aged children scored over 75% on their PIPS Baseline Assessments as opposed to 5.1% of children nationally. The National Literacy Project (Years 1,3,5) assessment results reveal that 80.4% of the home-educated children scored within the top 16% band (of a normal distribution bell curve), whilst 77.4% of the PIPS Year 2 home-educated cohort scored similarly. Results from the psychosocial instruments confirm the home-educated children were socially adept and without behavioral problems. Overall, the home-educated children demonstrated high levels of attainment and good social skills. (Rothermel, 2002)

She also notes that the children of working class, poorly-educated parents were doing significantly better than middle class children. While five and six year old children from middle class backgrounds scored only 55.2 per cent in the test, they scored 71 per cent. Dr Rothermel suspects the cause of this is that working class parents are much harder at pushing their children, even they are less obviously qualified to teach them at home (Rothermel, 2002).

What anecdotal evidence can be acquired is also broadly positive. Take, for example, the case of Farooq and Halimahton Yusof, who live in England. They taught all five of their children at home. Al five excelled in mathematics, and entered university several years before is normally the case (Petty, 1999). Or take the case of Anthony Dixon, already mentioned. Though he was taught at home not because his parents positively chose home schooling, his progress at home was reported to be excellent (Cohen, 2002).

Against this, take a case just reported to the author of this paper by a friend in conversation. His sister, who like him, was educated at a technical school in Kent during the 1970s—technical schools were set up after 1944 to prepare children for careers in engineering and the other technical sectors—decided to educate her three children at home. She had no educational qualifications and no particular skills as a teacher. She did not really teach her children. Instead, "they were left to drag themselves up." The results were not impressive. They were perhaps no obvious advertisement for home schooling. But they were not that badly either.

The children are now in their early 20s. The eldest runs his own business, and is literate and numerate enough to handle all the administration of the business. The middle child is presently training as a physical education instructor. The youngest—her only daughter—is pregnant and considering marriage to the father. All three children are said to be remarkably self-confident in their dealings with the world. While they had, during their education at home, little contact with children of their own age, they did mix with a wide circle of people from other age groups. The author's friend has sent his own children to the local school. He is not unhappy with the quality of education, but he worries about the "negative attitudes" of the children with whom they mix. He complains about their "poor sense of values and aspirations, especially in the educational field."

This is the least favorable anecdotal evidence the author can find of the effects of being educated at home. To repeat, it is not that bad. Doubtless, there are terrible cases known to various social workers—cases, for example, where children are taken out of school or never sent there in the first place, and who run wild. This, however, brings us to the unmapped frontier that divides some kind of "suitable" education from outright truancy.

It seems that the main disadvantage of educating children at home is the often very high opportunity cost. Usually, one of the parents must stay at home part of the time to supervise the education. Often, one parent must stay at home all the time. This means the loss of part or all of one salary—a considerable sacrifice in a country like Britain which, though very rich overall, has a high cost of living and relatively high taxes. There are the costs of seeking the necessary materials. There are the costs of sending children for examination at special centers—costs that, assuming nine GCSEs and four of the new modular A Levels, may run to around £1,000 per child.

See Mrs. E.J. Keele, writing to a national newspaper in January 2004:

> I'm a "stay-at-home mum" who is in the happy position of being able to afford not to work. But that freedom does come at a price.
> My family doesn't have lavish holidays, and my husband and I are often forced to go without for the sake of our children.
> My husband's salary keeps a roof over our heads, food in our mouths and pays the bills, and the family allowance of £150 a month keeps our three children clothed and in shoes. (Keele, 2004)

Unless one of the parents is in an occupation that pays an income well above the national average, the decision to educate children at home involves considerable sacrifice for the whole family.

CALLS FOR THE REGULATION OF HOME SCHOOLING

While the law, in England at least, has never placed any barriers to the right of parents to educate their children at home, and while there is no significant evidence to suggest that children are suffering by not going to school, there are the beginnings in Britain of organized opposition to home schooling.

In June 2004, Kim Tomsett spoke at the conference in Bournemouth of the Professional Association of Teachers, which is one of the main teaching trade unions. She called for home schooling to be regulated. In particular, she called or a change in the law to make it compulsory for parents to submit to external monitoring. She explained:

> These are the only group of children who have no consistent level of monitoring or inspections yet are the only group taught in the main by those with no qualifications. (quoted in Blair, 2004)

Tomsett appears to be a lone voice in England. There are ugly stories to be found in the newspapers. It seems that some authorities are trying to conflate home schooling with truancy. Individual officials have been accused of threatening parents known to be educating their children at home—saying that their children would be put on the at-risk register. There is one story of a school that informed a mother that it was illegal for her to take one child out of school following the suicide of another who had been bullied there (Freely, 2000). But none of this yet reflects official policy. The official policy remains the statement, already given, of the relevant minister:

> Parents are allowed to educate their children at home instead of school if they choose to do so. Under English law, it is education that is compulsory, not schooling. A Labour government should be taxing the wealthy to pay for a state education system we can all be proud of, not pandering to people like the McKays who think our teachers are unfit to educate their children. (Brown, 2002)

Judith Gillespie, development manager of the Scottish Parent Teacher Council,[22] agrees:

> Part of the point of school is that children learn to cope with what the world will throw at them in a comparatively safe environment.... They need to learn to deal with the awkward squad, because, at some time in their lives, they are bound to meet people like that.

She feels there is a danger that children who are educated at home will be influenced by their parents' "prejudices":

> One of the most important things is that children need space away from their parents to find out who they really are.... At secondary age, children are generally embarrassed by their parents, mortified if they turn up at the

school gates—and that's how it should be.... If in later life they turn out to share the same values as their parents then that's fine, but they need to have the chance to find out for themselves. (Garavelli, 2002)

There is an official attempt in Scotland to make home schooling less easy for parents. In 2002, the Scottish Executive, which is the devolved government of the country, proposes that local authorities should be able to use details from the United Kingdom Census, from birth registers, from medical records, and from other confidential sources, to identify those children being educated at home. Members of the Scottish Parliament also tried to change the law so that parents who took their children out of school and then moved to another area would be required to inform the authorities in the same way as if they had stayed in the original area. Not surprisingly, these proposals have been bitterly fought by the home schooling movement—not just in Scotland, but also in the United Kingdom as a whole, and also from America, where there is a far larger and more organized movement. The law remains unchanged, but the proposals have not gone away.

One reason given for hostility to home schooling has already been discussed—that children educated at home may not receive a "suitable" education. Another reason given is the general welfare of the children. According to John Stodter, who is the director of education in Aberdeen,

The issue here is about the protection, safety and welfare of children.... It's about making sure every child is known to the authorities. Some parents are worried that the new legislation means they're going to be subject to all sorts of checks but that's not the case. Our responsibility is simply to ensure some education is being provided and that the general welfare of the child is being looked after. (Lindsay, 2002)

The natural implication of this is that children who do not go to school may, unless inspected by the authorities, suffer some kind of abuse by their parents. However, while there is reasonably full and undoubtedly sad evidence from schools and other institutions run by the state, there has to date been not one instance reported of bullying, or sexual abuse, or suicide or murder within a British family that educates its children at home.

It is an incompetent—and even immoral—mode of argumentation to oppose a point of view by simply looking for psychological or other interested reasons for advancing that view. It is far better on all grounds to take the view in itself and to oppose it as incorrect in itself. This being said, the case against home schooling is so weak, and yet—in some places—so firmly advanced, that it is necessary to look for other reasons than whether it is incorrect in itself. Three reasons almost suggest themselves.

There is the professional jealousy of teachers. There is an abstract passion to regulate. There is an ideological agenda.

Professional Jealousy

Teaching seldom brings much in the way of material reward. Teaching in the state sector is often morally unrewarding as well. Not surprisingly, teachers may feel personally offended when they learn that some parents do not value their contribution to enlightenment and civilization. As Mark Brown puts it, home schooling "is an absolute insult to Scotland's teachers." As the number of children educated at home grows, and as discussion of that option becomes more frequent, the various teaching unions and other interest groups will become more opposed to home schooling. They will emphasize its alleged deficiencies, and call for regulations. These may be light in the first instance. They may simply involve the identification and accurate counting of children educated at home. But, as has often been the case, to identify something can be the prelude to its strict regulation or even its effective prohibition.

The Passion to Regulate

As in the rest of the English-speaking world, Britain is subject to a heavy and growing weight of regulation. This is not the place to discuss whether any specific regulation is justified. It is enough to say that there is a general assumption among those who matter that everything that is done by the people must be known to the authorities and controlled by them.

Going back 10 years from September 23, 2004, the phrase "completely unregulated" occurs 153 times in the British newspaper press. In all cases, unless used satirically, the phrase is part of a condemnation of some activity. We are told that the advertising of food to children (Frith, 2004), residential lettings agents (Bagnall, 2004), funeral directors (Page, 2004), rock climbing (Parri, 2003), alleged communication with the dead (Curtis, 2003), salons and tanning shops ("Will You Sleep," 2003), contracts for extended warranties on home appliances (Hunter, 2002), and anything to do with the Internet—that these are all "almost completely unregulated" or just "completely unregulated," and that the authorities had better do something about the fact.

Now, home schooling falls straight into this category. Though so far left alone by the authorities in England, it is surprising that this has been left alone for so long, and perhaps astonishing that there have been so few calls for its regulation.

Ideological Agenda

A strand of neo-Marxist thinking claims schooling to be the means by which capitalism reproduces itself: it instills in working class children a set of values hostile to their true interests (see, e.g., Bowles & Gintis, 1976[23]). In its specifics, this is an unlikely claim. It is true, however, in its generality. As with most neo-Marxist theory, it says little about what is being attacked, but much about the intentions of those making the attack. State schools do not turn out adults who believe in the rule of law and in free enterprise. But they often do their best to turn out adults who are inclined to believe in the opposite. Though state education seems in the urban areas of Britain to be approaching the point where little seems to be taught either good or bad, and the popular media has largely taken over the job, state education has for as long as it has existed been the reproduction mechanism for various kinds of statist ideology. Until the middle of the twentieth century, it was the means by which people were made into good nationalists: would 10 million young men have marched semi-willingly to their death in the Great War without the prior conditioning of state education? Since then, it has been captured by the radical socialists.

Since the 1980s, Dennis O'Keeffe, now professor of sociology at the University of Buckingham, has been analyzing the capture of education by the neo-Marxists. They dominate teacher training. They run the institutions, and they determine the modes of instruction. Student teachers are required to read and discuss and thereby absorb the works of Antonio Gramsci and Louis Althusser and Michel Foucault, among others. Professor O'Keeffe describes teacher training as

> a missionizing ideology. The world is [said to be] intolerable. It is full of unacceptable hierarchies. It is the duty of teacher education, at least so far as the school-world is concerned, remorselessly to combat these hierarchies. All cultures are equal, all histories equally valid.. God is dead, but the religions of equal opportunity more than make up the inspirational deficit. (O'Keeffe, 1990)

Perhaps, as with the indoctrination of any established ideology, students pass without reading or read without absorbing. Even so, enough gets through to the classroom. Professor O'Keeffe finds that

> socialist ideas pervade education.... These ideas are dangerous in their universalist form, when they propose Utopian equalities, and in their latest,

separatist incarnations, where equality is reserved for insider groups like women, blacks [sic] and non-western cultures, everything male, white [sic] or western being derided and opposed as inferior or oppressive. (O'Keeffe, 1999)

This being so, it is natural that the neo-Marxists should see home schooling as a challenge to their own hegemony in education. To be sure, these are not pantomime villains, and they do not sit about complaining how their conspiracy risks being frustrated. Instead, they believe they are doing a good and necessary job, and are concerned that at least some children are missing the benefits that they dispense.

We see this explicitly in the writing of Michael W. Apple, an American academic. He claims that the educational policies promoted by a coalition of "rightist" groups—he calls them the forces of "conservative moderniza-tion": neoliberals, neoconservatives, authoritarian populists, and "the managerial and professional new middle class" (Apple, 2001, p. 11)—entail terrible consequences, which, if left unchecked, threaten all but to destroy public education in America. In particular, home schooling is an example of "individualized behavior" that "threatens to undermine the quality of public education" (p. 14).

He is still more explicit in a shorter work:

While it is quite probable that some specific children and families will gain from home schooling, my concerns are larger. They are connected to the more extensive restructuring of this society that I believe is quite dangerous and to the manner in which our very sense of public responsibility is wither-ing in ways that will lead to even further social inequalities. In order to illu-minate these dangers, I shall have to do a number of things: situate home schooling within the larger movement that provides much of its impetus; suggest its connections with other protectionist impulses; connect it to the history of and concerns about the growth of activist government; and, finally, point to how it may actually hurt many other students who are not home schooled....

I have used this essay to raise a number of critical questions about the eco-nomic, social, and ideological tendencies that often stand behind significant parts of the home schooling movement. In the process, I have situated it within larger social movements that I and many others believe can have quite negative effects on our sense of community, on the health of the public sphere, and on our commitment to building a society that is less economically and racially stratified. I have suggested that issues need to be raised about the effects of its commitment to "cocooning," its attack on the state, and its grow-ing use of public funding with no public accountability. (Apple, 2000)

Parents who choose home schooling are taking children away from schools where they might otherwise be taught how to help build a new kind of society in which everyone will accept the common doctrines of political correctness.

CONCLUDING REMARKS

There can be no doubt that—whatever may be the numbers overall—the number of children educated at home has increased and is increasing. During the next few years, it is also at least reasonable to believe that there will be a debate over whether the numbers ought to be diminished.

On the one side will be the supporters of an activist state, divided as to their motivation, but united in their belief that education should be supervised by the authorities. On the other will be the home schooling parents. Most of these may be hiding, and they will continue to see safety in concealment. Those who are visible can be expected to fight all efforts at regulation with a passion not seen in British politics within living memory. We may, then, be returning to something like the debates of the middle and late Victorian years, when education was considered more than just a matter of funding and standards.

NOTES

1. From a biography provided at http://www.online-literature.com/agatha_christie/

2. The full text of the Education Act 1996 is available online at: http://www.hmso.gov.uk/acts/acts1996/96056-za.htm

3. Reported as *Harrison & Harrison v Stevenson* (QB (DC) 729/81).

4. Reported as *R v Secretary of State for Education and Science, ex parte Talmud Torah Machzikei Hadass School Trust* (1985) (Law Report in *The Times*, London, 12 April 1985).

5. The act provides:

   If it appears to a local education authority that a child of compulsory school age in their area is not receiving suitable education, either by regular attendance at school or otherwise, they shall serve a notice in writing on the parent requiring him to satisfy them within the period specified in the notice that the child is receiving such education. (s 437 (1))

6. Reported as *R v Gwent County Council ex parte Perry* (1985) 129S.J. 737:CA

7. *Phillips v Brown*, Divisional Court (20 June 1980, unreported). See this statement from Lord Donaldson:

   Of course such a request is not the same as a notice under s 37 (1) of the Education Act 1944 [now s 437 (1) of the Education Act 1996] and the parents will be under no duty to comply. However it would be sensible for them to do so. If parents give no information or adopt the course... of merely stating that they are discharging their duty without giving any details of how they are doing so, the LEA will have to consider and decide whether it "appears" to it that the parents are in breach of s 36 [now s 7 of the Education Act 1996].

8.   Available online at: http://www.legislation.hmso.gov.uk/si/si1995/Uksi_19952089_en_1.htm.

9.   Education Act 1996, ss 444(3)(a), 444(9)

10. The relevant law is the Education (Scotland) Act 1980. Section 30 of the act states:

It shall be the duty of the parent of every child of school age to provide efficient education for him suitable to his age, ability and aptitude either by causing him to attend a public school regularly or by other means.

This is qualified by Section 28(1):

In the exercise and performance of their powers and duties under this Act the Secretary of State and education authorities shall have general regard to the principle that, so far as is compatible with the provision of suitable instruction and trabining and the avoidance of unreasonable public expenditure, pupils are to be educated in accordance with the wishes of their parents.

11. Education and Libraries Northern Ireland Order 1986 SI 1986/594. There is an unofficial summary of the law available on line at: http://www.hedni.org/legal.html

12. He runs Educational Heretics Press, which publishes works that "question the dogmas of schooling in particular, and education in general, and to develop the logistics of the next learning system." The Website is at: http://edheretics.gn.apc.org/

13. The Home Education Advisory Service Website is: http://www.heas.org.uk/

14. The Education Otherwise Website is at: http://www.educationotherwise.org

15. The Website of the Otherwise Club is at: http://www.safran26.freeserve.co.uk/OCFrontpage.htm

16. The Schoolhouse Home Education Association web site is at: http://www.schoolhouse.org.uk/

17. See, for example, this from a U.S. Website:

How does this kind of research affect homeschooling?

It leads to increased control and regulation of homeschools, it forces homeschools to become more like conventional schools, and it weakens the grassroots homeschooling networks and organizations that are the foundation of the homeschooling movement. (Larry & Susan Kaseman, Does Homeschooling Research Help Homeschooling available at: http://www.homeedmag.com/INF/FREE/free_rsrch.html)

18. This is advertised as "based on recent research, relevant experience, and current legislation. Co-ordinated by Professor Peter Smith (Goldsmiths College, University of London)." Available on ine at: http://www.dfes.gov.uk/bullying/pdf/dfee%20bullying%20insideNEW.pdf

19. From statistics published in August 2004 by Department of Education and Skills, discussed in MacMahon (2004).

20. For a summary of the unschooling position, see the Website of unschooling.com, available online at: http://www.unschooling.com/index.shtml. Though this is an U.S. site, there are British unschoolers. One of these is a friend of the author. See the Taking Children Seriously Website maintained by Sarah Fitz-Claridge: http://www.takingchildrenseriously.com/

21. Dr. Rothermel finds that 14% of parents who educate their children at home followed the National Curriculum in 2002. At the least, this shows that some parents do try to duplicate the normal school syllabus.

22. The Website of the Scottish Parent Teacher Council is at: http://www.sol.co.uk/s/sptc/

REFERENCES

Alpress, M., & Turnbull, E. (2000, July). Education Otherwise—A positive choice? Paper presented at the International Conference, Education for Social Democracies: Changing Forms and Sites, Institute of Education. Available online: http://www.worldzone.net/lifestyles/homeeducation/mapap.htm

Apple, M. W. (2000). Away with all teachers: The cultural politics of home schooling. *International Studies in Sociology of Education*, 10(1). Retrieved September 2004, from http://www.asu.edu/educ/epsl/EPRU/resources/Apple.Away.Tchrs/Apple.Away.rtf

Apple, M. W. (2001). *Educating the "right" way: Markets, standards, god, and inequality*, New York: Routledge Falmer.

Bagnall, M. (2004, May 15). Just don't let them get away with it. *The Guardian*. Retrieved September 30, 2004, from www.athens.ac.uk

Blair, A. (2004, July 30). Teachers want curbs on home education. *The Times*. Retrieved September 30, 2004, from www.athens.ac.uk

Bowles, S., & Gintis, H. (1976). *Schooling in capitalist America: Educational reform and the contradictions of economic life*. New York: Basic Books.

Brown, M. (2002, September 2). Why these parents have got it wrong. *The Mirror*. Retrieved September 30, 2004, from www.athens.ac.uk

Cohen, D. (2002, Oct. 22). Do you call this parent choice? *The Evening Standard*. Retrieved September 30, 2004, from www.athens.ac.uk

Cook, S. (2002a, December 10). Home front. *The Guardian*. Retrieved September 30, 2004, from www.athens.ac.uk

Cook, S. (2002b, December 18). Home front. *The Guardian*. Retrieved September 30, 2004, from www.athens.ac.uk

Curtis, N. (2003, September 12). And if you want to find a psychic. *The Evening Standard*. Retrieved September 30, 2004, from www.athens.ac.uk

Department for Education and Skills. (2004). *Bullying: Don't suffer in silence—An anti-bullying pack for schools.* London: Author. Available online: http://www.dfes.gov.uk/bullying/pdf/dfee%20bullying%20insideNEW.pdf

Duguid, H. (2003, June 30). Women: We want to change the world. *The Guardian.* Retrieved September 30, 2004, from www.athens.ac.uk

Freely, M. (2000, May 7). Home is where the class is. *The Observer.* Retrieved September 30, 2004, from www.athens.ac.uk

Frith, M. (2004, May 26). With one in four children overweight, the experts explain what can be done about it. *The Independent.* Retreived September 30, 2004, from www.athens.ac.uk

Gathorne-Hardy, J. (1977). *The English public school phenomenon, 597-1977.* London: Hodder and Stoughton

Grant, G. (2004, August 10). Record numbers of parents teach their children at home. *The Daily Mail.* Retreived September 30, 2004, from www.athens.ac.uk

Garavelli, D. (2002, September 1). A class of their own. *Scotland on Sunday.* Retrieved September 30, 2004, from www.athens.ac.uk

Hartley-Brewer, E. (1997, December 11). Governesses: Are they the answer to parent' prayers? *The Independent.* Retrieved September 30, 2004, from www.athens.ac.uk

Holmes, T. (2003, April 12). In order to keep the faith, these parents want their children to learn some home truths. *The Times.* Retrieved September 30, 2004, from www.athens.ac.uk

Hunter, T. (2002, October 27). Travel agents and electrical retailers ordered to play fair. *The Sunday Herald.* Retrieved September 30, 2004, from www.athens.ac.uk

Keele, E. J. (2004, January 19). I'm so proud to be a stay-at-home mum. *The Daily Mail.* Retrieved September 30, 2004, from www.athens.ac.uk

Kenrick, J. (n.d.) *Noel Coward: Biographical sketch.* Retreived September 2004, from http://www.musicals101.com/noelbio.htm

Kingsley, M. (1998, February 28). In a class of their own. *The Times.* Retrieved September 30, 2004, from www.athens.ac.uk

Lewis Foundation, C. S. (n.d.) Retrieved September 2004, from http://www.cslewis.org/resources/chronocsl.html

Lindsay, M. (2002, February 8). Check on kitchen classrooms. *The Aberdeen Press and Journal.* Retrieved September 30, 2004, from www.athens.ac.uk

MacMahon, M. (2004, August 1). Sexual jealousy whets the schoolboy's blade. *The Sunday Telegraph.* Retrieved September 30, 2004, from www.athens.ac.uk

A matter for debate. (2004, June 3). *This is Hampshire.* Retrieved September 30, 2004, from www.athens.ac.uk

Mcauley, R. (1995, October 3). Home win. *The Guardian.* Retrieved September 30, 2004, from www.athens.ac.uk

Meighan, R. (n.d.). *Natural learning.* Retrieved Septermber 2004, from http://edheretics.gn.apc.org/EHT001.htm

More parents choose to educate children at home. (2004, July 30). *The Guardian.* Retrieved September 30, 2004, from www.athens.ac.uk

Newell, C., & Lock, A. (2003, August 31). Exam stars flop at 1950s school. *The Times.* Retrieved September 30, 2004, from www.athens.ac.uk

Oborne, P. (2004, August 21). How Labour ministers lie about the world and their opponents. *The Spectator.* Retrieved September 30, 2004, from www.athens.ac.uk

O'Keeffe, D. (1990). *The wayward élite: A critique of British teacher-education.* London: Adam Smith Institute.

O'Keeffe, D. (1999). *Political correctness and public finance.* London: Institute of Economic Affairs.

Page, C. (2004, May 11). Shocking cost of dying. *The Daily Record.* Retreived September 30, 2004, from www.athens.ac.uk

The Parent Centre (n.d.). *Educating children at home* Retrieved September 2004, http://www.parentcentre.gov.uk/publishContent.cfm?topicAreaId=61&c=generic&r=8&do=list#97

Parri, I. (2003, December 31). Feedback. *The Daily Post.* Retrieved September 30, 2004, from www.athens.ac.uk

Petty, M. (1999, April 1). Brains of Britain. *The Times.* Retrieved September 30, 2004, from www.athens.ac.uk

Redwood, M. F. (2004, May 4). When mum is miss, too. *The Daily Mail.* Retrieved September 30, 2004, from www.athens.ac.uk

Rothermel, P. (2002). *Home-education: Rationales, practices and outcomes.* Retrieved September 2002, from http://www.dur.ac.uk/p.j.rothermel/Research/Researchpaper/BERAworkingpaper.htm (Checked September 2002)

Rousseau, J. J. (n.d.). *Emile, ou l'éducation, 1762* [Émile or education]. Retrieved Septermber 2004, from http://projects.ilt.columbia.edu/pedagogies/rousseau/contents2.html

Turner, J. (2002, February 9). Education system has a lot to learn. *The Evening News.* Retrieved September 30, 2004, from www.athens.ac.uk

West, E. G. (1965). *Education and the state: A study in political economy.* London: Institute for Economic Affairs.

West, E. G. (1974). The economics of compulsion: The twelve-year sentence. Retrieved September 2004, from http://www.ncl.ac.uk/egwest/pdfs/economics%20of%20compulsion.pdf

Will you sleep well after sessions on sunbeds? (2003, April 14). *The Batch Chronicle.* Retrieved September 30, 2004, from www.athens.ac.uk

CHAPTER 14

HOMESCHOOLING

The Case Against
Compulsory School Attendance Laws

Tom Burkard and Dennis O'Keeffe

But for compulsory school attendance laws, homeschooling would hardly be an issue. Although the vast majority of children would still attend a school of some description, parents who chose to homeschool would be free to direct their energies toward their children's education, instead of keeping one eye out for the truant officer. At present, homeschoolers must seek exemption from attendance laws, and this process can be highly arbitrary and unfair. One of the authors of this chapter homeschooled his child in England with the full approval of the local education authority—granted after one perfunctory home visit—yet less educated parents in Britain have spent time in prison because of their children's absence from school. Considering that parents legally possess no coercive power over truculent children, and that truancy has reached epidemic proportions in the United Kingdom (even in middle-class schools, about 20% of 15- and 16-year-olds will be AWOL on any given day) this law is monstrously unjust. Since the abolition of military conscription, school attendance is

Home Schooling in Full View: A Reader, 229–249
Copyright © 2005 by Information Age Publishing
All rights of reproduction in any form reserved.

the last form of involuntary servitude left in the United States and the United Kingdom, and it is clearly time that the issue was re-examined.

THE ORIGIN OF COMPULSORY SCHOOL ATTENDANCE LAWS AND THE "PROFESSIONALIZATION" OF TEACHING

Historically, school attendance laws were a byproduct of the industrial revolution. Large-scale industry introduced a phenomenon without precedent: industrial slums full of masterless men from the lower orders. There was very genuine concern for the lack of moral and religious instruction for workers' children, as well as fears for social stability. In the United States, laws compelling parents to send their children to school were almost as old as the first English settlements, but in general this was a matter for township government. It is not entirely coincidental that compulsion was first enforced by state statute in Massachusetts in the 1840s, when English capital and Catholic Irish immigrants transformed the scale of industrial enterprise. The Irish, who through no fault of their own were lacking in the traditions of democracy, were seen as a danger to an overwhelmingly Protestant society.

Undoubtedly most middle-class people saw education as a powerful redemptive force. This statement by Horace Mann (as quoted in Coulson, 1999) in 1841 expressed contemporary wisdom: "Let the Common School be expanded to its capabilities, let it be worked with the efficiency of which it is susceptible, and nine tenths of the crimes in the penal code would become obsolete; the long catalogue of human ills would be abridged."

As Andrew Coulson (1999) wryly added, "In 1998 the Los Angeles County School Board voted to arm its public school police with shotguns." No doubt Mann was as sincere as he was mistaken, but this should not blind us to the fact that he was the first major empire-builder in American education. Mann is also regarded as the first major advocate of progressive education in the United States, as well as being responsible for the introduction of the disastrous "look-and-say" method of beginning reading instruction.

Compulsory school attendance laws were an essential component of Mann's projected New Jerusalem. What is less well-recognized is the importance of his efforts to establish teaching as a profession through the establishment of Normal Schools, or the first American teacher-training colleges. Previously, it was generally assumed that anyone could teach, and the only qualification needed was an understanding of the subject that was being taught, and a willingness to stand in front of a class.

Whether an individual was a good or bad teacher was thought to depend on temperament, not training. The Lancastrian schools in England went so far as to employ older pupils as "monitors" to teach basic literacy and numeracy skills to younger children, thereby bringing the cost of education down to an extremely low level. Needless to say, Joseph Lancaster was not especially popular with teachers, whose salaries were already so low as to preclude all but the shabbiest pretenses at respectability.

Therein lay the rub. The human instinct to instruct youth and to pass on one's values, knowledge ,and experience is so basic that there is never a shortage of persons willing to teach. By establishing Normal Schools, Mann was in a position to control entry to the newly-created "profession"; and he was also able to dictate how teachers were trained. Because entry was restricted, Massachusetts teachers' salaries rose throughout the 1850s, and the loyalty of those teachers who had jumped through hoops was assured. They now had money and social status, which they had not previously enjoyed, and it was very much in their interest to maintain the myth that teaching was an arcane art requiring specialist training. And of course, this in turn provided a powerful argument for compulsory schooling, one that is still central the current debate on homeschooling.

Ironically, the "professionalization" of teaching is one of the main reasons why homeschooling has become so popular. As Lancaster demonstrated, anyone can teach if teaching only implies the transmission of knowledge and skills. Once the focus of teaching shifts from the material to be learnt to the "development" of the child, it becomes possible to pretend that teachers are experts in child development and psychology. The effrontery of this argument is amply demonstrated by Andrew Coulson's comment, and indeed one of the major reasons why parents homeschool is because our "child-centered" classrooms can be such dangerous places.

THE RATIONALIZATIONS USED TO JUSTIFY COMPULSORY SCHOOL ATTENDANCE LAWS

However, to decry the dreadful state of our schools does not, in itself, answer the arguments for compulsory schooling. Nor is it enough to show that the professionalization of teaching was bogus and corrupt. If we are unfortunate enough to buy a car, which constantly breaks down, from a crooked car dealer, we are not forced to conclude that we should never buy another car. The case for compulsory schooling must be answered in detail. In the first instance, we will look to the pragmatic issues, which are the common currency of public debate. Second, we will look to the theoretical issues. These are perhaps the most important; it would be impossible to underestimate the power of ideas, or the influence of the intellectual elite who understand how these ideas set the agenda for the public debate.

Most people in the education reform movement, those who seek to turn back the tide of progressive doctrine, seek only to fix our schools. They still think of schooling as an incontestable public good. They believe that an efficient school system is essential to a nation's economic health; indeed, compulsory schooling was first introduced in England in the 1870s because of concern that Germany and the United States were threatening Britain's position as the dominant industrial and trading nation. This measure, it should be noted, did nothing to reverse Britain's relative decline. Schools are also viewed as the means by which the state creates a common culture, or at least instills the civic virtues necessary for the survival of a democratic society. Schooling is deemed to be essential to children's social development, giving them the team working skills needed to function in today's complex society. It as seen as a protection against the pernicious influence of cults. Lastly, we have the legacy of Charles Dickens: the fear that children will be exploited economically if they are not in school.

THE PHILISTINE FALLACY:
EDUCATION AND THE ECONOMY

Taking the first objection: it has become a political mantra that *we need a highly educated workforce if we are to remain competitive*. As dubious (and as Philistine) an argument for compulsory schooling as this may be, most people accept it unquestioningly. Politicians and educators who are seeking to justify the upward spiral of spending on schools bleat out this message endlessly. Even education reformers, those flinty-eyed guardians of our intellectual heritage, believe it. Indeed, they are often the first to repeat it. Yet the economic argument is absurd. No demonstrable relationship exists between a nation's economic performance and the efficiency of its educational arrangements. Were this the case, the postwar economic performance of the United States and the Soviet Union would have been reversed. During the industrial revolution, Britain led the world, despite the lack of government schools or laws that forced parents to send their children to school; whereas Prussia, France and the United States—countries where schooling had long been mandatory—lagged almost a century behind in industrialization.

We are now turning out far more graduates than we need. For instance, in Britain, less than 25% of our information technology graduates actually find jobs in their chosen field, and about a third of our recent graduates are either unemployed or are working in jobs that do not require a degree. When employers specify a degree for a given position, in most cases it is only because graduates are presumed to be brighter than average, and because they have demonstrated their ability to *play the game*. Relatively few graduate vacancies demand skills or knowledge that have been imparted in tertiary education.

Indeed, it is worth noting that one of the reasons why governments of the 1970s and 1980s spent so much money expanding tertiary education was to reduce unemployment by shrinking the labor force. Now that employers find it difficult to fill vacancies, both Britain and the United States are flooded with illegal immigrants, without which our economies could not function. The overschooling of our children is socially destabilizing. Educators, in their efforts to build their empires, relentlessly disseminate the message that pupils should *aim high* so they will not end up in a *dead-end job*. Pupils are taught to despise manual work, and that to settle for a low-level job in the retail or service industries is contemptible; hence our need for large numbers of immigrants, often from cultures which are openly hostile to the host nation.

The simple (and for educators, unpalatable) truth is that technological advances are created by a tiny number of geniuses; and these are exploited in countries that have the lowest taxation and the most liberal and adaptable economic arrangements. Technologically, England was a relatively backward nation in the seventeenth century; but the wealth of English agriculture—itself a product of a prosperous peasantry enjoying security of tenure, and working in a cash economy—was liberated by Oliver Cromwell's abolition of Royal monopolies, and the re-admission of Jews. After the conquest by William of Orange, the Whig administrations created a secure environment for enterprise and finance—and (despite the unenforceable Test and Corporation Acts) a relatively tolerant religious regime.

Security of property and an independent judiciary ensured that prosperous new businesses would not find their assets sequestered or stolen by greedy or hostile governments, and it allowed entrepreneurs to plan for the long term. Hence, England attracted some of the most talented immigrants: Dutch engineers, German miners, Flemish textile finishers, French metalworkers, and (perhaps most crucially) Jewish bankers. The remarkable advances in science, industry, commerce and technology in eighteenth and nineteenth England all occurred without the slightest governmental involvement in the nation's educational arrangements.

The globalization of the economy has ensured that no nation will remain backward for a lack of scientists and technically-trained personnel; the backward countries of Africa suffer not from a want of schools, but from kleptocratic elites, which bleed all honest enterprises, dry. Which brings us to a question, which will be explored in greater detail later—

What is in fact the relationship between education and schooling? Is education truly related to a nation's economic viability only because the educated elite, the philosophers and thinkers, understand the nature of the open society—and its enemies? England created the industrial revolution because it followed Locke, and not Hobbes. In this sense, it is difficult to see how compulsory schooling in any way contributes to education in America or Britain.

Indeed, it would be far easier to make a case that *homeschooling* contributes to our economic well-being. Schools, despite all their rhetoric about encouraging independent investigation, are far more apt to encourage conformity and discourage innovation. If we ask one of today's schoolchildren whether they have ever heard a teacher or pupil express doubts about the reality of global warming, they will be genuinely puzzled. It is not so much that they have been brainwashed into accepting it—rather, they understand that asking awkward questions is not the way one gets good grades, or for that matter how one gets ahead in the world. The homeschooled child is highly unlikely to have this inhibition. What could be more natural, after all, than arguing with one's parents?

THE 'MELTING POT' FALLACY: COMPULSORY SCHOOLING HAS NOT UNITED US INTO A COHESIVE AND DEMOCRATIC SOCIETY

If the economic argument will not wash, what about civic virtue? Leave aside, for the moment, the hollow laughter of the 11th grade civics teacher fresh from another desperate encounter with the rump that bothered to show up for his or her class. Forget Andrew Coulson's cynical remark about armed school police. Surely, one might object, the older generation attended schools, which taught us to be proud of our country and to understand, cherish and protect our free and democratic society. Alas, the use of compulsory schooling to create a culturally cohesive society has become something of a can of worms because multiculturalists, with their wonderfully Orwellian way of thinking, are doing everything they can to create a society consisting of mutually hostile and isolated subcultures.

Bureaucrats whose responsibility it is to enforce racial equality and justice would be out of jobs if their actions actually created a color-blind society, so it comes as no surprise to find them fanning the flames of racial grievance and resentment. Yet education reformers would argue that if yesterday's schools could bind us together in civic virtue, there is no reason why today's schools should lack the same potential. The Core Knowledge Foundation is built on this noble ideal.

Unfortunately, this ideal is built on an illusory view of the past. It is often argued that Mann's Common School was the melting pot in which immigrant communities were integrated into American society. This is nonsense. Until the last generation, most Roman Catholics made considerable financial sacrifices to keep their children out of schools where they feared their children's faith would be compromised. Garrison Keillor's, *Lake Woebegon,* with its perpetually squabbling Lutherans and Catholics from Norway and Germany, is a portrait of the American Midwest which anyone who grew up there before 1960 will recognize instantly as *exactly what it was like back then.* Immigrant groups tended to stick together for generations, and it took the postwar suburban flight to integrate Germans, Swedes, Poles, Italians, and Irish into the mainstream culture. Unfortunately, this American suburban culture is defined by racial exclusion. Even with forced bussing, schools have failed to create a common culture for all Americans.

Although we believe that a common culture is a desirable goal, we also believe that it is both wrong and unwise to use the power of the state to ensure conformity, even in a democratic society. A country cannot be considered truly free when men and women cannot obey their consciences, nor can it be stable. The problem is exacerbated when, as in Britain, the antinomian elite succeeds in creating a curriculum which many if not most parents would find objectionable, were it not so effectively camouflaged with reassuring rhetoric. In *Market Education,* Andrew Coulson (1999) has demonstrated how attempts to use schools to enforce cultural norms have actually exacerbated tensions and even provoked violence. People with differing beliefs can normally coexist quite happily as neighbors—and perhaps even find some common grounds for understanding and friendship—but if one were forced to educate their children to the other's beliefs, they would soon become enemies. It is, for instance, quite possible to have homosexual friends and strongly oppose the persecution of homosexuals while objecting quite strenuously to having homosexuality portrayed as a *positive lifestyle* in school.

Homeschooling is more conducive to building a peaceful and cohesive society than Mann's Common School. Homeschooled children will almost certainly meet a much wider range of people than those who attend a public school. Indeed, school children's social contacts are pretty much limited to those who live in the same area and share the same year of birth. In the United States, and to a lesser degree in Britain, primary schools generally have a highly homogenous population. The contacts of homeschooled children, by contrast, are more likely to reflect their parents' social and work contacts, which inevitably will be far more varied. Since they will not be compelled to accept views, which they or their parents find repugnant, they are more likely to be accepting. A basic law of life is that when people feel threatened, they are far less likely to be tolerant. The intense homophobia and misogyny of underclass males—the most marginalized group in modern society—is a result of this vulnerability.

THE DILBERT FALLACY: DOES OUR "KNOWLEDGE ECONOMY" REALLY NEED MORE TEAM WORKERS?

What about social adjustment? Do we not agree that one of the main purposes of school is to turn out children who are capable of the team working, which lies at the heart of modern management theory? Can it be right to bring up children in isolation from their peers? All these questions deter the potential homeschooler, and they form a superficially attractive argument in favor of compulsory school attendance.

Yet any adult who has ever met homeschooled children will agree that there is something different about them. They are almost invariably polite, cheerful, and full of curiosity. The "in-yer-face" style of their peers seems to pass them by. And it is in no small part due to the fact that they are far more in control of their environment and their education than children who attend school. They do not have to worry about studying a curriculum determined by political rather than academic considerations; they do not have attend schools where scheduling is a matter of administrative convenience; and they do not have to sit in classrooms that must accommodate pupils of wildly varying ability. Nor, it must be added, do they have to worry about bullying.

They do not learn much about teamwork. It would be possible to argue that schooling is a good preparation for working in large organizations, and children should learn how to maximize their chances within them. In particular, the lower echelons of corporate America and Britain require that recruits work in teams—nothing new about this. In William Whyte's, *The Organization Man*, first published in 1956, we discover how modern management was born. In prewar America, businesses and industry had minimal management superstructures organized strictly by top-down rules. Each individual had clearly-defined responsibilities to clearly-identified superiors. However, the capitalist barons of the early twentieth century sought respectability by sending their sons (and daughters) to Ivy League universities, where they imbibed the dubious wisdom of the early sociologists. As they began to take over their parents' enterprises, they re-created management in a new democratic image, replacing authoritarian structures with ones based on consensus.

But as Whyte pointed out, the change was more style than substance: the alpha males still climbed to the top. They of course spoke a new language; the one now taught at Harvard Business School. Management became far less efficient, as actions, which once required a simple decision made by one man expanded into problems requiring endless committees and reports. However, wartime spending created an unprecedented boom for American corporations, and many of them grew to such a size that management became increasingly independent of shareholders. Management became a cult in its own right, and Enron represents the ultimate evolution of the corporation where the primary activity is satisfying the greed and megalomania of managers.

Parents who want their children to climb up the greasy pole in the modern corporation—in either the private or public sector—are well-advised to send them to school. At a very early age they will learn that teamwork is really a screen for manipulation. Sitting at tables in groups of six, they soon learn how to cajole the weakest members into doing all the work, while of course taking their share of credit for the project. They will learn whom they should cultivate, and whom it is safe to patronize or to openly despise. They will learn that presentation and style are far more important than substance. Above all, they will learn to take the *safe* option, and to think conventionally.

Fortunately, a very large part of the economy is still relatively immune to the management disease. Virtually all the new jobs in America are created by smaller and newer enterprises where ownership and management are, if not one and the same thing, still closely related. Without the enormous advantages conferred by size, political influence, brand names, and quasi-monopoly status, these firms must employ people who are truly productive. In such an enterprise, the homeschooled child will be at no disadvantage at all, for he or she will have been judged from a very early age on what has been learnt or accomplished.

The assumption that homeschooled children will suffer from a lack of contact with children their own age is nonsense. The age-determined peer group is the most unnatural social construct imaginable, and it would not exist but for educators' insistence on grouping children by age, instead of by educational achievement and ability, and by interests and inclinations. These days, most children suffer from a lack of contact with people who are *not* their own age. In practice, very few homeschooled children are socially isolated, as most parents actively seek out fellow homeschoolers or after-school activities that involve other children.

OVER THE MOONIES: KIDDIES AND CULTS

Compulsory schooling is also seen as a safeguard against cults. If we knew a child who was inducted into a hierarchical cult where strict obedience was enforced, children were made to pray for hours on end, and where almost all contact with the outside world was discouraged, we would be very worried indeed. However, this is exactly how Tibetan monasteries operated prior to the Chinese invasion in 1950. Curiously enough, the fashionable thinkers who now revere the Dalai Lama would be the first to condemn a cult which remotely resembled real Tibetan Buddhism. But who is to say that the austere life of Tibetan children was necessarily inferior to the daily existence of the pampered American teenager, who plays sadistic video games and worships misogynist and murderous rap stars? Who is to say what is a cult, and what is a valid lifestyle? And why is it that liberals suddenly become fiercely judgmental when it comes to how other people raise their children?

SAVING CHILDREN FROM THE HORRORS OF PAID EMPLOYMENT AND USEFUL ACTIVITY

Historically, one of the most effective proponents of mandatory schooling, Charles Dickens, almost single-handedly popularized the sentimental modern concept of childhood. Dickens was nothing if not sentimental; as Oscar Wilde was reputed to say of Little Nell's death, "It would take a heart of stone not to laugh." Dickens remembered his own childhood employment in the bottle-blacking factory with great bitterness not because the working conditions were onerous, but because he was a middle-class boy who was cut out for better things. Society has paid a terrible price for young Dickens' humiliation; now it is almost impossible for children to get a legal job. To deny them the opportunity to make a worthwhile contribution to society is to deny them the one experience which would truly enhance their sense of self-worth, and give them a sense of connection with society.

Anyone who has taught the bottom sets in any high school will, if honest, admit that the exercise is a total waste of time. The pupils hate being there because their primary school teachers were so concerned about their development that they forgot to teach them anything useful, such as how to read and write. They know that school is a dead end, and that they are being kept there only because adults say they must. But they also take adults at their word: if, in this nonjudgmental age, they are entitled to choose their own lifestyle, well then that lifestyle is going to involve systematic truancy.

We are either ignorant or hypocritical if we insist that these children are better off in school than they would be if they were working. And of course by infantilizing them so, we are in danger of teaching them that they are not responsible for themselves. If we deny them the chance to make money and insist that they spend their time in an activity, which is profitless in more ways than one, we should hardly be surprised when they become hostile, alienated, or even criminal. We have in effect told them that they are no use to anybody, in school or out. If there is an immediate and pressing argument for the abolition of mandatory school attendance laws, it is their demoralizing effect on the least academic children. There is good evidence to support this contention: when the school-leaving age in England was raised from 14 to 15 years in April, 1947, there was an immediate and substantial increase in reported rates of juvenile offences. But thanks to Dickens, there are few votes to be had in the very sensible proposal that illegal immigration be curbed by allowing our alienated youth to find work at an earlier age.

Admittedly, homeschooling could be used as a dodge by unscrupulous parents bent on economic exploitation. No doubt it does happen, especially in the case of illegal immigrants who would be in danger of deportation if their children were registered at school. In such cases, compulsory attendance laws are rather beside the point. But in most cases, the potential earnings of a small child are pretty small beer these days. In an age where nearly all young children, even those from the lowest social and economic groups, are showered liberally with DVDs and fashion accessories, this concern about exploitation borders on the grotesque. The only people who really do exploit children for their own economic benefit are educators whose comfortable salaries cannot possibly be justified by such knowledge or skills as are gained by their involuntary *clients*.

BEYOND UTILITARIAN ARGUMENTS: THE PRINCIPLED CASE FOR HOMESCHOOLING

Essentially, all of the above objections to compulsory school are based on Benthamite arguments. It is our contention that judgments based solely on utilitarian criteria are inherently dangerous. There can be no doubt but that the education policies of the Bush Administration are based on the best of intentions, and that the No Child Left Behind Act is an honest and even honorable attempt to rectify the manifold failings of the modern American public school. But basic principles were ignored. The Constitution, a document written by men to whom principle was all, nowhere justifies the intervention of the Federal Government in schooling. The sophistry (and fundamental ignorance) of activist Supreme Court Justices has bent the Constitution to serve utilitarian ends, and the result has been an enormous extension of government power. Arguably, many of the problems of American schools can be traced to Horace Mann, who instituted control of schools at the level of state government. Federal intervention in education has resulted in yet another layer of officials standing between parents and the schools where they send their children. This governmentalization of education may be stimulating for the growth of the homeschooling movement, but it most certainly is not good for any child forced to attend a District of Columbia public school.

WHAT IS EDUCATION?

One of the most elusive factors in educational controversy is a lack of an understanding of what education is and what purpose it serves in a liberal society. Elaborate teaching and learning are integral to modernity. This is not in dispute. But compulsory school attendance is a most problematic concept, witnessed—as we have seen—in a very problematic practice. We should start with the words *compulsory education* on the grounds that education is the most philosophically elevated of the words which imply the deliberate passing of information from one person to another, a list also including *training, instruction, schooling, indoctrination*, and so forth.

First of all, are the two components of compulsory education mutually contradictory, an oxymoron? Might one say, to parody Hobhouse on Rousseau, that: Insofar as it is educational, it is not compulsory? And insofar as it is compulsory, it is not educational? Well yes, one might. Perhaps, though, the case for or against compulsion may be governed by one's definition. There have been two principal definitions in general academic currency in recent years.

For R.S. Peters, one-time doyen of philosophy of education, education is the pursuit of knowledge for intrinsic purposes, in a voluntary spirit, and within an open cognitive perspective. Not much help comes the way of compulsion from this source, then. The unwillingly confined denizens of 11th grade are by definition not there voluntarily. Nor are they likely to take an open cognitive perspective. The point to remember, though, is that Peters was trying to tease out from a highly nuanced word, some quintessential meaning. He was not trying to mount a case for education, in that refined sense, to be put on a compulsory basis, or a voluntary one either. His definition may or may not convince. It points away from compulsion if anything.

We may be inclined instead, however, to an essentially *moral* definition of education. We may see it as the pursuit of goodness, an old a view—going back to Plato—and historically more common. It is now favored by the social democrat liberal, John White. It is bound to appeal today in modern societies threatened by lawlessness, and by the collapse of parental authority, both in a moral and intellectual sense. The failure of schools to deliver a moral education, and the implicit challenge to parental authority in educators' stated mission of guiding children's social and emotional development, are without doubt the major factors in the growth of homeschooling.

This *moral* definition, however, rather founders on doubts as to whether someone can be compelled to pursue the good. If I detain you I can perhaps prevent your doing such and such a thing; but can I really compel you to be virtuous?

SHOULD THE PREREQUISITES OF THE PURSUIT OF KNOWLEDGE OR VIRTUE BE COMPULSORY?

Another possibility is that it may be that only the prerequisites of education require compulsion. Both approaches, the cognitive and the moral, subsume training. Without a bedrock of skills, one cannot become an autonomous agent pursuing knowledge for its own sake. Children must be trained in these skills before they embark on genuine cognitive inquiry of an intrinsically motivated kind. Similarly, the forcible moral training of the very young is the prerequisite of what can later be articulated as real moral education. Thus, we may despair of finding grounds for compulsory education as such, but switch instead to justify *compulsory training* in its prerequisites.

We would argue that while public finance is the *fuel* of intellectual mediocrity, primary schools, because of the ideology they embody, are the principal *motor* of educational failure. The case even for compulsory basics fails, then, on the grounds that as presently constituted, the primary school system is not up to the task. We can make a justification for separating primary, secondary, and tertiary education conceptually, but a proper continuity between them is critical. This continuity simply does not exist. So badly does primary experience equip children that secondary education is a doomed enterprise from the start in the case of many of the students who experience it. And the longer-term effects of poor lower (K-12) education on higher education are too obvious to need pointing out.

Thus, even the basic training case does not do away with the libertarian argument against compulsion. One cannot claim, of course, that the libertarian argument has ever won much mileage. Nor is there any famous version of it. Anticompulsion is, however, quite easy to articulate and quite powerful.

THE LIBERTARIAN CASE

The libertarian case is that compulsion is *never* right for older children, teenagers, for example, and does not become viable even for little children, merely on the assumption that some homes are insufficient to the task. The libertarian will not hold that all homes are sufficient to the task. He or she will say, however, that if we think most homes are adequate, and yet we have compulsory education, we are left in an odd position. We are requiring all families to send their children to school on the ground that some families do not understand the importance of equipping their children with elementary cognitive and moral training. There are large numbers of parents whose own educational achievements are so meager as to preclude the possibility of effecting such instruction. But why should most people be forced to send their children to school when they would do this voluntarily, just because a minority will not or cannot comply?

This is surely an unsatisfactory basis for the learning arrangements of a free society. The very most that could be claimed is that *some* families are not up to the job and therefore must be compelled to send their children to school. This, however, has implications even more unpleasant and ethically improper than our present arrangements, insulting as these are. If we retained compulsion on these grounds, restricting it to this group, this would leave the state with the highly invidious, and politically explosive task, of deciding which people need compulsory schooling. There would be cases where compulsion and voluntary attendance would be separable only by a hair's breadth, or simply not at all. Hard cases make bad law. Enforcement at the margin would be manifestly impossible.

We suggest after this brief discussion that the philosophical case for universal compulsory education, though it may have some superficially attractive features, is fundamentally weak and contradictory. School cannot be made compulsory without insulting the maturity and capability of most citizens.

This is not an argument against public provision of the contested good, so-called education. There is a strong case against such public finance, but we are not making it central to our case, or anyway not at this point. Though financial and economic considerations do intertwine with jurisprudential ones in this debate, the two sets of issues are quite distinct conceptually. One can therefore perfectly reasonably make a case for public provision of a good, which will be taken up by a majority of parents on a voluntary basis. An even better case could be mounted for arguing that education cannot be compulsory and should not be publicly financed either. If education were solely the responsibility of the parent, there can be little doubt but that the market and the voluntary sector would respond very rapidly to provide this good very much as they did before schooling became compulsory. Children would experience schooling in many different forms, and some of them would almost certainly be a hybrid of home-schooling and part-time commercial or charitable provision. Let us leave that for the moment.

EMPIRICAL CONSIDERATIONS:
THE INSTRUMENTAL REALITY

If the philosophical vistas seem gloomy, what if we just look at the facts? After all, the law on speed limits is one thing, and the compliance of drivers another. So-called education is roughly comparable. In many instances school is not de facto compulsory, as we have stressed already. In many cities in countries all round the world secondary attendance is virtually on a voluntary basis. In many British high schools there is a level of truancy so high as to make attendance for some people effectively voluntary.

Even for many children who attend willingly, with their parents' active support, the reasons for their attendance are not such as to satisfy either of our two versions of philosophical reasoning. Rather few children may be seen as motivated by a pure thirst for knowledge. Nor is such a thirst on the part of their parents likely to be the reason for their requiring children's attendance during the early training stage. A few people may be driven all their lives by a desire to know; and there may be others who acquire such a desire, after they have learned to read, when they are trying to get into university, or at any point when they suddenly discover they have a real academic aptitude. In general, though, the trouble with the R.S. Peters line is that people do not follow it. People want knowledge mostly for instrumental purposes. When they want it for its own sake it is often a self-indulgent consumerism that is involved.

The goal of moral goodness seems a bit more promising. It certainly fits in with the popular perception that one goes to school to learn to behave properly. There are several catches though. The most obvious is that while it may be widely believed that prolonged study makes you good, the evidence is dubious, as the earlier citation from Andrew Coulson suggests. Most people think that schools teach moral decency but there are countless examples of people with long exposure to books and institutions of learning that were (are) morally repugnant. It may even be that education is in overall terms dysfunctional as well as mal-functional. Certainly, the behavior of homeschooled children does strongly suggest that that schooling does not impart moral standards.

OTHER ASSORTED ARGUMENTS

We may conclude that the behavior of individuals in institutions of learning does not correspond to the elevated notions philosophers entertain as to what those institutions are for. We are grappling here with the real difficulty that "education" is an overlapping terrain for the attention of an a priori subject, like philosophy and semi-empirical subjects like economics, sociology and politics. The question then is whether, insofar as compulsion is concerned, an instrumental case can stand in for the failed arguments from intrinsic love of knowledge or virtue. Can economic or sociological arguments stand in for (partially) unsuccessful philosophical ones?

Let us allow, for the moment, the suggestion that education produces economic growth and that this is a good reason for making it compulsory. We reply that knowledge must indeed in some sense be associated with economic advance but that unfortunately we cannot easily tell how. The fact that education is largely publicly financed makes it impossible to work out the relationship. Most people work for the private sector and yet they have to make career choices in a public sector context, in which the imperatives of scarcity and choice are unrealistically muted—as we have seen from the huge surplus of information technology graduates in Britain. Because the education system is publicly financed, the people who work or study in it are not making decisions on the basis of their own resources, but on the basis of other peoples'. In other words economic reality is partly stifled.

THE QUESTION OF EXTERNALITIES

Officialdom tends to argue for certain externalities involved in education, which discourage it under private finance. First, I cannot stop other people from benefiting from my knowledge, so I will not acquire it without some public recompense. Secondly I cannot stop others from benefiting from my virtuous behavior. Again, I will demand less education. Overall, citizens will undertake less education than is optimal. Therefore the state must step in, both funding the experience, and for a certain minimum number of years, making it compulsory.

All this is nonsense. Education is a private good which is over-demanded when it is publicly financed. Nor do we have any evidence that when it is compulsory, the stock of human capital formed by education is increased. Human capital depends on *a particular articulation between knowledge and markets*. The Soviet Union was rich in knowledge formation, but *not* in human capital formation. Russia, Cuba, and the other Communist societies were characterized by an economically useless accumulation of knowledge. So idle chatter about the theory of "human capital" or "human capital formation" cannot rescue compulsory education.

In any case, we find a much darker side to the question. For all the propaganda about the inexhaustible benefits of an ever expanding educational estate, it is at times nearer the truth to identify education as Joseph

Schumpeter (1962) and Paul Johnson (1996) have, as linked to insurrection and disorder. In Britain, for example, the huge expansion in secondary education has gone hand in hand with an equally significant increase in juvenile crime. At best the former (education) did not prevent the latter (crime) In our view, it *fuelled* it. The fact is that the socioeconomic case for compulsory schooling fares no better than the philosophical one.

Why should it fare better? It is after all only a variation on the instrumental skills argument, with no evidence that we would see an underinvestment in education if it were voluntary, and quite a good case for saying that there is *overinvestment now*. The philosophical case for education is at least a good one, in abstraction. We do surely mean when we speak of someone's being successfully educated that we are confronted with an individual who is intellectually accomplished, curious, open-minded, and virtuous.

We are skeptical, however, whether much of the philosophical prospectus has been achieved by our public arrangements for education. Mass culture seems philistine and the demand for good theatre and good music and art, though large, are minority tastes, which we may presume, do not need underpinning by compulsory attendance. Nor have we compensated for lack of culture by a superior performance in skill formation. Some highly skilled workers are in very short supply. The present government in Britain is anti-intellectual and hostile to high culture. It talks up *skills*, because they sound horny-handed compared to culture, but these skills are never well-defined. They are never defined in concrete terms, such as the ability to read and spell words or to perform simple calculations, almost certainly because such performance can easily be measured.

The sociology of education has little to offer by way of support for compulsory education. The greatest sociologist of education by far, Emile Durkheim, would have been profoundly in favor of compulsory attendance. If modern schools were as good at moral formation as Durkheim advocated, maybe the case for compulsion would look a bit stronger. But they are not. Juvenile crime is out of control, and as we have suggested antiracist education is designed to heighten racial antagonisms, rather than to ameliorate them.

TURNING HISTORY ON ITS HEAD: MAKING CHILDREN ASHAMED OF THEIR ANCESTORS

Above all, mass education seems characterized by the appearance of large numbers of mischief-making and antinomian intellectuals, people who could never admit that the nation which mounted the world's first industrialization, and maintained an innovatory dynamism across the whole range of human affairs, throughout the nineteenth century, did so with neither compulsory school attendance nor public finance. In the process the British set in motion the gradual freeing of much of the world's population from the ancient scourges of primary poverty, famine, and disease.

This stupendous achievement ought to fill British hearts with pride, and most foreign ones with admiration and gratitude. Instead, it has provoked envy and rage; instead of celebrating the achievements of great men and women, our history lessons demand that pupils "empath" with the poor and oppressed. This has a singularly evil effect, beyond the distortion of the past: if children identify with life's losers, they will think of themselves as powerless, when in fact they live in a free society where there are still relatively few obstructions to those who wish to better themselves, or to better the lot of others. They do not think of themselves as free citizens who shape their communities or their civic institutions to the dictates of their beliefs, or as creators of economic wealth, but rather as helpless cogs in a machine, and sullen slaves of the system. In no more than a generation, we have abandoned our free common law traditions for the mental enslavement of the Russian serf.

By contrast, homeschooled children are taught by parents who, by the very act of choosing to educate them, expressed a belief in their children's future. Even if the parent's ambition is no greater than to teach a child to take pride in work, however humble it may be, this is far better than the passive mentality engendered by compulsory schooling, and the negative attitudes created by a curriculum which dishonestly portrays evils such as slavery as being peculiar to Europeans in general, and Anglo-Saxons in particular—ignoring the fact that Britain ended the slave trade, going very much against the traditions and financial interests of Africa and the Near East.

SCHOOLING AND SOCIAL ORDER

The fumbling and incompetent educational leadership of America and Europe today does not supply a good case for the claims of mass education, compulsory or otherwise. As elementary education got going in the late nineteenth century, before and after compulsion, and up to the Second World War, the curve of British crime fell. With the huge growth of secondary, tertiary, and further education since then, crime has grown to levels previously unknown. One flinches from drawing mechanistic associations, but the contingent growth of antisocial activity side by side with the parallel expansion of mass schooling raises questions too obvious to be ducked.

Obviously we are more affluent today, but affluence is far from being the whole or even the core of human felicity. Since we want affluence and moral order, let us suggest to you that while the 1980s brought Britain economic redemption, they also short-changed us educationally. For example they gave us that symbol of a revived Oriental Despotism, the National Curriculum.

THE FATAL DIALECTIC:
EDUCATION AND ECONOMY IN 1980S BRITAIN

The late Basil Bernstein once observed that social life is characterized by a dialectic of openness and closure. What he meant is that there are historical periods of considerable duration, of freedom and openness. There are others of opposite tendency, when closure and restriction predominate.

Bernstein may also be read as meaning that this distinction also characterizes *short-term* movements in the life of society as a whole, or of groups of people. There may be transient public moods of freedom or clamp-down. Families, friendships, churches, schools, and other institutions, too, share with society as a whole, the tendency to oscillate between periods of freedom and periods of repression and restriction. The dialectic on the smaller scale may, or may not, coincide with the dialectic on the societal scale. Sometimes a whole subsector of society, of government and economy, may move in a different way from the overall polity and economy.

This is what happened in the 1980s in Britain. The commercial economy as a whole became comprehensively more free and open. That very important subsector of economic life, the education system, by contrast, became more rule-bound, more interventionist, more bureaucratic, more restrictive, more closed. It also became almost certainly more inefficient.

There were portents for this discontinuity between the overall economy and economic subsystem. From the late nineteenth century in Britain and America, and many decades earlier in some parts of Europe, educational practices took hold which did not conform to the traditional conditions of education as these are explained by E.G. West (1965) and more recently by Andrew Coulson (1999). Coulson's observation is that in all the cases in history where education has been efficiently conducted, it has been conducted on the basis of private finance.

Considerations of compulsion versus voluntary attendance point in the same direction. We hypothesized that voluntary attendance would have improved the results by retaining power on the demand-side of production. It would not have been risk free or painless. There would have been casualties. But compulsion too has those. How many school-classes are ruined for the well-disposed by the ill-disposed? We do not have to be as rude as Murray Rothbard, who said that compulsory education forces bright children into the company of morons. How many teachers live in dread of hateful and unmanageable pupils? There is no risk-free policy. If school were voluntary some people would not go; but effective attendance, that is attendance where people learn something useful, would almost certainly improve. No one who has taught at an inner-city high school would dispute this.

THE EDUCATIONAL CONFUSION OF FREEDOM VERSUS COMPULSION

In fact, compulsion does not stand or fall by a calculus of crude majoritarian social physics. Our views on education, compulsory or otherwise, diverge widely. Some of us are fervent believers, others are mild observers, others could not care less, and yet others are positively hostile. Compulsory education has 130 years of habit reinforcing it in this country. Habit may be no bad thing. Aristotle says that through its courtyard we gain access to the palace of virtue.

It is a fair guess too that for the present, voluntary school is a nonstarter. But habit may not continue indefinitely to underpin compulsion. The antinomy of freedom versus compulsion need not anyway be settled on an all or nothing basis. In Britain, for instance, lowering the school-leaving age from 16 to 14 is a real possibility, as truancy levels in that age group have grown to such a level that authorities may well be forced to bow to the inevitable. Certainly the right of parents to homeschool their children should be enshrined in law, and the threat of prosecution removed.

Even more to the point, if compulsory schooling laws were repealed, it would allow for the growth of alternatives which met the needs of students, as opposed to those who have a vested interest in maintaining existing schools. As we have suggested, homeschooling does not imply that a child will sit at home all day, every day, being taught personally by a parent. The provision of educational services, be they part-time courses or educational materials, is cheap. Schools, which are in loco parentis, are not.

There seem to be two contemporary drifts. On the one hand, the educational elite has succeeded in the last half century in vastly increasing the scope of secondary education. It has also conspired with a series of educationally incompetent governments, for the last 30 years, to give us expanded higher education, which the state cannot afford and the public, overtaxed, do not want to pay for. Terence Kealey, the vice chancellor of the University of Buckingham (Britain's only private university), believes the middle classes could pay if they chose. Well they choose not to, and it would probably take a big tax reduction to alter their determination. The elite would probably like, on top of sending half the population of school-leavers to university, to extend compulsion down to 3 years of age and upwards to 18. On the other hand the money has run out, and the old joke about raising the school leaving age to 35 has run out of gas.

The case for compulsion is demonstrably weak and not proven, and it is high time more scholars and reflective people took a long, hard look at it. In all probability, events will force us to do so in the not-so-distant future. Already, there is something of a boom in businesses supplying educational services to parents—most of whom are not homeschoolers—who are dissatisfied with state provision of schooling. In a free society, these services are almost impossible to regulate if they are not full-time schools. The utilitarians are demanding ever increasing levels of state control of everything from hamburgers to nail scissors, in the name of public safety, but short of imposing a police state, it is almost impossible to stop determined parents from educating their children as they see fit. But ultimately, the argument for homeschooling must rest on the principle that governments are only justified in using compulsion out of necessity. Otherwise, the right to homeschool will forever be contestable.

REFERENCES

Coulson, A. J. (1999). *Market education: The unknown history.* New Brunswick, NJ: Transaction.

Johnson, P. (1996). *Modern times: The world from the twenties to the nineties.* New York: Harper & Row.

Schumpter, J. A. (1976). *Capitalism, socialism and democracy* (5th ed.). New York: Harper Torchbooks.

Whyte, W. H., Jr. (1956). *The organization man.* Garden City, NY: Doubleday.

ABOUT THE AUTHORS

Michael W. Apple is John Bascom Professor of Curriculum and Instruction and Educational Policy Studies at the University of Wisconsin, Madison. He has written extensively about the relationship among knowledge, power, and education in such books as: *Ideology and Curriculum, Education and Power, Cultural Politics and Education, Official Knowledge,* and *Educating the "Right" Way.*

Clive R. Belfield is assistant professor of economics at Queens College, City University of New York. He is also associate director of the National Center for the Study of Privatization at Teachers College, Columbia University. He has published widely in the *Economics of Education*; and his most recent books are *Privatizing Education in America* and *Economic Principles for Education: Theory and Evidence*.

Tom Burkard is the director of The Promethean Trust, a British charity for dyslexic children. With his wife Hilary, he has developed Sound Foundations, a "user-friendly" basic literacy program designed for use by parents. He has written two studies on reading policy in England for the Centre for Policy Studies. He homeschooled his own son from the age of 8.

Bruce S. Cooper is professor and chair of the Division of Educational Leadership, Administration & Policy at Fordham University's Graduate School of Education, and former president of Associates for Research on Private Education (ARPE). He has written widely on private and public school policies and finance, and is editor of *The Private School MONITOR*. His most recent book is *Better Policies, Better Schools*.

Steven F. Duvall, PhD, received his doctoral training at the University of Kansas. After working as a school psychologist in the public schools for 21 years, Dr. Duvall began directing the School Psychology Training Program at Fort Hays State University in Hays, KS. His research interests involve homeschooling, low-achieving students, and program delivery models.

Sean Gabb is a lecturer in the Department of Social Sciences at the University of Buckingham. A former adviser to the Slovak prime minister, he is a frequent broadcaster in the British media and the author of three books.

Charles D. Glenn teaches education policy and history at Boston University. His most recent book (with Jan DeGroof), *Balancing Freedom, Autonomy, and Accountability in Education*, profiles 40 national educational systems.

Nicky Hardenbergh received her BA in political science from Bryn Mawr College and an MAT in social studies from Boston College. While teaching in a classroom for 11 years, she found that her ideas about education changed radically after a few years of homeschooling her two children. She is currently researching and writing about the history and effects of compulsory attendance policies.

Joy A. Marean is a doctoral candidate in educational leadership at Teachers College, Columbia University. Her professional experience and research interests have focused on private and international education.

Marc F. Ott is a doctoral candidate in educational leadership at Teachers College, Columbia University. Currently employed in admissions at the Leysin American School in Switzerland, an international boarding school with students from 50 nations in grades 9 to 12, Ott is primarily interested in international private school education.

Brian D. Ray has been studying the homeschool movement for 22 years and is internationally known for his research and writings. He has been a classroom teacher in public and private schools, taught children and youth from public schools, private schools, and homeschooling, and served as a professor in the sciences, research methods, statistics, and education at the undergraduate and graduate levels. Dr. Ray earned his PhD in science education from Oregon State University, his MS in zoology from Ohio University, and his BS in biology from the University of Puget Sound. Among other things, he currently does research, speaking, writing, and consulting, and serves as president of the National Home Education Research Institute.

Rob Reich is assistant professor of political science and ethics in society at Stanford University. He is the author of *Bridging Liberalism and Multiculturalism in American Education*, which contains an extended discussion of the ideas developed in his chapter in this volume, and other articles that stand at the intersection of political theory and education.

Matthew J. Rush is director of the Middle School at North Cross School, a coed independent K-12 day school in Roanoke, VA. A master's degree recipient from Columbia University's Klingenstein program, he has been in independent school education for over 20 years as a student, teacher, and administrator. He is also a member of Kappa Delta Pi, an international honor society for educators.

Tom Smedley, a freelance technical writer and editor, lives with his wife Vicky and daughters Beth and Laura in Durham, NC. Their two older children, Greg and Dori, finally went to a public school—the nearby North Carolina State University in Raleigh, NC. His seminal thesis, "Social Maturity of Home Schooled Children: A Communication Approach," is posted at http://mysite.verizon.net/res0iqde/

Scott W. Somerville, Esq. has helped teach his six children at home since 1985. A graduate of Dartmouth College and Harvard Law School, he has served as a staff attorney at the Home School Legal Defense Association since 1992.

Venus Taylor currently uses her EdM from Harvard University to homeschool her two children, ages 10 and 7, in Massachusetts, with the support and assistance of her husband, Hycel. She is founder of a support group, the Association for Diverse Homeschoolers of Color (ADHOC), Website: www.adhocsupport.net

Printed in the United States
66394LVS00002B/262

9 781593 113391